W9-DHI-676

Spurious Issues

Spurious Issues

Race and Multiracial Identity Politics in the United States

Rainier Spencer

Westview Press
A Member of the Perseus Books Group

Copyright © 1999 by Westview Press, A Member of the Perseus Books Group

Published in 1999 in the United States of America by Westview Press, 5500 Central Avenue, Boulder, Colorado 80301-2877, and in the United Kingdom by Westview Press, 12 Hid's Copse Road, Cumnor Hill, Oxford OX2 9JJ

Find us on the World Wide Web at www.westviewpress.com

Library of Congress Cataloging-in-Publication Data
Spencer, Rainier.
    Spurious issues : race and multiracial identity politics in the
United States / Rainier Spencer.
        p.   cm.
    Includes bibliographical references and index.
    ISBN 0-8133-3677-5
    1. United States—Race relations—Government policy.   2. Racially
mixed people—United States—Race identity.   3. Categorization
(Psychology).   4. Race—Social aspects—United States.   Title.
E184.A1S73   1999
305.8'04073—dc21   99-24420
                                                                              CIP

The paper used in this publication meets the requirements of the American National Standard for Permanence of Paper for Printed Library Materials Z39.48-1984.

10   9   8   7   6   5   4   3   2   1

To Pat

Contents

Acknowledgments

It is a difficult thing to separate oneself from one's work, and it is difficult also to separate the people and experiences that have contributed to who one is from the people and experiences that have contributed directly and indirectly to the work one does. Recognizing this, I shall nonetheless make the attempt to acknowledge those persons who have been especially important to me in my writing this book.

Happily, though, the question of where to begin presents no problem. The most important people in my life have been two women whose assistance and guidance have been so fundamental that I literally cannot imagine having arrived where I am without them. The first is my wife, Jackie, without whose help and support I would not have even entered the realm of scholarly pursuits. Her sacrifices, and those of our daughter, Nicole, especially during the difficult and trying doctoral program years, represent a debt I can only hope to one day repay.

The single most important person in my professional life has been my teacher, mentor, adviser, critic, and good friend Patricia Penn-Hilden. Through her personal example and the scholarly rigor she demands in her work as well as in the work of others, and by showing more genuine care and concern for students than any other professor I have ever known, she has opened for me a vast array of intellectual doors whose existence I had not even imagined. In terms of the manuscript itself, it was Pat who unfailingly and mercilessly sent me back to the drawing board time and time again when the present book existed as a dissertation-in-progress. Her persistence was the best thing that could have happened to me, though, and my writing has benefited immensely from her attention and consideration. She also graciously provided reviews as the project moved toward finally becoming a proper book manuscript. Both Pat and her husband, Timothy Reiss, hold a special place in my heart for all they have been to me.

Certainly, I owe a great debt to Emory University, especially to its Graduate Institute of the Liberal Arts. I did the vast majority of my library research, particularly relating to government documents, at Emory's Robert W. Woodruff Library. I want to especially recognize the very fine government documents section there and to personally thank the library's excellent and indomitable interlibrary loan staff, particularly Marie Hansen.

I received indispensable assistance from the federal government as well. From mailing me copies of contemporary and archival documents to providing current updates of assorted policies, various federal offices proved to be invaluable resources. The Library of the Executive Office of the President saved me on more than one occasion when I was in need of obscure government publications that I could not find elsewhere. For special praise I must single out Suzann Evinger of the Statistical Policy Office of the Office of Management and Budget's Office of Information and Regulatory Affairs. She put up with frequent telephone calls from me and was always obliging with her very valuable time. Although her office was in the midst of dealing with potential revisions to federal racial classification, and my constant requests were surely a distraction for her, she nonetheless kindly provided me with information and references to other sources that were of immense help to me.

I would be remiss if I did not give humble thanks to Ramona Douglass, president of the Association of MultiEthnic Americans, for her generosity in sharing with me many of the details regarding the negotiations and inner workings of the move to add a multiracial category to the federal scheme. Although we remain apart philosophically on some of our positions regarding the idea of multiraciality, I continue to have only the utmost respect and the highest admiration for her both personally and professionally.

There are several individuals whose work and friendship have been especially helpful as I pursued this project. The idea for this book originated out of my reading an excellent essay by Cynthia Nakashima that inspired me to take the path I did. Two colleagues of Cynthia's, Becky King and Kim DaCosta, who have also become dear friends of mine, offered ideas, criticism, and friendship through conversation, correspondence, and the happy (though all too few) occasions of appearing on conference panels together. Another friend, Lise Funderburg, has done a great deal to inspire me with her calm precision and objectivity. And Aubyn Fulton never backed down from a logical challenge, forcing me, via his pointed and relentless dialectic, to constantly rethink and restate my arguments in the best ways possible.

I want to thank my colleagues in the Department of Anthropology and Ethnic Studies of the University of Nevada, Las Vegas, for their encouragement and support as I completed this book. I am indebted as well to the staffs of the interlibrary loan office, especially Victoria Hart, and the faculty copy service of UNLV's James R. Dickinson Library for their invaluable assistance.

Thanks also to Mari Shullaw, who reviewed and commented upon an early version of the manuscript. Thanks especially to Karl Yambert of Westview Press for his support and confidence. The task of writing is rendered so much easier when one knows one is in good hands. Those hands also include Jennifer Chen, Lisa Wigutoff, Michelle Trader, and Cathleen Tetro of Westview. I want to explicitly acknowledge the invaluable contribution of Norman Ware, whose copyediting of the manuscript was simply superb.

Finally, while recognizing the important assistance of the individuals named above, I take full responsibility for the contents of this book and for any factual errors or technical mistakes contained herein.

Rainier Spencer

A Note About Electronic Sources

Electronic sources such as mailing lists and World Wide Web pages have been known to change their addresses, sometimes quite frequently. For the sake of historical accuracy and since there is no guarantee that updated addresses would remain valid for long, I have chosen to give electronic addresses that were valid on the dates I utilized them. In particular, readers will note two different addresses for the Interracial Individuals Discussion List, the maintainership of which changed hands in the spring of 1996. The two addresses for that mailing list are reflective of that change.

Acronyms

ACLU	American Civil Liberties Union
AMEA	Association of MultiEthnic Americans
B+MATA	Box + "mark all that apply"
CNSTAT	Committee on National Statistics
CPS	Current Population Survey
EEOC	Equal Employment Opportunity Commission
ERIC	Educational Resources Information Center
FICE	Federal Interagency Committee on Education
GAO	General Accounting Office
HEW	Department of Health, Education, and Welfare
HIV	Human Immunodeficiency Virus
HMDA	Home Mortgage Disclosure Act
MATA	"mark all that apply"
NAACP	National Association for the Advancement of Colored People
NCS	National Content Survey
NCT	National Content Test
OCR	Office for Civil Rights
OE	Office of Education
OFSPS	Office of Federal Statistical Policy and Standards
OMB	Office of Management and Budget
RACE (Project)	Reclassify All Children Equally
RAETT	Race and Ethnic Targeted Test

The author and his family on his seventh birthday.

Identity is not what we are but what we are passing for.

—Samira Kawash, *Dislocating the Color Line*

Introduction

"You're not worried about me marrying your *daughter," James Baldwin told a white southerner during a television debate. "You're worried about me marrying your wife's daughter. I've been marrying your daughter ever since the days of slavery.*[1]

Mulatto, quadroon, octoroon, zebra, half-breed, spurious issue, multiracial, biracial, mixie. These are a few of the terms that have been used to describe persons of so-called mixed racial ancestry in the United States. Some of these terms are relatively new whereas others are centuries old, reflecting the fact that although issues of mixed race may be a current concern they are by no means a new one. Historically, mixed-race matters have gone hand in hand with questions of race itself. Soon after the earliest Native American–African–English contact in what would become the United States of America, such persons began to exist and began to multiply. For the most part, however, they and their descendants have been assigned, relegated, categorized, and classified racially in ways that deny or otherwise ignore portions of their ancestry, especially any European component. They have generally been required by prevailing racial understandings to identify with a single non-white racial group.[2] In the case of Afro-Americans especially, the willingness to accept singular racial categorization despite a history defined in large part by extensive population mixture is one of the most puzzling and illegitimate aspects of the race concept.

As a result of federal requirements to comply with antidiscrimination laws stemming from the civil rights movement of the 1950s and 1960s, the last quarter of the twentieth century witnessed the codification of American popular understandings of race into a government-mandated system of racial classification and statistics that extended to every government agency, every activity or institution receiving federal funds, every business of more than 100 employees, and every American citizen.[3] Michael Omi and Howard Winant provide a partial summary of the breadth of federal racial categorization in the United States:

> How one is categorized is far from a merely academic or even personal matter. Such matters as access to employment, housing, or other publicly or privately valued goods; social program design and the disbursement of local, state, and federal funds; or the organization of elections (among many other issues) are directly affected by

racial classification and the recognition of "legitimate" groups. The determination of racial categories is thus an intensely political process.[4]

During that inaugural phase of racial statistics–keeping, a look at most forms requiring racial identification confirmed that the federal system of racial classification was a monoracial one, which is to say that a person was either American Indian or Alaskan Native, Asian or Pacific Islander, black, or white. In the United States, all people had to be classed into one and only one of these categories. Mixtures of two or more races within a single individual were not recognized by the American system, leaving people to identify officially with only one of the above racial groups. For persons who considered themselves to be racially mixed or multiracial, however, this was often a frustrating and unsatisfactory situation.

One consequence of this frustration was an attempt by multiracial advocates to have a multiracial category added to the system of federal racial classification in time for the year 2000 census. As a result of that initiative, issues of race and multirace entered the national spotlight in such a way as never before, as groups and individuals on all sides of the debate presented their views to the public and to the government. Collecting and considering all this testimony was the U.S. Office of Management and Budget (OMB), which would make the ultimate decision on whether federal racial categorization would be changed to include a multiracial category, changed some other way, or not changed at all.

On October 30, 1997, OMB announced its decision regarding the way race would thenceforth be conceived of, utilized, and reported by the federal government. This announcement was the result of a four-year, multimillion-dollar review of federal racial classification, which was the center of a national debate over race, identity, and the exigencies of civil rights compliance monitoring. The essence of the announcement was that "respondents who wish to identify their mixed racial heritage should be able to mark or select more than one of the racial categories . . . but that there should not be a 'multiracial' category."[5] Thus, when marking one's race on forms requesting it, a person would no longer be constrained to mark one box only. Although the proposal to add a specific multiracial category to federal racial designations was rejected by OMB, it would nonetheless now be permissible to mark as many boxes as one felt applied. The instruction to "mark one only" was transformed into an invitation to "mark all that apply." The significance of that modification, and of the debate that both led to it and continues beyond it, is the subject of this study.

This book is an analysis of race, multirace, and identity in the context of federal racial classification. It is an examination of multiracial identity politics in the United States and of the specific issues surrounding OMB's review and decision—the stakes involved, the parties concerned, the history of federal racial categorization, and the significance of the new rules on race in America. It is also a book about race generally, an extended argument that invites and challenges readers to assume a skeptical position in regard to one of the most widely accepted but rarely analyzed components of life in the United States. Antiracialism is the filter through which I conduct my analysis of multiracial identity, federal racial categorization, and OMB's modifications to this categorization, and as such it serves as the conceptual framework on which this book rests. Racial skepticism, then, is the first principle of my general argument, informing my discussions of race, identity, and federal policy.

My methodology is interdisciplinary, which is only fitting since part of what I am doing is challenging the practice of assigning people to distinct and exclusive biological groups. I utilize a philosophical approach tempered by an appreciation of the serious practical realities associated with racial categorization in the United States. In other words, I use philosophical analysis as a means with which, and logical consistency as a standard against which, to critique the historical and sociological phenomenon of the American racial paradigm. A multifaceted approach is especially called for here, as issues of race are usually not addressed adequately when treated in disciplinary isolation. A sociological approach only tells us where we are; a historical approach only tells us how we got there; a philosophical approach only tells us if it makes logical sense to be where we are; and a practical approach only tells us the real-world implications of where we are.

All too frequently, people treat race as if it were not a historically contingent concept. Too frequently, commentators treat race as if a sociological phenomenon were the same thing as a biological fact. And too frequently, people criticize federal racial classification in the United States without an adequate understanding of its history or its implications for monitoring bigotry and discrimination. In other words, a full understanding of what the multiracial category debate truly entails requires the integration of various kinds of knowledge in a more complex way than commentators usually provide, for it is precisely that point where personal identity, racial loyalty, group entitlements and concerns, and federal racial categorization appear to meet—the tiny space of a check-box on a form—that has been the flash point of heated debate and political lobbying about race and identity, extending far beyond the form itself.

Identities imply categories, for if a person has an identity (or identities), that person must then identify as something (or some things). There are some categories to which we can assign people that are uncontroversial, perhaps indisputable. For instance, to be categorized as human and placed in the set *humans* should bring no argument from anyone. One can easily imagine other such uncontroversial categorizations. For example, it would be difficult to regard being placed in the set of left-handed persons a violation of autonomy, so long as one is indeed left-handed, since everyone with working hands is either left-handed, right-handed, or ambidextrous. When membership in a group is not, because of the facts of the matter, at the discretion of the individual, such as in the case of left-handedness or being human, there is no conflict. It is a different case, however, when the existence of the category itself is contested. When it is not merely the facts of the matter that are at issue but the existence of the group itself, there can be grave implications involved in assigning persons to it. Race is the category I want to contest, problematize, and otherwise call into question here.

The American racial construct has long been and continues to be the organizing principle around which people conceptualize themselves, the groups they see themselves as belonging to, and others whom they see as different. However, there is a phenomenon occurring with the potential to challenge America's way of thinking about race, racial categorization, and race mixing. We are now witnessing the emergence of a discourse that questions the idea of race, focusing on fundamental flaws in the system of classification on which it depends. This discourse, which is not monolithic and which includes competing multiracial and antiracial ideologies, threatens to disrupt the ability of race to continue to act as a primary mechanism of social ordering in the United States. Popular magazines, television talk shows, political activism, an expanding scholarly literature, and the multiyear review of federal racial classification by OMB all point to the spread of this critique.

Racial categorization in the United States has in general been, with the notable exceptions of antebellum Charleston (South Carolina) and New Orleans, a monoracial exercise. For as long as monoracial classification has existed in America, there have been people who have been mixtures of two or more supposedly distinct racial groups and who have been necessarily classified inaccurately in the monoracial scheme. At the time of OMB's review, millions of people felt that they were classified inaccurately and that they did not fit into any single racial category; these so-called multiracial individuals were growing increasingly dissatisfied with the ways race had been constructed traditionally. Some of these people joined together, becoming aware that their personal dissatisfaction with the American racial construct was shared. Many voices were raised in this new, though fragmented, movement. Some sought radical change in the form of a new, separate multiracial category for themselves; others merely sought some form of recognition. What unified this population, if only on one central point, was a conviction among its members that a monoracial system of classification did not adequately provide a means for their accurate identification. It remains to be seen whether OMB's modifications to federal racial categorization will satisfy this group ultimately, especially those who most strongly advocated the adoption of a federal multiracial category.

What is at issue goes beyond mere personal recognition. Racial classification provides a framework within which people who are mixtures of two or more supposedly different races may be faced with troubling and contradictory questions of identity and belonging. In the past, people who have been identified as multiracial have been characterized negatively by terms such as *half-breed* and through a host of tragic mulatto figures in literature and film. These pathological characterizations have been based on such persons' traditional positionality between two supposedly distinct racial groups. Given a system of racial classification that can hope to approach philosophical validity only if race refers to distinct and mutually exclusive categories, how can mixed-race or multiracial persons place themselves with consistency and meaning within that system?

In this book I consider two responses to the above dilemma: (1) ending the practice of placing multiracials in one of the traditional racial categories by advocating a new racial category specifically for them, or (2) challenging the racial paradigm itself. The former response, that of modifying the system of racial classification in order to accommodate the explicit placement of multiracials within it, requires acceptance of that system, although advocates of this position argue that short-term acceptance will yield long-term destabilization of the race construct. In contrast, the latter response of challenging the paradigm resituates the locus of the problem by removing it from the individual and placing it on the notion of race itself.

The ambiguousness and irony of OMB's modification of federal racial classification lie in the fact that for all the time, effort, and cost that went into producing the modification, the decision neither resolves the dilemma nor satisfies the opposing sides of this heated debate. The modification allowing persons to mark more than one race is not and cannot be the ultimate resolution of this contentious issue. It is instead a small dressing applied to a gaping wound, a measure that will at best merely quell most debate until after the 2000 census. Indeed, not long after OMB's announcement, the more vocal advocates of a separate multiracial category attacked the decision as being wholly inadequate.

The conflicting ideologies of multiracialism and antiracialism will continue their philosophical struggle regardless of OMB's "mark all that apply" decision, since it satisfies neither of them. This is because multiracial ideology strives for the addition of a stand-alone multiracial category alongside the traditional racial classifications, whereas antiracial philosophy argues for an eventual full and total rejection of racial categorization altogether. Both of these perspectives recognize that monoracial categorization and monoracial identity do not provide an acceptable framework for the self-identification of many Americans, and both of them find the "mark all that apply" compromise of OMB to be an inadequate solution as well. These points of agreement, however, do not translate into further concordance about ultimate goals or matters of strategy and tactics.

Cynthia Nakashima has provided a useful description of three "approaches or voices" dominating multiracial discourse: (1) "the struggle for inclusion and legitimacy in the 'traditional' racial/ethnic communities," (2) "the shaping of a shared identity and common agenda among racially mixed people into a new multiracial community," and (3) "the struggle to dismantle dominant racial ideology and group boundaries and to create connections across communities into a community of humanity."[6]

While considering all three of these perspectives, this book focuses particularly on the last two. Principally this is because the impulse and the pressure for nonwhites to identify with a minority community, especially when the minority community in question is the Afro-American one, has long been a commonplace in American society. The vast majority of Afro-Americans are of mixed ancestry, whether the element of mixture derives directly from a white parent or from a white ancestor or ancestors farther removed. Since the decade prior to the Civil War, and especially since the end of the civil rights era and the beginning of the black militancy era, there has been strong social pressure for Afro-Americans having all manner of ancestral diversity to identify monoracially as black. The monoracial inclusion approach is currently the standard method of personal identification for most Afro-Americans who acknowledge mixed ancestry.

Second, a great deal of support for the American racial paradigm comes from the traditional civil rights organizations in the United States. Pressure to conform to the monoracial schema is exerted by these groups in an attempt to maintain Afro-American political power. Nakashima's approaches (2) and (3) above (which I categorize as multiracial and antiracial, respectively) both differ from approach (1) in that they seem to challenge, rather than support, monoracial classification. A particular focus on the multiracial and antiracial approaches will allow me to isolate these two voices, which, while both purporting to challenge monoracial categorization, differ significantly from each other in a philosophical sense.

The central concern of this book, then, is the idea of multiracial identity—its appropriation, its expression, its advocacy, and its recognition in the United States. As a type of racial identity, multiracial identification would seem vulnerable to the same criticisms as monoracial identity, which are many. However, its most vocal proponents claim for it a power, specifically as multiracial identity, to destabilize the racial structure of U.S. society. On the other hand, this alleged destabilization may be challenged on the ground that all racial classification is problematic. On this view, multiracial identification becomes as illogical and untenable as any of the traditional racial categories. I shall explore the tension between multiracial and antiracial ideologies through an analysis of the failed attempt, at the close of the twentieth century, to add a multiracial category to federal racial designations.

The thesis I am advancing in this book derives directly from a position of racial skepticism: Because racial categorization is an impossible myth that we must move away from (while making sure not to undermine federal antidiscrimination efforts in the process), the assertion of multiracial identity (which necessarily requires acceptance of biological racial classification) is therefore every bit as untenable and inconsistent as the monoracial myth on which it is founded.

As in many scholarly debates, especially the more passionate ones, as author I have had a personal relation to my subject matter. It has been my own personal journey through the racial landscape of the United States, my own engagement with constructions and deconstructions of race and mixed race in my life, that have led me to my position as well as to the desire—the need—to write this book. In my work, my reading of multiracial literature, and my numerous discussions with multiracial activists, I have learned that one of the first responses to criticism is the charge that the critic does not know what it is like to be between two races, does not understand the pain and frustration of being multiracial.[7]

I understand these all too well, however. If my personal philosophy on race did not take me in the direction it did, I might well have donned a multiracial identity myself, for under the racial framework on which multiracialism depends, I qualify as a first-generation multiracial individual. As I like to put it, my mother thinks she is white and my father thinks he is black. I grew up believing I was a little colored boy, and believing I was mixed (long before multiracialism came to be in vogue), until, for lack of a better term, *critical consciousness* demonstrated to me that race is an impossible myth and that multirace is necessarily a myth as well.[8] My personal journey has taken me beyond the artificial constraints of race. The pain and frustration of multiraciality will remain for others, unfortunately, as long as people continue to believe in the myth of race. My thesis is a controversial one, and I expect both unreflective censure and considered critical commentary. Of all the potential criticisms, however, the claims that I lack authenticity or that I do not understand what it feels like to think of oneself as multiracial cannot be among them.

My examination of multiracial identity will begin with an analysis of racial categorization and popular understandings of race and race mixture in America, before turning to the specific issue of a multiracial category. The first two chapters are concerned with laying out the traditional American racial paradigm as the context for understanding multiracial identity politics. My elaboration of the race concept in Chapter 1 involves seeing it in two different, though interrelated, aspects: the scientific construction of race and the social construction of race. I argue that the historical construction of a scientific basis for racial distinctions is a fallacy that has for the most part been discarded by modern scientists. It has not disappeared, however. Rather, it has gone underground, to reemerge in the guise of a socially constructed idea of race. Because of this often covert connection, there is no practical difference between the two constructions of race. To appeal to the social construction is at the same time to invoke the scientific construction.

I undertake to provide a brief overview of race in America, which will of necessity be capsular and selective, in order to offer the context out of which I shall present my arguments regarding multiracial identity. This particular historical review is intended to be neither comprehensive nor exhaustive, but rather aims to highlight several select and specific historical moments in order to illustrate what I see as major turning points in the evolution of race in America. I am consciously avoiding a continuous, linear, historical rendering because I intend for the review to provide a context for my thesis without overshadowing it or detracting from the main points I am endeavoring to make.

In addition to filling in the historical backdrop, this review expresses an idea of the American race construct as being rooted in an interconnected complex of historical events. The high points of these are what is commonly termed the Age of Discovery (and, especially, particular scenarios of contact), the rise of science and scientific measurement, and the era of American slavery. From an examination of these points I argue that race in America is and has always been, from the earliest period of the invasion of the Americas by Europeans, primarily a hierarchical binary opposition between white and black. Although some will doubtless resist the way I have chosen to highlight the black/white duality, I nevertheless contend that these two perceived extremes make each other possible, and in turn make the American racial paradigm possible.

In Chapter 2, I turn my focus away from race in general and move to a consideration of federal racial classification in particular. My goal in this chapter is to bring coherence and accuracy to the often misreported history of federal racial classification and to describe the ways such classification is used for the positive purpose of antidiscrimination compliance monitoring while paradoxically serving to segregate American society statistically. Much criticism is leveled at federal racial classification without due consideration for the ways it has made institutional and covert racism harder to commit and easier to detect. It is vital to understand why federal racial classification exists and why, though we must move beyond it eventually, it cannot simply be terminated out of hand. There is a need to reconcile philosophical and empirical arguments against racial classification with the practical reality that U.S. civil rights laws have produced a vast, interlocking web of mandated racial statistical tracking that is perhaps our best weapon in the battle against continuing racial discrimination. This reality presents a major dilemma for the racial skeptic, who must nonetheless chart the eventual course away from racial classification. The content of Chapter 2 therefore foregrounds my discussion in Chapter 6 of the need to think seriously about moving away from federal racial categorization without weakening antidiscrimination efforts.

Having provided an overview of the American racial paradigm in general, and federal racial classification in particular, I then undertake an explicit analysis of multiracial identity politics. Chapter 3 is concerned with multiracial identity and its relationship to biological racial classification, which I take to be a philosophically necessary one. I question whether multiracial identity can—as its advocates claim—destabilize the race construct, or whether multiracial identity needs the idea of race in order to even be considered as an identity choice.

A major deficiency in multiracial scholarship has been the lack of historical context, together with the concomitant error of viewing mixed-race identity as an exclusively recent phenomenon. For the sake of correcting this problem I have drawn extensively on the work of Edward Reuter, the most prominent scholar of mixed-race issues in the first half of the twentieth century. An analysis of Reuter's work is especially useful in providing a fuller context for the arguments of today's multiracial advocates. In several important ways, including a reliance on biological race, the ascription of pathological psychologies, and the manipulation of mixed-race people, today's multiracial ideology is, in a structural sense, not far removed from that of the 1920s.

Through a rigorous examination of this ideology I present a critique of multiracial identity that strives to achieve a deeper and more substantive level of analysis than the usual, simplistic tropes of multiraciality conceived of as alternately being "caught between two races" and "exemplifying the best of both worlds." In this chapter I extend the general antiracial critique undertaken in Chapter 1 to the idea of multiracial identity in particular, assessing whether it is simply another arbitrary and contingent social construction.

In Chapter 4, I consider the specific argument for a multiracial category in the context of federal racial classification. The previous chapter's exploration of the underlying identity dynamic that fuels the movement for a federal multiracial category provides the context for my discussion of more formal initiatives. I see these efforts as indicative of Nakashima's community approach orientation to multiraciality. I examine the movement to institute a federal multiracial category in terms of the claims that proponents of such a category make for its ability to destabilize the American racial paradigm, exploring these claims and balancing them against the explicit goals of political recognition and group identity that multiracial advocates use as rallying points. I further consider whether these two different goals—destabilization of the race construct and political recognition of multiracial people as a distinct racial category—are likely to each be met by a federal multiracial category, or whether they are inherently contradictory. This chapter includes a close examination of two different types of multiracial category proposals submitted by multiracial advocacy organizations in 1993 and 1995. These different proposals will foreground my later discussion of the significant ideological divergence within the multiracial movement.

In Chapter 5 I consider a final proposal submitted to OMB by one of the two major multiracial advocacy organizations, which was endorsed by the other—a proposal that did not include a separate multiracial check-box. Some very significant differences between these two organizations will become apparent in this chapter, differences that are suggestive of a major ideological split in what has been referred to consistently as the "multiracial community." I also provide an analysis of OMB's final decision on the matter. This is especially important as the OMB decision allowing people to check more than one race will surely not signal the end of agitation for a federal multiracial category.

Chapter 6 is the concluding chapter, in which I synthesize the important issues of the preceding chapters and argue for the importance of plotting a course for moving the United States away from federal racial categorization as opposed to deepening our investment in it. In this chapter I argue that we must look to the future, as opposed to the past or present, in considering racial identity and federal racial categorization. Although each of the earlier chapters makes connections with the others in terms of the overlapping of certain issues, in Chapter 6 I explicitly bring the separate conversations surrounding biological race, ordinary public understandings of race, federal racial categorization, civil rights compliance monitoring, and multiracial identity together and evaluate the multiracial category debate in a way that takes them all into account.

My goal in writing this book has been to provide the fullest account of multiracial identity politics that has yet been compiled. Thus, I have striven to integrate historical and current conceptions of race in the United States, the dependence of multiraciality on biological race, the significance of federal racial categorization and its relation to civil rights compliance monitoring, and discussions of the need to move away from racial classification eventually, into a comprehensive work that delves into far more detail than any article and that has more conceptual weight and thematic unity than any anthology. The effort has been worth it in terms of my own determination to write sincerely and forcefully about the problem of racial categorization in the United States, but if it contributes in some way to eroding the race concept in America, it will have been well worth it many, many times over.

Notes

1. Quoted in Eugene D. Genovese, *Roll, Jordan, Roll: The World the Slaves Made* (New York: Vintage Books, 1974), 414.

2. Race terms in this book are always a reference to people's misguided belief in the illogical American racial paradigm. Given that my topic concerns the notion of racially distinct and racially mixed people in the United States, my use of such terms in some instances is necessary as I endeavor to engage the current racial paradigm and provide evidence of its shortcomings. Race terms in this text, therefore, should always be read as if preceded by the words *so-called*. It was my original intention to illustrate the contested and problematic nature of race terms by always presenting them in italics, and up until my final revisions that is how the manuscript read. However, I found the resulting number of italicized words in the text somewhat distracting, and so in a concession to practicality I let that idea go. Some will no doubt take issue with my use of *Afro-American* as a substitute for *black*. I acknowledge this criticism and can only offer that at the very least *Afro-American* is somewhat farther removed from the notions of race and biology that the term *black* invokes. The only other alternative would have been to deploy a cumbersome phrase such as "persons who are perceived as, or who consider themselves to be, black or Afro-American," which would have been even more distracting than the italicized terms.

3. Unless otherwise noted, references to *America* and *American* apply specifically to the United States.

4. Michael Omi and Howard Winant, *Racial Formation in the United States: From the 1960s to the 1990s,* 2d ed. (New York: Routledge, 1994), 3.

5. Executive Office of the President, Office of Management and Budget, "Revisions to the Standards for the Classification of Federal Data on Race and Ethnicity," by Sally Katzen, *Federal Register* 62, no. 210 (October 30, 1997): 58782, 58784. With regard to the multiracial category question, OMB announced that it was accepting the recommendation of its Interagency Committee for the Review of the Racial and Ethnic Standards. For the full report of the interagency committee, see Executive Office of the President, Office of Management and Budget, "Recommendations from the Interagency Committee for the Review of the Racial and Ethnic Standards to the Office of Management and Budget Con-

cerning Changes to the Standards for the Classification of Federal Data on Race and Ethnicity," by Sally Katzen, *Federal Register* 62, no. 131 (July 9, 1997): 36874–36946.

6. Cynthia L. Nakashima, "Voices from the Movement: Approaches to Multiraciality," in *The Multiracial Experience: Racial Borders As the New Frontier,* ed. Maria P. P. Root (Thousand Oaks, Calif.: Sage Publications, 1996), 81.

7. In addition to drawing from my own lived experience, I have had extended conversations, and arguments, with the leaders of the major national multiracial advocacy organizations.

8. I discuss in more detail these personal matters and how they led me to my particular position on race and multirace in the essay "Race and Mixed-Race: A Personal Tour," in *As We Are Now: Mixblood Essays on Race and Identity,* ed. William S. Penn (Berkeley: University of California Press, 1997), 126–139.

1

The American Racial Paradigm

Black man, black woman, black baby,
White man, white woman, white baby,
White man, black woman, black baby,
Black man, white woman, black baby.

—*Lyric of a Public Enemy rap recording[1]*

Power, Purity, and Hypodescent

As the twentieth century draws to a close, it is clear that although more overt forms of racial oppression may have declined, obsession with color—race—remains one of America's preeminent problems. A belief in the existence of race and a corresponding belief in the possibility and accuracy of racial categorization is, for Americans, as significant and as culturally self-limiting a myth as was the mistaken belief in a flat Earth for many medieval Europeans. In the United States, this acceptance of race has manifested itself as a complex of social and political constructs, all based loosely on selected phenotypic traits. The American racial paradigm utilizes arbitrary somatic differences to separate people into two main groups, one white and one composed of several subcategories of non-whites. This system constitutes a multifaceted ideology, which serves as the engine for a larger system of racial and class hegemony. Its breadth is such that it would not be unreasonable to argue that racial classification is the most important tool of social organization in the United States. At the very least, joined by gender and class, it stands among the top three.

This opening chapter is grounded in two interconnected arguments in support of my main thesis. Together, these two arguments articulate the origin, use, and fallacy of the race construct in the United States and set the stage for an elaboration of federal racial categorization in Chapter 2. First, I argue that race as an accurate and meaningful system of biological classification does not exist. Second,

I suggest that this myth of biological race serves as the foundation for what is known as the social construction of race. It is not my goal in this chapter to develop my arguments regarding multiracial identity and a federal multiracial category. I attend to those matters in Chapters 3 and 4 respectively. My intention here is to map the history and present understandings of race on which the notion of multiraciality necessarily depends. My discussion of the history and current formulation of race in America is therefore the foundation for everything that follows.

Although race terminology in the United States does not refer to any consistent, scientifically valid system of classification, this fact says nothing about people's proclivity nevertheless to believe in race and, perhaps more importantly, to act on those beliefs. Many Americans would reply by asserting that they have no difficulty identifying blacks, whites, and Asians, for instance (or any difficulty understanding other Americans when they do so), and that biological race is therefore a reality. The problem with this reply, however, is that it fails to account for the way somatic distinctions are learned responses that, when challenged, cannot be made the basis for consistent racial groupings. It is akin to claiming that the Earth cannot be spherical by arguing that no matter how far one walks, one never turns upside down and falls off.[2]

It also takes for granted the arbitrary somatic characteristics that American society has fixated on and accepts the structure of white superiority from which they are derived. By this I mean that the general racial construct in the United States is based on the division of society into one white and several non-white categories. An important aspect of American socialization is the indoctrination process that teaches that certain cues are indicative of blackness or Asianness but that there are no physical cues to tell that a person is incontestably white. There are no somatic cues, no phenotypic characteristics, that serve to mark one indisputably as white. Someone can have blue eyes and still be black; someone can have paler skin than most whites and still be black. That this indoctrination is passive diminishes neither its impact nor its effectiveness.

A simple thought experiment will illustrate the irrational nature of the race concept in the United States.[3] We can imagine ninety-eight people who would routinely be labeled in the United States as black, arrayed in chromatic order from darkest to lightest in skin color. Distributed among the members of this group is a wide range of skin tones and other phenotypic features. To complete the picture we imagine a dark-skinned person from West Africa and a pale-skinned northern European standing at either end of this group, the European at the light end and the West African at the dark end. Taking a close look at the variety of phenotypic features present, what reason is there for categorizing everyone but the European as black? What logical reason is there for not categorizing everyone but the West African as white? Some persons in this group will be much closer to the northern European in skin shade and features than they are to the West African, and for others the opposite will be true. Indeed, some will be extremely light skinned, with West African phenotypic features, whereas for others the reverse will hold, and of course many people in this group will simply fall somewhere between the two. Nevertheless, most Americans will deem it obvious and take for granted that only the European is white and all the others are black. In fact, the above illustration is nothing less than a visual representation of what the term *black* signifies.

Yet how can this be? Reason dictates that if we are going to divide these people into two groups based on biology or ancestry, we should utilize some sort of reliable and consistent means of doing so. If skin color does not result in a sensible binary grouping (and it clearly does not), we could substitute an alternative criterion such as nose shape. Using that as our criterion we would discover that like skin color, the noses change shape from wide and flat to long and narrow—but very importantly, they change shape completely independently of skin color, so we may well have an extremely dark person with a nose as thin and narrow, or even thinner and narrower, than the European's. Using a single criterion, there is no way to justify the traditional racial groupings. Adding more criteria, such as combining skin color, nose shape, and hair texture, makes it even more impossible to arrange people consistently, based on appearance, into the traditional racial groups. Even an explicit focus on so-called black Africans yields immediate difficulty for traditional racial grouping, for the typical Somali or Ethiopian phenotype will differ markedly from the typical West African phenotype, which will again differ radically from the typical Khoisan phenotype.[4]

What does it mean if such counterintuitive cases pose no problem for the American racial paradigm? What it means is that racial categorization is not a logical activity but rather a learned response to particular, selected, visual cues. All of our original ninety-eight people have some amount of African ancestry, and most of them have significant amounts of European and other ancestries as well. It is no more justified to class them as black than it is to class them as white. It is necessary to situate oneself outside the race construct in order to appreciate the tremendous degree to which it is lacking in logical consistency and classificatory validity. Marvin Harris argues that "all racial identity, scientifically speaking, is ambiguous. Wherever certainty is expressed on this subject, we can be confident that society has manufactured a social lie in order to help one of its segments take advantage of another. By what ingenious computation is the genetic tracery of a million years of evolution unraveled and each man assigned his proper social box?"[5]

The answer to this question, in the history of the United States, can be found in the form of *hypodescent,* also known as the *one-drop rule.*[6] In the context of a society characterized by superordinate and subordinate groups, hypodescent works to ensure that the offspring of any union between these several different groups always assumes the identity and status of the lower-ranked group (*hypo* meaning *under* or *lower*).[7] Moreover, in the United States specifically, hypodescent refers to the social mechanism whereby, in order to preserve the illusion of a bipolar racial structure, anyone with any known or detectable African ancestry, no matter the extent of European or other ancestry, is categorized as all and only black. Although hypodescent could in theory be deployed in other scenarios of racial mixture, it effectively comes into play in the United States only in cases of black/white mixture. From the perspective of the overall social schema in America, what matters most is neither mixture among non-white groups nor mixture between whites and Asians or Native Americans (although these mixtures may certainly prove problematic in the first and immediately succeeding generations); rather, what is crucial is that whiteness not include any trace of African ancestry.[8] In other words, the revelation that an ostensibly white individual has a Native American or Asian grandparent would in no sense engender the depth and urgency of identity questioning and calls for recategorization that would accompany the revelation that the grandparent in question was instead Afro-American.[9] The primary function of hypodescent is to guard against this latter possibility.

Gunnar Myrdal, although writing a generation prior to the first use of the term *hypodescent,* nevertheless provides a perfect definition of the word by explaining that "the 'Negro race' is defined in America by the white people. It is defined in terms of parentage. Everybody having a *known* trace of Negro blood in his veins—no matter how far back it was acquired—is classified as a Negro. No amount of white ancestry, except one hundred per cent, will permit entrance to the white race."[10]

Under hypodescent, the problem of categorizing racially mixed offspring is resolved by their being assigned to the lower-ranking group. In this way the artificial racial categorization of the black group is reproduced over and over, despite mixture with whites and others, while the myth of biological racial purity is thereby simultaneously maintained for the white group. As Harris points out: "That a half-white should be a Negro rather than a white cannot be explained by rational argument. . . . The rule of hypo-descent is, therefore, an invention which we in the United States have made in order to keep biological facts from intruding into our collective racist fantasies."[11]

Ultimately, a person is white if she has no distinguishing markers (especially those perceived as African-derived) that point to non-whiteness. Although physical characteristics such as nonkinky hair, a narrow nose, and a relatively low level of melanin may provide cumulative evidence for whiteness, a serious suggestion of African ancestry, whether observable in a physical way or not, is always enough to overcome the somatic presentation and to paint the person as black. Thus, only in the absence of any disqualifying criteria is a person safely white. This strict code ensures that whiteness remains invisible, and makes problems of race the problems of other (non-white) people. The function of the American racial system is to maintain this exclusionary distinction between whites and non-whites, and especially between whites and blacks. Arguing for an understanding of whiteness as a form of property, Cheryl Harris links the two by asserting that "whiteness and property share a common premise—a conceptual nucleus—of a right to exclude."[12] The notion of exclusivity is echoed by Stephen Satris's argument that "this racial system is not a matter of classifying people according to their predominant ancestry but rather a matter of screening the population for those who will be admitted into an exclusive 'white' group."[13]

Unpacking and analyzing the notion of race reveals the way people place this hegemonic engine of exclusivity into operation without even realizing what they are doing. For instance, common opinion has it that a so-called black/white racially mixed person is obviously black. One just has to look to see the black or African features. Whether it is skin tone or hair texture or the shape of the eyes, the evidence is supposedly clear that the said person is black, and therefore not white. Yet how sensible is this common perception? I would argue against the rationality of this belief by asserting that it is neither natural nor obvious that such a person is black, but that the categorization is instead an artifact of the way Americans *learn* race. Americans learn to see that a khaki-colored person with a narrow nose and slightly kinky hair is obviously black. They learn to see that this person looks more black than white, and obviously so. Yet the only obvious conclusion should be that such characterizations are nonsense. The decision to place a person who shares features or has intermediate features, for instance, in one but not both groups is in no sense obvious or natural. Here I realize that I am arguing against what appears to be common sense, and I have selected the following several examples in order to demonstrate the irrational way we allow race to cloud what should be our better judgment.

Suppose we have a white parent, a black parent, and their child. Suppose as well that we choose to focus on three phenotypic features. The white parent is extremely pale, with a thin nose and very straight hair. The black parent is extremely dark, with a broad nose and very kinky hair. I want to propose two hypothetical scenarios here. First, imagine that the child is exactly intermediate between the two parents in each of the selected phenotypic features. Her skin color is a light-to-medium brown, her nose exactly intermediate in shape, and her hair loosely curly. Now by what logic is it possible to assert that the child is obviously black and obviously not white? If phenotypic features determine race, there is no consistent way to place this child in one race or the other. Yet in the United States there is no problem whatsoever in doing so. Furthermore, if we suggest a second scenario in which the child's features are not evenly divided but instead are weighted by two-thirds on the side of the white parent, it will still be obvious in America that the child is black. In fact, the only way the child's race could possibly be ambiguous is if she appears to have inherited practically no phenotypic features at all from the black parent.

What is operating here is, of course, hypodescent, and far from being a commonsense way of categorizing people, it is instead an expression of power mediated through the myth of white racial purity. Because of the way whiteness is mythologically pure and invisible, it takes only a single black phenotypic feature—any hint of African descent—to cause otherwise reasonable people to deem it obvious that the subject is not white. I purposely fashioned the above examples using a child with one white and one black parent in order to make the point clear, but the example extends to practically all Afro-Americans, the vast majority of whom no longer look like their West African ancestors of roughly 200 to 400 years ago. Their current wide range of phenotypic features is the result of population mixture and continuous internal miscegenation. Were we to ask an alien observer unfamiliar with the American system of racial categorization and hypodescent whether each of the ninety-eight Afro-Americans in our earlier example more closely resembled the West African or the northern European, most Americans would undoubtedly be surprised by the resulting objective classifications.

Reversing the current racial power relation will bring the irrationality of race into even sharper focus. Imagine a civilization of very dark-skinned people marginalizing a pale-skinned minority who perhaps in times past were their slaves. Imagine that these people call themselves blacks and whites respectively. Should children be born of occasional intergroup liaisons, would those children be assigned to the white group or the black? If this civilization has the same race concept Americans do, the answer is obvious. The black group is in power and will marginalize the pale group based on nothing more than physical appearance and ancestry. The best way to ensure that current relations of power and privilege are retained is to declare any mixed persons white, no matter what in-between shade of color they actually are.

It is important to see that, in this hypothetical scenario of power and abuse, the dominant blacks, whose skin color might vary but would still tend to be rather dark (the way the skin color of American whites varies but is still relatively light), would find it obvious that their mixed offspring are white, since it is the pale portion of the offspring's genetic constitution that makes them lighter than the dominant black group and that gives them their in-between features. Those in-between features would be interpreted as cues of whiteness, so that the same person who is obviously black in America would be obviously white in our example here. That these hypothetical offspring are the result of population mixture is indisputable. What is arbitrary is their being assigned to the lower-status group based solely on the evidence of that mixture. The issue for our hypothetical civilization, and for Americans as well, is relative power.[14]

Race and Racism: Connections and Disconnections

Even though biological race does not exist, its ideological deployment has had, and continues to have, real and significant effects on people's lives. In the United States, people's lives merge together and are torn apart by race every day. Although there may be some question as to precisely when race acquired the pseudobiological meaning it possesses today, somatic and ancestral differentiation have been used to enslave, murder, and otherwise oppress Native Americans, Africans, Afro-Americans, and others in North America for hundreds of years.[15] I want to be quite explicit here in acknowledging the evil that has been and is still being done because of the idea of race. Real people are hurt and real people suffer because of hatred and discrimination based on the false notion that persons belong to different racial groups. However, to deny that race exists is neither to deny people's pain nor to pretend that there is no phenotypic variety in humans based on ancestry.

I want to be clear as well that antiracial philosophy is not a call to ignore the reality of racism but rather a challenge to cease giving credence to the false belief that makes racism possible. That darker-skinned people in the United States are more often the victims of discrimination based on phenotype is indisputable. What must be disputed is the idea behind this discrimination that it is somehow reasonable to classify people based on an inconsistent appeal to phenotype. This will not by itself eliminate racism, of course, but given that race is a scientific fallacy, it is surely more productive to move away from the false idea of race than to continue endorsing it. Frankly, this is where many well-meaning critics of antiracialism simply miss the point. Being themselves so wrapped up in the idea of race, they cannot conceive of challenging it or of making the conceptual distinction between race and racism. So they reply, "But if we simply ignore race, we won't be able to know when racism is being practiced, because by saying that race doesn't exist there would then be no Afro-Americans and no racial statistics." This typical response is worth considering in greater detail.

The statement is inadequate for three reasons. First, it presents antiracial philosophy in the false guise of ignoring race, when in fact antiracialism is concerned with eliminating the false idea of race, not ignoring it. The subtle difference is that the stance of ignoring race presumes that race really exists but should be ignored, whereas the stance of eliminating the false idea of race takes into account the fact that race is a myth that must be exposed for the fallacy it is.

Second, the response fails to distinguish between the unreality of race and the reality of racism. By failing to understand that the hatred and bigotry of racism are based on a biological fallacy, the statement thereby reifies the racial myth. Race could in theory exist without racism, but racism certainly cannot exist without a prior notion of race. Would the same critics of antiracialism assert that there really was a species of being in Salem, Massachusetts, that could be classified under the category *witch,* and that witches actually existed with all their supposed powers, just because there was antiwitch paranoia in 1692? If the answer is "no," then why do these critics insist that race must be real because of racism, or that racism cannot be fought without giving credence to race?

Finally, the criticism that antiracialism would lead to the disappearance of Afro-Americans is simply not credible. There would obviously still be the same phenotypic diversity among Americans that we witness now. The difference is that we would finally be informed enough to understand that the very fact of this diversity argues conclusively against the notion that Americans can each be placed into a singular, mutually exclusive, and distinct category, as if massive genetic mixing had not occurred in the former British North American colonies. The indisputable genetic fact is that the people categorized as black in the United States are not just Afro-American; they are also Euro-American, often with more European ancestry than African. Rather than being forced to pretend that they are all and only African-descended, those now considered black would be able finally to claim the full range of their various heritages. Such a paradigm shift might also encourage white-appearing persons to acknowledge African or other heritages, should such be the case.

It is worth asking, however, whether there is any substance to concerns that certain kinds of data obtained via racial statistics may become unavailable should race finally be eliminated. This is a valid concern, and as I will argue in Chapters 2 and 6, it imposes on racial skeptics the responsibility of finding a way to move beyond race without undermining the ability to track discrimination and other important social phenomena. But there is a counterconcern as well: the danger of reinscribing race through the use of racial statistics, which so often obscure the real causes of social problems.

From the incidence of Human Immunodeficiency Virus (HIV) to low birth weights, racial statistics too often screen other, more important factors. In the case of low birth weight, for instance, how much do racial statistics reveal about class, education, or region? Popular opinion holds that Afro-American women have smaller babies due to genetic factors. It may be true statistically that Afro-American women as a group tend to give birth to babies with lower weights, but what do such data mean when issues of class and education are factored in? What proportion of upper-class Afro-American women have low birth-weight babies compared to lower-class Afro-American women? What proportion of upper-class Afro-American women are knowledgeable about and have easy access to prenatal health care compared to lower-class Afro-American women? Although racism is certainly a significant factor when considering health outcomes, it is not the only factor and may not even be the most important one, while race is not a factor at all (although specific family history might be, as I will discuss more fully in Chapter 4).

There is also the concern that an individual's disavowal of race will not necessarily result in sudden freedom from racist oppression. This is of course true, but racial skepticism is not an overnight cure for racism. The goal is not just to have minorities acknowledge the emptiness of race but for the concept's fallaciousness to become a universal principle, just as the Earth being neither flat nor the center of the universe are now universal principles. If we imagine initial medieval European reactions to the Earth's roundness and position in the universe, and compare them to our geological and astronomical understandings today, we see how even the most deeply ingrained beliefs can be changed through education and the passage of time.

People will not instantly disavow the race concept, but children can be taught the scientific truths that their parents never accepted, and they can then develop a firm basis for maintaining that knowledge as they grow older and teach their own children. Individuals who reject the race concept will of course continue to suffer from racism as long as persons who do not reject the concept remain, but this obscures the larger picture. Such cases of lingering racism are not a compelling argument for endorsing the notion of race but rather are an incentive to redouble efforts to upend and supersede the racial false consciousness that is the foundation of racist ideology. In the end we must ask if we would really rather continue to validate a fallacy merely because a diminishing number of holdouts insist on clinging to an erroneous pseudoscientific paradigm that was established more than a quarter-millennium ago and that has remained unchanged ever since.

Racist discrimination can be fought without giving further credence to the idea of race. The antiracialist is not interested in ignoring racism, but rather is vitally concerned with opposing racism. One of the many tools used in this fight is the exposure of race as a biological myth. It is true that Afro-Americans statistically are more likely to suffer various social ills, ranging from higher unemployment to a vastly disproportionate representation in the penal system to lower incomes. But, far from proving the existence of race, these prove instead that the false idea of race combined with racist hatred can be mediated through the social and political structure to produce huge inequalities and horrors. The attempt to undermine the basis of this hatred—the fallacious racial paradigm—should be considered neither questionable nor controversial, but should be seen as the very least we can do in the fight against racism. Amy Gutman says as much when she warns that "human psychology being what it is, the moral case against racial injustice is unlikely to be effective if people continue to believe in the fiction of distinguishable human races."[16]

In reality, it is impossible to construct a workable taxonomic system with which to consistently capture and arrange the marvel of human diversity. This inability is a logical and scientific fact. That people nonetheless attempt to do so, and that they utilize the resulting fallacious racial classifications to express their fear and hatred, is indisputable. It is critical, however, not to slip from this very important realization into a corollary acceptance of race itself as a reality. To do so is to fall into *reification,* the "fallacy of taking abstractions and regarding them as actually existing entities that are causally efficacious and ontologically prior to and superior to their referents."[17] This is precisely what people who assert the reality of race do.

Although the effects of people's belief in race, and the effects of racism, are real and often violent, it is crucial to maintain a distinction between belief and reality, between mythology and the effects of mythology, between the process of reification and the phenomenon reified. The reality of racism does no more to validate the existence of race than the reality of Galileo's censure by the Roman Inquisition for teaching Copernican theory did to validate the notion that the

Earth is the center of the universe. At the same time, it is abundantly clear that hatred—indeed, entire belief systems—need not be based on truth in order to have profound effects. Witch-hunting paranoia and murder no more required actual witches than did Southern lynching require Afro-Americans who were actually criminals. Racism and other forms of bigotry are no proofs of the false belief, hatred, ignorance, and intolerance they feed upon and spread. To assert that race is real because of racism, or that antiracialism should not be pursued because of racism, is to fall victim to the most perfect hegemony, for far from being the proof of the race concept, racism is instead its ugly result.

Nevertheless, it is often said in regard to the claim that race does not exist that such a view implies that racism is imagined and that one is therefore not properly concerned with issues such as discrimination, economic disparity, hatred, self-hatred, and violence. But this is an inaccurate criticism because it treats race and racism as interchangeable when they are in fact quite different from each other. This criticism of antiracialism misses the very important distinction between a false belief and the evil undertaken as a result of that belief. Indeed, racism and race are as different as two things can be, for one exists while the other does not.

It is critical to maintain the distinction that I am drawing between race and racism. These are not the same thing, but are bound together in a particular relation to each other. Racism depends on a belief in race but not in any sense on the reality of race. Just as people once hated who they thought were witches, many people today hate who they think are members of different racial groups. Popular opinion and conventional wisdom may recoil initially from such a pronouncement of contingency, but when the concept of race is interrogated, and belief separated from reality, race emerges as a fantasy—no more real than a winged horse or a view of fifteenth- and sixteenth-century North America as an unpopulated wilderness.[18] Race is as nonexistent as sea monsters, the flat Earth, and the geocentric universe. These are all things that people have at one time believed in, and they highlight that the reality of the belief and the unreality of the physical phenomenon are two wholly different things.

At the close of the twentieth century, many debates grounded in the subject of race are raging in the United States. Some of them, such as the ethics of affirmative action and hiring preferences, and the constitutionality of racially configured voting districts, involve serious economic and social consequences. What these disputes all share is the presumption that race is a meaningful method of categorizing human beings. The underlying logic is the idea that what we call racial differences can tell us useful things about people and can help us sort people into distinct, exclusive, and logically consistent categories. In regard to this book's thesis in particular, any consideration of a federal multiracial category requires a thorough interrogation of the race concept on which such a category would necessarily rest. A historical review of how race has developed in America will facilitate this critical examination.

American Racial History

What is race? There are a variety of definitions and criteria to which one can appeal: breeding population, gene structure, geographic ancestry, skin color, head shape, ethnic group, and blood quanta are but a few of the many paradigms people have employed to categorize the diversity of human types we see around us. They are all inadequate, of course. There is no single criterion, or any possible group of criteria, that can categorize people into what we take to be the traditional racial groups in the United States. These groups are, in hegemonic descending order: whites, Asians, Native Americans, and blacks.[19] At times, Native Americans (based on the theory that they are descended from Asians who embarked on Ice Age migrations across the Bering land bridge) may be subsumed under the Asian group, and at other times both Asians and Native Americans may disappear completely from the American racial landscape, leaving only blacks and whites in a seemingly never-ending binary opposition. Indeed, in the United States, blacks and whites are in a binary opposition even when the other racial groups are recognized, since the American racial construct is a hierarchical scale, with whites most valued at one end and blacks least valued at the other. Although not representing a true symbiotic relationship, the twin ideas of whites and blacks are nevertheless fully dependent on each other for their existence. In similar fashion, the idea of race in America is absolutely dependent on them both.

The particular relation of blacks and whites in America finds its genesis in slavery, for when the American unfree labor system evolved from being one that was part slavery (both indigenous and African) and part indentured servitude to one that contained only slaves, it gradually became a system in which only Africans and their descendants could be enslaved. Whiteness as an identity, as a category that superseded other categories such as Englishness or class status, was therefore created simultaneously as the antithesis to perpetual, hereditary bondage, and thus to blackness. As Cheryl Harris puts it: "The ideological and rhetorical move from 'slave' and 'free' to 'Black' and 'white' as polar constructs marked an important step in the social construction of race."[20]

Whereas Englishmen in the North American colonies had once made a distinction between themselves and Africans on the basis of religion (i.e., *Christian* versus *heathen*) the institution of chattel slavery provided the means to shift the distinction to one residing in physical appearance rather than religion.[21] Thus, as Winthrop Jordan notes, as a result of the institutional solidification of American chattel slavery, whites were in a sense begotten by the creation of blacks: "Most suggestive of all, there seems to have been something of a shift during the seventeenth century in the terminology which Englishmen in the colonies applied to themselves. From the initially most common term *Christian,* at mid-century there was a marked drift toward *English* and *free*. After about 1680, taking the colonies as a whole, a new term appeared—white."[22] Adding support to this view,

Ashley Montagu reports that "the first recorded use of the phrase 'Negro slave' occurs in a document issued 30 March 1660."[23]

It would be a mistake to see this as the sole beginning of racial classification, however. This particular kind of designation, which might be termed *popular,* would find itself bolstered eventually by European natural philosophers working in the Enlightenment field of natural history. The classificatory schemes resulting from their work were the genesis of what would later, after a shift from Enlightenment natural history to post-Enlightenment biology, become scientific racial classification. So, although the English in America may have begun to distinguish themselves from their African slaves solely on the basis of color, it would take the respected endeavors of European natural philosophers to provide the empirical content for these popular distinctions and transform them into "true" racial classifications. Therefore, even while noting the emergence in the late-seventeenth-century English North American colonies of what we would today term racial language, it is nonetheless justified to begin an inquiry into the scientific construction of race in the United States by locating the origins of American racial classification in early-eighteenth-century Europe.

Michel Foucault provides insight into this post-Renaissance era, which he terms the "Classical age":

> In the eighteenth century, the historical *a priori* that provided the basis for inquiry into or controversy about the existence of genera, the stability of species, and the transmission of characters from generation to generation, was the existence of a natural history: the organization of a certain visible existence as a domain of knowledge, the definition of the four variables of description, the constitution of an area of adjacencies in which any individual being whatever can find its place. Natural history in the Classical age is not merely the discovery of a new object of curiosity; it covers a series of complex operations that introduce the possibility of a constant order into a totality of representations.[24]

It was during this period that Carolus Linnaeus, in his *Systema Naturae* (1735), began placing virtually every living thing into a category. The world of the western Europeans was expanding rapidly as an ongoing result of an era of intensive voyaging and exploration. During this period (which arguably began with the Portuguese defeat of the Moors at Ceuta in 1415, initiating the chain of events leading to extensive Portuguese exploration of West Africa), western European intellectuals, their horizons broadened by the explorers' discoveries, as well as by the artifacts brought back as trophies of Europeans' burgeoning imperial ambitions, had a strong urge to compartmentalize the swiftly growing store of knowledge from around the world. This urge can be seen in Linnaeus, who, as Jordan notes, categorized plants, animals, people, diseases, and clouds, among other things.[25]

In the case of humans, Linnaeus theorized four existing types: (Native) American, European, Asiatic, and African; and two fanciful types: Wild Man and Monstrosus.[26] Linnaeus was certainly influenced by an ethnocentric bias in making these classifications; yet, although the characteristics that Linnaeus gave the African were at the farthest remove by modern standards from those of the European, Jordan argues that "Linnaeus' categories were not hierarchical; they were merely confusing. . . . Thus while there were hints of ranking in the Linnaean approach, the concept of hierarchy was never really developed."[27]

The significant thing about Linnaeus's system of classification as opposed to the types of scientific classification that followed it was that, except for hints that humans stood above the apes in the classification of living things, his system was concerned with categories, not hierarchy. Nor was his famous follower, Johann Friedrich Blumenbach, intent on constructing a system of racial hierarchy via scientific classification. Blumenbach did, however, make certain refinements to Linnaeus's work that opened the door to subsequent scientific racial hierarchies.

Blumenbach thought that Caucasians must be the original people of the divine creation and that other racial groups were departures from this original form.[28] So, in revising the four-race Linnaean system, he added a category (Malays), placed Caucasians at the center, and posited two symmetrical lines of departure: on the one hand, Asians with Native Americans intermediate, and on the other, Africans with Malays intermediate. What came out of this European-centered structure and remains with us to this day was a sense of somatic distance between Europeans and Africans that would prove essential to later formulations of the race concept. From the perspective of northern Europeans especially, the sense of somatic distance on the European–Native American–Asian side was never as great or as persistent as the perceived distance between Europeans and Africans on the other. In Blumenbach's defense, it can be said that he "believed in the mental and moral equality of all peoples" and evinced only a slight ethnocentrism in the design of his symmetrical system.[29] As Jordan puts it: "The white man was the 'primeval' type and stood at the center; but there was no indication that he was on top."[30]

However, the historical implication of Blumenbach's revision was to prove more ominous when, several generations later, Western epistemology moved out of the era of natural history and into the era of biology. Arguing that "natural history, in the Classical period, cannot be established as biology," Foucault explains that until "the end of the eighteenth century, in fact, life does not exist: only living beings."[31] There are no absolute demarcations among these differing epistemological frameworks, however, and one may therefore see occasional traces of biological fixity in the natural history era as well as remnants of Enlightenment epistemology in the scientific era. Still, partly as a result of this shift, the practice of categorizing groups of people by their visible characteristics was ultimately transformed in the nineteenth century into a more permanent differentiation among these groups—which, while still appealing to somatic cues, went much deeper to claim both permanence and a timeless hierarchy. What is important to note here is that what would ultimately be termed scientific racial categorization originated under the framework of the earlier era and made the transition to the modern era, changing along with the epistemological background of the period. The ease with which racial categorizers adapted their fictions to newer paradigms, even as the older ones they had previously depended on fell away, is a key to the dogged survival of the race construct even today.

From the European perspective, cultural differences between Europeans and Africans were seen to be as great as the perceived somatic differences between them. For some, this alone was proof that Africans and Europeans were two distinct species, despite the difficulty presented by the fact that the two could mate and produce fertile offspring. It was somatic distance, however, that determined the future course of racial ranking, for phenotype alone came to serve as the criterion for categorization and ranking, standing as a sign for all other important traits, such as intelligence, temperament, and industriousness. Thus was ushered in an age of almost frantic measurement and categorization, as natural philosophers and protoscientists worked feverishly to find differences between blacks and whites. As Western epistemology began to move beyond the natural history period, racial philosophy would find itself shackled to two centuries of seeking to prove a priori racial conclusions in the name of scientific objectivity.

It will be useful to pause and take note of the effects of this obsession with categorization. Audrey Smedley provides the following account of the consequences of European racial categorization:

1. [The categories] gave an aura of permanence and rigidity to conceptions of human group differences. Once something is classified, it is set irretrievably in time and space, with a tendency to be transmitted to others as a fixed and unalterable entity.
2. The categories, as drawn up, seem to accept without question the linkage of physical characteristics with behavioral ones, along with such psychocultural features as temperament, disposition, and moral character. Such fusion, we have seen, was a trend in the general popular thought of the times; hence it documents the growing strength of this component of the racial worldview in the minds of both the classifiers and their readers.
3. [The categories] ignored, as Jonathan Marks has pointed out, "the geographically gradual nature of biological diversity" as well as the cultural realities that do not accord with presumed biological boundaries.
4. The classifications easily lent themselves to hierarchical structuring, fostering an impression of inequality among the different groups, with the most positive and progressive cultural features associated with Europeans and the least positive ones associated with those called "savages." This clearly fit well with the still expanding racial worldview and accorded with social, economic, and political realities.

5. Finally, such classifications by reputable and highly renowned scientists (naturalists) as Linnaeus and Blumenbach made mankind part of the natural order of things. They thus legitimized as "natural" and God-given the inferior qualities ascribed to non-Europeans and helped to justify their lower positions in world societies. In other words, they tended to provide scientific sanction and scholarly credibility for prevailing popular images and stereotypes of non-Europeans.[32]

I have sought to situate the origins of the contemporary American racial construct in earlier centuries because the racial thoughts and ideas that carried the day in the eighteenth century, and that evolved into the racist ideas of the nineteenth century, were still the driving forces well into the twentieth century. Although the specific debates of earlier centuries may not themselves have still been in vogue in an overt sense, the implications derived from them—hierarchical human ranking, separate creation or massive retrogression, and the like—still operated as a background fabric in the minds of the scientific and lay communities. Gunnar Myrdal points out that it is difficult to escape such cultural assumptions, since:

There must be still other countless errors of the same sort that no living man can yet detect, because of the fog within which our type of Western culture envelops us. Cultural influences have set up the assumptions about the mind, the body, and the universe with which we begin; pose the questions we ask; influence the facts we seek; determine the interpretation we give these facts; and direct our reaction to these interpretations and conclusions.[33]

The northern European natural philosophers who worked so determinedly to distance themselves from Africans had come into large-scale contact with them much later than their southern European and Mediterranean counterparts. Perhaps because these latter had, in some measure, been in contact with sub-Saharan Africans for close to a thousand years, they did not share the northern obsession to *explain* the African. After all, the Mediterranean slave trade from antiquity through the late Middle Ages included North Africans, sub-Saharan Africans, and southern Europeans as principal participants. Moreover, the centuries-long hostilities between Christian Iberians and the Moors (who, in their periods of dominance in Iberia, would have imported a considerable number of sub-Saharan Africans as domestic servants) ensured further that southern Europeans would not suffer the same kind of culture shock as their northern counterparts upon voyaging to West Africa.[34]

Frank Snowden reports that:

In the Mediterranean world the black man was seldom a strange, unknown being. In this respect the ancient situation differed strikingly, for example, from that in coun-

tries such as England, where the powerful impact the Africans' color made upon sixteenth-century Englishmen resulted from the abrupt nature of their contacts with
blacks: one of the fairest nations on earth was suddenly brought face to face with one
of the blackest of mankind.[35]

Jordan makes a similar point regarding African-English contact, arguing that "the
most arresting characteristic of the newly discovered African was his color.
. . . Englishmen actually described Negroes as *black*—an exaggerated term which
in itself suggests that the Negro's complexion had powerful impact upon their
perceptions."[36]

Jordan argues that the reactions of English colonists to Negroes (which led to
the unique form of racial slavery that existed in America until the end of the Civil
War) were predetermined by the reactions of Englishmen to Africans at the time
the English first became involved in the African slave trade, more than fifty years
before the sustained English influx into North America. Jordan also suggests that
before the English general public became familiar with Africans, they had such a
negative predisposition to the color black that unfavorable personal comparisons
with dark-skinned West Africans were practically inevitable. He posits the English negative predisposition to the color black as one of the primary reasons for
the distinct character of English slavery in North America vis-à-vis that of the
colonial settlements of other European powers in the Americas.[37] The
black/white binary hierarchy, the relative difficulty of manumission and consequent integration into the dominant society, and the lack of intermediate racial
categories (except in Charleston, South Carolina, and New Orleans, which were
heavily influenced by free and slave immigration from Barbados and Santo
Domingo, respectively) were distinctive of English North American slavery. Contemporary U.S. formulations of race are the legacy of that distinctiveness.

In addition, Cheryl Harris links property, race, and oppression in the early English colonial period. She argues that "the origins of property rights in the United
States are rooted in racial domination. Even in the early years of the country, it
was not the concept of race alone that operated to oppress Blacks and Indians;
rather, it was the *interaction* between conceptions of race and property that
played a critical role in establishing and maintaining racial and economic subor-
dination."[38]

Seeing protoscientific racial categorization as rooted in a specific set of circumstances—including European exploitation of material and human resources,
differing scenarios of contact, a European-felt need to categorize the enormous
amount of information becoming available as a result of exploration, and the rise
of North American slavery—demystifies the concept, allowing us to analyze and
challenge it. Without a sense of the race concept's contingent character, it can
seem a natural and unquestionable part of our world. One aspect of this contingency is the fact that the race concept and racial prejudice are relatively recent
ideas, coming into real focus only in the past 400 years or so.[39] Michael Omi and

Howard Winant make explicit the link between the dawn of racial categorization and the beginnings of rapid and extensive European exploitation of West Africa and the Americas: "The identification of distinctive human groups, and their association with differences in physical appearance, goes back to prehistory, and can be found in the earliest documents—in the Bible, for example, or in Herodotus. But the emergence of a modern conception of race does not occur until the rise of Europe and the arrival of Europeans in the Americas."[40]

The biological categorization of humans into racial groups is not inevitable, nor is it necessary for a logical understanding of the world. In Snowden's view, "nothing comparable to the virulent color prejudice of modern times existed in the ancient world. . . . The ancients did not fall into the error of biological racism; black skin color was not a sign of inferiority; Greeks and Romans did not establish color as an obstacle to integration in society; and ancient society was one that for all its faults and failures never made color the basis for judging a man."[41]

This is not to suggest that these ancient cultures ought to be emulated in all respects, for they certainly generated their share of injustice and inhumanity; rather, I am pointing to the fact that while the ancients dealt with each other on friendly and also on hostile terms, they never developed the sense of biological-protobiological race that so defines the history of the United States. Jack Forbes relates a similar view for a later period in Europe:

> It seems quite likely that most Christian Europeans of the late medieval period paid relatively little attention to human skin color, except as an aid in the identification of a fugitive or as one of several ways to describe an individual. Human beings were still understood to be all descended from Adam and Eve. Thus all human beings, in the biblical tradition, were of the same "race" or stock. Some had become tanned or burned by the sun of the equatorial zone, but the variations were not of fundamental significance. Most slaves and serfs were "white" and of the same color (at birth) as were the ruling classes. . . . Concern was directed towards developing a very few terms to describe people of intermediate color (between black and white). There was apparently no concern or need to identify persons of "mixed race" since the concept of "race" (as we know it) did not exist and "race" mixture among humans was not an existent concept.[42]

A great deal of work was done by natural philosophers in their attempts to measure and prove the foreordained conclusion of Negro deficiency and, therefore, racial difference, and I again wish to draw attention to the movement from the epistemology of natural history, in which, according to Foucault, "the critical question concerned the basis for resemblance and the existence of the genus," to that of biology.[43] Commenting on this movement away from the natural history frame of reference and toward a modern notion of biology, Robyn Wiegman argues:

The epistemology of the visual that enables natural history is thus displaced (though not abandoned) by an emphasis on the organic nature of the body, on its invisibly organized and seemingly definitive biological functioning. It is this emphasis on race as a constituted "fact" of the body—as a truth that not only can but must be pursued beyond the realm of visible similarities and differences—that characterizes the methodological proclivities of the modern episteme, and it is under its disciplinary gaze that an elaborate discourse purporting the African's inherent inhumanity is most productively, though not originally, waged.[44]

The shift from a natural history view that, although classifying different human groups, nevertheless saw their constitutions as somewhat flexible and open to mutability, toward a biologistic view that operated from the premise that the different human groups were fixed and hierarchical, was a significant step in further cementing the notion of race in the Western consciousness. Wiegman continues: "In the ascendancy of biology . . . the concept of 'race' will undergo significant transformation, losing the kind of fluidity it achieved in natural history as a product of climate and civilization, as a variation within the human species, to become a rather stable and primary characteristic for defining the nature of the body, both its organic and ontological consistency."[45]

For an account of scientific thought about race in mid-nineteenth-century America that serves to illustrate the depth of the idea that race was a fixed phenomenon, we can turn to the noted physician Samuel Cartwright, who in an 1851 article in *De Bow's Review* (an antebellum magazine that published articles on economic as well as political issues) asserted that "it is not only in the skin that a difference of color exists between the negro and the white man, but in the membranes, the muscles, the tendons, and in all the fluids and secretions. Even the negro's brain and nerves, the chyle and all the humors, are tinctured with a shade of the pervading darkness. His bile is of a deeper color, and his blood is blacker than a white man's."[46]

Cartwright extended his analysis beyond the medical field to the cultural arena as well:

It is this defective hematosis, or atmospherization of the blood, conjoined with a deficiency of cerebral matter in the cranium, and an excess of nervous matter distributed to the organs of sensation and assimilation, that is the true cause of that debasement of mind, which has rendered the people of Africa unable to take care of themselves. It is the true cause of their indolence and apathy, and why they have chosen, through countless ages, idleness, misery and barbarism, to industry and frugality,—why social industry, or associated labor, so essential to all progress in civilization and improvement, has never made any progress among them, or the arts and sciences taken root on any portion of African soil inhabited by them; as is proved by the fact that no letters, or even hieroglyphics—no buildings, roads or improvements, or monuments of any kind, are anywhere found, to indicate that they have ever been awakened from their apathy and sleepy indolence, to physical or mental exertion.[47]

This passage serves to illustrate one of the central flaws of biological racialism—that racial science has always been illegitimatized by the failure to acknowledge that it originates in sociocultural presumptions that cannot help but be proven correct because biased, a priori value judgments are taken for granted by the researcher. One can hardly expect to conduct objective research if one believes that one's subject is a hopelessly degraded race that has wasted the perfection of God's creation. Likewise, one cannot expect to achieve objective results when instead of asking "What is the difference between the Negro group and the white group?" one asks "What differences can we find to explain why the Negro group is so absolutely degraded as compared to the white group?"

It is precisely this kind of thinking, begun by those northern Europeans who had had the least prior experience with sub-Saharan Africans and who had to travel the farthest to reach Africa (the result of these two factors being a culture shock that emphasized the somatic distance between the northern European explorers and the indigenous sub-Saharan Africans), that remained the basis of racial science well into the twentieth century. Most of Cartwright's conclusions may now be in disrepute, but his assumption that there are separate races that can be arranged hierarchically is still accepted widely today. As we shall see, racist science may since have been supplanted by other paradigms, but *racial* science, the presumption of categorical and consistently classifiable differences between groups of people, is still at the heart of popular opinion.

From the time of Cartwright's article to the end of the nineteenth century, science continued to use numbers and measurements to shore up its foregone conclusions. Craniology and criminal anthropology rose to take their places alongside prognathism and atavism in the halls of racial science. These developments led to what was likely the zenith of racist science in the late nineteenth century in terms of its public credibility and pervasiveness. In Smedley's analysis:

The wedding of scientific and folk beliefs was now complete. From the mid-nineteenth century on, science provided the bases for the ideological elements of a comprehensive worldview summed up in the term "race." Numerous scholars of the late nineteenth and early twentieth centuries occupied themselves not only in tediously researching the nature of human differences but also in interpreting how these differences reflected the inequality of the races.[48]

The twentieth century witnessed the toppling of the racist biological paradigm. A number of factors were involved, including (but certainly not limited to) the rise of sociology as a field of study, scientific reaction to the explicit racism of Nazi ideology, and especially the advent of genetics, which has found ways to

turn traditional racial categorizations on their heads. Discussing the effects of sociology and ethnicity on race theory, Omi and Winant conclude:

> By the early decades of the twentieth century biologism was losing coherence. It had
> come under attack by adherents of progressivism, and had also been called into
> question by the work of the "Chicago school" of sociology. . . . In contrast to biolog-
> ically oriented approaches, the ethnicity-based paradigm was an insurgent theory
> which suggested that race was a *social* category. Race was but one of a number of de-
> terminants of ethnic group identity or ethnicity. Ethnicity itself was understood as
> the result of a group formation process based on culture and descent.[49]

In the work of the Chicago school of sociology, and in Gunnar Myrdal's mon-
umental tome *An American Dilemma,* we see the displacement of the overtly biological conception of racial traits by a sociological conception. Herman Hoetink
argues a similar case by pointing out that it was American researchers and intellectuals in the immediate aftermath of World War II who hastened the downfall
of racist science by finally studying the Negro culturally in the context of a segre-
gated society:

> Probably most important of all, interest was now focused on the effect of the social
> structure (in the Deep South) on the formation of certain psychic and social charac-
> teristics of the Negro. The term "caste structure" began to be used with reference to
> whites and Negroes who form separate worlds, each with its own social gradations,
> in the Deep South. . . . With this approach, novel at the time, the "problem of race"
> was reduced to that of the social structure of a society with a heterogeneous popula-
> tion. . . . The separation entailed by this unequal distribution gives rise to myths
> about the groups, myths which serve to maintain the *status quo.* The colour of the
> skin, and other racial characteristics, are thus reduced to mere symbols of social sta-
> tus. Their importance lies not in themselves as such, but in their social significance.[50]

Although the sociological argument has never taken over completely as the operative intellectual paradigm, its rise, especially when considered against the centuries of belief in the biological-protobiological theory, is phenomenal indeed. It
is important to note, however, that sociology never displaced biology but rather
only modified the mechanism that was thought to generate racial group traits. In
other words, it was not the case that biological race was rejected as much as it was
that supposed racial group characteristics were beginning to be located socially as
opposed to biologically. The idea of distinct races was still accepted, and it is very
much a mistake to see sociology as supplanting a conception of distinct and exclusive biological racial groups. What had changed was the notion that behavioral and social traits were biologically based.[51]

   That the idea itself of biological racial groups remained unchallenged by sociologists during this time is made plain by Myrdal:

It should by this time be clear that it is the popular beliefs, and they only, which enter directly into the causal mechanism of interracial relations. The scientific facts of race and racial characteristics of the Negro people are only of secondary and indirect importance for the social problem under study in this volume. In themselves they are only virtual but not actual social facts. . . . The definition of the "Negro race" is thus a social and conventional, not a biological concept. The social definition and not the biological facts actually determines the status of an individual and his place in interracial relations."[52]

Myrdal argues that social prejudice rather than biology determined the social status of Negroes in his time. He is, of course, writing about character traits and behavior, however. The fact that a person was in the first place considered Negro or non-Negro was still eminently a matter of biology. It is important to see two separate levels in regard to race in this discussion. One level involves the assignment and understanding of character traits and social behavior, while the other level concerns the prior establishment and legitimization of racial classification itself. Racist science essentialized individual and group behavior under the rubric of biological race. The transition to a sociological understanding of group behavior involved accepting environment and socialization as more important factors than simple biological racial group membership.

However, the sociological understanding of racial group behavior nonetheless necessarily operated by first assigning individuals to biological racial groupings. It is important to see, then, that the movement from racist science to sociology was not a movement away from *racial* science but only a separation of behavior from racial group membership. Racial science and racial group membership remained the basis for the social groupings on which sociologists, and psychologists as well, conducted their studies. It is only the advent of more conclusive proof that the traditional racial categories are not supportable scientifically that has instigated movement away from an overtly stated biological conception of race.

Science and Race

The development of genetics and the continuing advances in technology have ushered in a new age of discovery; but rather than coming into contact with new bodies, now the discoveries are being made within the human body itself. Scientists and anthropologists have used these advances to displace notions of racial difference based on traditional phenotypic observations.[53] The advent of genetic studies has led to a greater understanding of the similarities among members of different so-called races, as well as the significant differences among persons within those socially defined groups. It is now recognized as a mistake to assume that all members of a particular socially defined race are alike, either in their cultural orientations or their physical structures. There are no biological criteria we can apply consistently that will yield the traditional racial groups that Americans have as a society established. It is the racist history of the United States and the continuing popular belief in biological race that allow people to accept uncritically the racial structures still operating in the country.

Skin color alone does not act as a valid marker of biological race. Using skin color as a criterion, there is no reason to class people into one group or another except by virtue of preconceived notions of racial grouping, since the variation of skin color in the United States represents an unbroken continuum.[54] As I stated earlier in this chapter, many blacks are lighter in color than many whites. America's history of population mixing and "racial passing" has ensured that, in the Afro-American case especially, the notion of biological purity is indefensible. In pointing out that the attempt to define races traditionally becomes even more impossible when one increases the number of racial traits used as criteria, Stephen Molnar contends that "the lack of association between traits and boundaries when several traits are used to distinguish between groups of populations renders any search for racial purity a futile and often silly exercise."[55] Yet if race (especially whiteness) is to mean anything at all, it must by definition refer to distinct and exclusive groupings.

It is always an arbitrary decision when someone decides what criterion to use as a racial marker. Each time a different set of criteria are used, if they are used objectively, a different racial grouping is the result. Grouping people even by the most generally accepted popular criteria is fruitless. An objective grouping of people by one combination of phenotypic characteristics leads to an outcome that is totally different from a grouping based on a different set of traits. Rejecting the race tradition, Alan Goodman makes very clear that racial thinking is an erroneous exercise, pointing out that human variation is "generally continuous" and "highly nonconcordant" and that there is "greater variation within than among purported races."[56]

Science has discovered not only that biology fails to support the traditional race concept but that if one must classify people, the results of modern science point to groupings that would be unimaginable to Linnaeus or Blumenbach. In a special issue of *Discover* magazine devoted to problematizing race, Jared Diamond demonstrates that if one constructed truly objective groupings (but focused on varying racial criteria), the result would be different groupings that contrast wildly with common understandings. Using the sickle-cell gene as a criterion, "Swedes are grouped with Xhosas but not with Italians or Greeks"; while lactase retention results in a racial grouping of "northern and central Europeans, Arabians, north Indians, and several milk-drinking black African peoples."[57]

One of the bases that allows the race concept to maintain its grip is the fact that individuals perceive selected somatic differences and then reify those differences, forcing them to fit into the illogical and untenable traditional racial categories. Thus, the same phenomenon that caused Linnaeus and the natural philosophers of his time to classify humans based on arbitrary physical traits is still predominant among the general population in modern America, although it has for the most part fallen into disfavor among scientists, who recognize that population intermixture by itself negates the possibility of traditional racial groupings. According to Molnar:

> Group classification based on some single attribute, such as geographic origin (e.g., Asian), language (e.g., Hispanic), or skin color (e.g., white versus nonwhite) ignores all other attributes and neglects to consider degree of admixture. . . . The confusion over "color," origins, and genetics is even more extensive when the ethnic group African American is considered. Their ancestry is a mixture of African and European with a contribution of Native American genes, forming, in some areas, triracial hybrids. . . . In addition, African ancestry is anything but homogeneous.[58]

Attempts to affirm race are usually attempts to prove a priori conclusions. Although the trajectory of science continues to move away from race as a meaningful concept, there are still some who remain committed to it. Significantly, though, scientific studies claiming to prove some form of racial data inevitably begin by precategorizing subjects or subject data into racial groups. Either individuals will self-identify racially, or researchers will assign racial groupings based on precisely the kind of arbitrary physical categorization that scientific inquiry is supposedly attempting to transcend. This occurs in sociological and psychological studies as well as in scientific studies. In a humorous but nonetheless accurate reformulation of this process, a researcher admits, "I wouldn't have seen it if I had not believed it first."[59]

A notorious example of the tendency to build a priori conclusions into racial analysis comes to us from Richard Herrnstein and Charles Murray in their controversial book *The Bell Curve*. In discussing their procedure for assigning people to racial groups for the purposes of assessing racial and ethnic differences in cognitive ability, they ask: "What does it mean to be 'black' in America, in racial terms, when the word black (or African-American) can be used for people whose ancestry is more European than African?"[60] This is an excellent question, of course, and suggests that the two authors recognize the disjunction between social group assignment and the possibility of a consistent racial taxonomy. The actual procedure they follow, however, is considerably less insightful than their initial question: "The rule we follow here is to classify people according to the way they classify themselves. The studies of 'blacks' or 'Latinos' or 'Asians' who live in America generally denote people who say they are black, Latino, or Asian—no more, no less. . . . We want to call people whatever they prefer to be called, including their preferences for ethnic labels."[61]

Thus, although Herrnstein and Murray seek to highlight cognitive differences between racial groups, they provide no consistency in their own method of defining these groups. They utilize no criteria other than social self-identification, making it impossible for the two authors to come to any valid conclusions about the supposed biological racial groups they are claiming to study.

To make their arguments, Herrnstein and Murray cite Stephen Gould, who, in criticizing the race concept, states:

> First, the very concept of race is illegitimate, given the extensiveness of interbreeding and the imprecise nature of most of the traits that people think of as being "racial." Second, the division of races is recent, occurring only in the last tens or perhaps hundreds of thousands of years, limiting the amount of time that groups of humans could have taken separate evolutionary paths. Third, developments in genetics demonstrate that the genetic differences among human beings are minor.[62]

In attempting to dismiss Gould's criticisms of the race concept, Herrnstein and Murray commit the same error they made when classifying people based on self-definition: "Our difficulty with this position is not that Gould (or others who make similar arguments) is wrong about the blurred lines between the races, or about how long the races have been separated, or about the number of genes that are racially distinctive. All his facts can be true, and yet people who call themselves Japanese or Xhosa or Caucasians or Maori can still differ intellectually for genetic reasons."[63]

But this conclusion is preposterous, for there may well be disjunctions between what race people say they are (which may have little to do with their actual biology) and what their genetic heritage truly is. A person who has only one Afro-American and three white grandparents might self-identify as either black or white, while a person who has one white and three Afro-American grandparents might possibly do the same.[64] They could clearly, in American society, both self-identify as black. Should both these individuals self-identify in the same way, whether as white or black, there is no rational sense in which their personal identity choice (which might be politically or culturally motivated, or imposed by another) could be seen as equivalent to a biological racial designation that could legitimately form a basis for Herrnstein and Murray's racial conclusions. Should our hypothetical mixed-race individuals both self-identify the same way, the differential nature of their respective grandparent sets makes it impossible to consider them as members of the same racial group, for such a racial group would make no classificatory sense.

Even if it were possible to classify in a consistent way what Americans take to be the traditional racial groups, self-identification would work to delegitimize any attempt to attain racially valid data. This is the fundamental error upon which Herrnstein and Murray erect their arguments for racially differentiable cognitive ability. They attempt the impossible—to base their research on sociological data obtained from members of self-identifying social groups and to then recast their results as genetically valid racial conclusions.

Furthermore, if Herrnstein and Murray are willing to accept Gould's criticisms of the race concept, especially the imprecision inherent in determining racial groups and the relative recentness of human phenotypic diversity, then there can be no substance whatever to people identifying themselves as members of particular races in the first place. Therefore, "people who call themselves Japanese or Xhosa or Caucasians or Maori" are saying nothing in a racial sense when they do so, for we've already determined that the lines between peoples are too blurry to accept the race concept. To further imply, as Herrnstein and Murray do, that such racial self-identification can be a source for validating genetic cognitive differences is ludicrous.

On the other hand, objective experiments that do not utilize racial precategorization result in groupings that conflict wildly with the received view, such as Diamond's objective categorizations, one of which places Norwegians and black Africans in the same group.[65] Americans, however, are for the most part not interested in scientific evidence that fails to verify their preconceived racial ideas. The irony is that although science tends to refute the American racial paradigm, people continue to appeal to a notion of biological difference when making sociological racial categorizations. Even when race is moved out of the biological milieu and into a different one, at base what is appealed to is a sense of biological difference.

The Social Reality View of Race

The race concept in America has moved from justification to justification with each successive delegitimization. It has moved from a purely biological conception in which character traits were seen as a function of race; to a sociological conception in which races were still taken to be biological categories but character traits were seen as a function of environment; to (as we will see in this section) a social reality conception which asserts that, although there is no biological basis for racial categorization, it nevertheless is the case that people are grouped and group themselves phenotypically in accord with the traditional racial categories, which should therefore be accepted as legitimate. When racist science became untenable in part due to the rise of Nazism and the emergence of sociology, racial groups were maintained but group characteristics were attributed to environment and socialization. When modern genetics demonstrated that the traditional racial groups were not justified by science, it became necessary to resolve the conflict between this new information and the deeply entrenched racial beliefs held by American society. This has been accomplished by asserting that race is a social construction—meaningless biologically, but relevant socially.

However, if race is a social construction, of what precisely is it constructed if not the scientifically invalid false consciousness of biological race? It is as vitally necessary to problematize the social construction of race as it was to question its scientific construction. Many people believe erroneously in a biological conception of race, but it is critical to see that even for those people who claim to eschew the biological conception in favor of a social one, the basis for their social construction view is an underlying conception of biological race, whether acknowledged consciously or not. This false consciousness serves to keep Americans fixated on what are thought to be racial differences, exaggerating and ultimately reifying such differences into a so-called social reality, as Omi and Winant describe:

> Our ongoing interpretation of our experience in racial terms shapes our relations to the institutions and organizations through which we are imbedded in social structure. Thus we expect differences in skin color, or other racially coded characteristics, to explain social differences. Temperament, sexuality, intelligence, athletic ability, aesthetic preferences, and so on are presumed to be fixed and discernible from the palpable mark of race. Such diverse questions as our confidence and trust in others (for example, clerks or sales people, media figures, neighbors), our sexual preferences and romantic images, our tastes in music, films, dance, or sports, and our very ways of talking, walking, eating, and dreaming become racially coded simply because we live in a society where racial awareness is so pervasive.[66]

Today's racial false consciousness is a direct result of the success achieved earlier by the old racist science. Because of the enormous energy and effort that scientists and natural philosophers of days gone by put into proving racist a priori conclusions (which reached a peak in the late nineteenth century before being displaced by a formulation of racial group characteristics as a function of socialization), and because of the willingness of the public to accept those earlier conclusions of science (which were themselves mere defenses of social prejudice), the myth of racial biology is now entrenched deeply in the public consciousness and in the social institutions of the United States. The idea of essentialist racial attributes was displaced by a notion of socialization, but the underlying acceptance of distinct and exclusive racial groups remained. Much of the essentialist baggage of racist science has been discarded, but what remains is a firm belief at some level in biological racial categories. Kwame Anthony Appiah is exactly right in his analysis of the dependence of social upon biological racial thinking when he asserts that "current ways of talking about race are the residue, the detritus, so to speak, of earlier ways of thinking about race; so that it turns out to be easiest to understand contemporary talk about 'race' as the pale reflection of a more full-blooded race discourse that flourished in the last century."[67]

So firmly established is this submerged notion of biological race that modern science has been incapable of making its own case to the general public, despite the tremendous advances in technology and methodology since the days of racist science. The success of biased, racist, nonobjective science in the eighteenth and nineteenth centuries was so great that the conclusions of modern science are viewed with virtual incredulity. In fact, Hoetink warns pessimistically that something more than a demonstration of the falsity of biological race is required to reverse its effects, remarking that merely pointing out that social prejudice is based on myths will likely have no positive effect as long as society's overriding goal is the delineation of people into different social groupings:

> The sociologist's exposure of racial prejudices as mere myths will not put an end to their psycho-social reality, nor will his diagnosis of these prejudices as a mere defense mechanism spell their doom. On the contrary, now that we understand that these myths stem from the human desire to make social distinctions and are an ideological defence of acquired positions, we are in a position to realize that optimism is not the most natural reaction to the race problem.[68]

The concept of race—insupportable biologically—has been salvaged, or perhaps transformed, by its reincarnation as a social reality. The idea behind this formulation is that although race does not exist as a biological phenomenon, people nevertheless continue to order their social lives in accord with the traditional notion of biological race. Therefore, the argument goes, since so many people in the United States act as if race were real, it ought to be considered a social reality in view of the impact it has on people's lives. People's belief in biological race (whether conscious or unconscious) has resulted in the continued acceptance and use of the concept in both the private and public spheres of American life.

In an effort to distance the acceptance of race from biologistic notions, race is recast as a social construction, suggesting—wrongly—that as such it is independent of, and not informed by, an underlying belief in biological race. In other words, a racial false consciousness has led to an acquiescence in the notion of race as a social construction—a social reality—making it then possible to claim that race is a legitimate phenomenon. It is vital, though, to recognize that the mere fact that a false consciousness has an impact does not make the false consciousness itself real in any sense. It remains a false notion, belief in which might cause or allow some individuals to harm others. There is no denying the harmful effects of the mistaken belief in biological race, yet it seems to me that referring to such a false consciousness as a social reality goes far beyond recognizing the impact the actions of its adherents have, and serves further to reify the concept itself in ways that critical thought ought not to allow.

That this particular formulation of race as a social reality is dubious hardly needs pointing out. It is the same as knowing that witches are a myth but acting as if they really exist merely because many people think they do.[69] It is likewise akin to knowing that the Earth is spherical but continuing to order one's life as if it were flat. Using this logic, a sailor might know that the world was not flat but still plan his sea voyages so that he would not fall off its edge. The analogy between belief in race and belief in a flat Earth is especially illuminating here, and I want to take a moment to emphasize it.

People who are critical of antiracial philosophy resist the flat Earth analogy, but it is an absolutely valid parallel of their own racial arguments. I suspect that people are so quick to resist the analogy because even the youngest children understand the utter foolishness of the flat Earth theory, and it is therefore difficult to conceive of oneself being guilty of an equally false and ridiculous belief. Yet logical comparison demonstrates the structural equivalence of the two beliefs. In each case, one holds a belief that contradicts the reality of the actual, physical world. In one case the world is taken to be flat when it really is not, and in the other case different races are said to exist when in fact they do not. Crude, uninformed judgments about sense data, combined with received popular opinion, may lead one to such false beliefs. If one is unaware of the Earth's true form and is ignorant of certain physical laws, the idea of a flat world may seem reasonable. Likewise, if one is unaware of basic biological facts and has been socialized into believing that people belong to distinct and exclusive racial groups, the race construct may seem sensible. The difference between modern proponents of race and medieval European flat Earth advocates, however, is that people today have no excuse for maintaining their particular false belief.

So, the challenge really ought to be laid at the feet of antiracialism's critics, who should explain and justify their insistence on continuing to propagate the race concept in the face of its proven falseness. They should also be willing to assert the conclusion of their argument's structural parallel—that the Earth in essence really *was* flat in the Middle Ages because so many people believed it was. Moreover, just as they claim that race is an acceptable social reality that does not require correction, antiracialism's critics should also be willing to assert that medieval Europe's belief in a flat Earth was a social reality that should have been accepted—even by people who knew better—rather than corrected. In other words, proponents of race as a social reality should be willing to argue that it would have been appropriate for informed people who knew that the Earth was spherical to retrogressively deny their own convictions and act as though it were flat, merely because so many other people felt that way. If, however, defenders of the social reality view are not willing to make these parallel assertions, they should then explain the logical inconsistency between their relative positions on the structurally equivalent cases of race as a social reality and Earth as a flat entity. Despite it being often asserted (usually without argument) that the flat Earth theory is not analogous to the social reality theory of race, it is in fact a devastatingly accurate parallel.

Moreover, the concept of a social reality itself requires critical unpacking and interrogation before it can be accepted as a sensible notion. What does it mean to say that a construct or theory is a social reality? In what sense is that construct then real? Does the construct have an existence? Most importantly, what is the practical difference between the erroneous belief in biological race and the acceptance of the very same racial groupings as a social reality? To posit race as a social reality is to accept the unreal as real. It is a case of reification, an instance of the willful suspension of critical thought. Race is a biological falsehood, yet it permeates American society and is embedded deeply within its social and political structures. There are at least two ways of resolving this problem: either by accepting race as a social reality without challenging it as such, or by refusing to accept the race construct, thereby taking a revolutionary stance against the false consciousness. It is not the case that the only choice one has is to accept the idea of race in American society. One can also refuse to accept it.

Acceptance of race in some form, however, is clearly the easier of the two avenues. It is often deployed as half of a false dilemma by being contrasted with a naive kind of color blindness, as Omi and Winant do here: "So today more than ever, opposing racism requires that we notice race, not ignore it, that we afford it the recognition it deserves and the subtlety it embodies."[70] However, noticing that commonsense beliefs in race have damaging effects does not necessitate the further step of reifying race itself. It is possible to "notice" belief in race and to "notice" its attendant effects without accepting that belief oneself. As for the choice presented by Omi and Winant, it certainly is not the case that the only alternative to noticing race is ignoring it. The real choice is between noticing the idea of race and accepting it on the one hand, or noticing the idea of race and rejecting it on the other. As Yehudi Webster points out, "The realist or social constructionist characterization simply allows social scientists to continue to operate with a flawed racial classification."[71]

What seems to be lost in arguments favoring the acceptance of race as a social reality is a sense of the way the false consciousness of biological race is merely reproduced in the guise of the racial social reality. This so-called social reality is no more than traditional, crude myths of biological race reified through popular opinion, social convention, and legal structures. Appiah is again helpful in making explicit the connectedness of social and biological conceptions of race by pointing out that "most contemporary racial identification . . . most naturally expresses itself in forms that adhere to modified (and sometimes unreconstructed) versions of the old racial essences."[72]

The assertion of race as a social reality is nothing more than a filtering operation for the acceptance of race as a biological reality. Webster illustrates this circular process by noting that "sociologists do not generally seek to refute racial classification, although doubt is often cast on the scientific status of race."[73] The sociologist claims to eschew the idea of biologically defined racial groups, only to deploy a sociological conception that reproduces precisely the same racial groups as the bankrupt biological interpretation. Abby Ferber also sees the responsibility for this error as falling back on academics who purport to study the social reality of race, in arguing that "when researchers fail to discuss what actually constitutes a racial group, they reproduce race as a naturally existing category."[74]

Of course, the problem is that the racial groups making up the so-called social reality cannot be explained or defined except by appeal to traditional conceptions of biological race. Shifting the meaning of race from the biological to the sociological does not serve to make it any more logical or consistent. It is no more than the rationalization of a false consciousness, which Ferber illustrates by explaining:

> Today, many researchers acknowledge the social construction of race, and often a statement is offered, explaining that the authors do not believe in the existence of real biological races, and believe instead that they are socially constructed. However, it is often explained that because *others* (i.e., normal people "out there" in society) believe in the existence of races, race does exist as a subject of study. I do not believe this avoids the problems I have been noting. This form of research creates an artificial rift between sociologists, who merely represent society, and those people out there who are supposedly creating it.[75]

Rather than making the racial paradigm any more legitimate, the attempt to find alternative justifications for the traditional racial groupings is the sociological equivalent of looking back at medieval Europe and declaring that a flat Earth—not just people's belief in it, but the thing itself—is a legitimate subject of study. Ian F. Haney López provides an example:

> I define a "race" as a vast group of people loosely bound together by historically contingent, socially significant elements of their morphology and/or ancestry. I argue that race must be understood as a sui generis social phenomenon in which contested systems of meaning serve as the connections between physical features, faces, and personal characteristics. In other words, social meanings connect our faces to our souls. Race is neither an essence nor an illusion, but rather an ongoing, contradictory, self-reinforcing, plastic process subject to the macro forces of social and political struggle and the micro effects of daily decisions. As used here, the referents of terms like Black and White are social groups, not genetically distinct branches of humankind.[76]

It will be useful to unpack and analyze the above rationalization for accepting the race construct in its social reality guise, for it stands as a representative example of many similar arguments. López employs three elements commonly used in rationalizations of race as a social reality: (1) The biological falsehood of race is acknowledged ("not genetically distinct branches of mankind"); (2) There is an assertion that races are groups of another, nonbiological type ("the referents of terms like Black and White are social groups"); and (3) Phenotype and ancestry are nevertheless asserted as sources of racial identity ("bound together by . . . their morphology and/or ancestry"). Far from explaining what race is, López's "definition" merely serves to rationalize the move from biological race to what is in practical terms the same thing—social race.

Despite claiming to deny the validity of biological race, López appeals to morphology as a criterion of social racial classification; and far from providing a nonbiological explanation of race, his linkage of social race to morphology is erected on and validates hundreds of years of misguided racial science. It is true that people take morphology to be a racial indicator, and it is true that people may align themselves inconsistently in groups based on these traits, but the researcher and the academic must do more than simply reproduce the false consciousness of their society. Ferber lays this charge squarely at the feet of sociologists by asserting that "there is no recognition of the complicity of social scientists in producing and defining specific racial categories."[77]

López describes race as a process, "an ongoing, contradictory, self-reinforcing, plastic process," yet this is surely a category error. In no sense is this an explanation of purported social race. To claim that people are "loosely bound together by historically contingent, socially significant elements of their morphology and/or ancestry" is to appeal to the same simplistic notions of biological race that science has since discarded. We must distinguish between recognizing the illogical and imposed system of racial classification in the United States, and being complicit with that system by uncritically failing to challenge its notoriously irrational premises. To make this critical distinction is to understand the difference between a thing that does not exist and people's irrational belief in that thing. Significantly, López's statement is loaded with contingency—"loosely bound," "historically contingent," and "socially significant" are all qualifications that point to the impossibility of systematizing a nonexistent construct. López shifts from race-as-categorization to race-as-process, but how can people be said to belong to a process? Finally, López opts out of defining social race, providing instead an untenable construction of race-as-process that is itself "contradictory and self-reinforcing," while appealing to morphology—which is precisely what biological race is based on—as a criterion of social race.

Walter Benn Michaels provides a far more critical and satisfactory analysis of race as a social reality, as he enjoins us to challenge, rather than acquiesce in, the fallacy:

> One way that we might characterize this reality is as the reality of a mistake. Even if race is not a biological fact, many people have believed in it as such, and some people, no doubt, continue to do so. And this belief, mistaken though it may be, has obviously had and no doubt continues to have significant consequences. So we might think that the reality of race consists in the fact that we live in a world that is still organized along racial lines. And the point of our new knowledge—the knowledge that there are no biological races—would be to undo the consequences of our old ignorance, to produce a world in which race was not a compelling reality.[78]

Perhaps the best rendering of the social reality argument can be found in Omi and Winant's influential *Racial Formation in the United States,* in which they argue for a view of race as a "complex of social meanings constantly being transformed by political struggle."[79] Noting, correctly, that a biological conception of race is inadequate, they hope to develop an alternative theory for understanding race; however, this very undertaking leads them to invest in race rather than challenge it. In the following critique of their work, I wish to point out that they are both right and wrong in the sense that although they correctly capture a certain view of the American racial terrain, they are wrong to naturalize this view. It is worth taking an extended look at a number of arguments from *Racial Formation*, as it is the most cogent articulation to date of the social reality school of thought.

To begin with, Omi and Winant involve themselves in the inevitable contradiction of basing the social construction of race on a biological foundation, arguing:

> Although the concept of race invokes biologically based human characteristics (so-called 'phenotypes'), selection of these particular human features for purposes of racial signification is always and necessarily a social and historical process. In contrast to the other major distinction of this type, that of gender, there is no biological basis for distinguishing among human groups along the lines of race. Indeed, the categories employed to differentiate among human groups along racial lines reveal themselves, upon serious examination, to be at best imprecise, and at worst completely arbitrary.[80]

It is difficult to see how such considered judgment regarding the uselessness of phenotype as a racial marker can simultaneously justify its reinscription through the filter of "social and historical process." If phenotype is a hopelessly inaccurate and unsatisfactory criterion of racial group membership, then it cannot stand as the basis for a legitimate social construction of race. It is at the critical juncture of distinguishing between recognizing the operation of the false consciousness and naturalizing it that Omi and Winant's presentation falters. Rather than explaining people's belief in race as the fundamental mistake it is, the authors instead describe the workings of the false consciousness of race and then validate that consciousness:

> If the concept of race is so nebulous, can we not dispense with it? Can we not "do without" race, at least in the "enlightened" present? This question has been posed often, and with greater frequency in recent years. An affirmative answer would of course present obvious practical difficulties: it is rather difficult to jettison widely held beliefs, beliefs which moreover are central to everyone's identity and understanding of the social world. So the attempt to banish the concept as an archaism is at best counterintuitive. But a deeper difficulty, we believe, is inherent in the very formulation of this schema, in its way of posing race as a *problem*, a misconception left over from the past, and suitable now only for the dustbin of history.[81]

Two points present themselves here: the possibility of change, and the responsibility for change. Claiming that race is too big or too pervasive a problem to tackle is both short sighted and ahistorical. Were we, in 1820, to have considered the possibility that not only would slavery end in the South in only forty-five years, but that a century later the new capital of the South, Atlanta, would have a succession of Afro-American mayors, the idea would have seemed inconceivable. Yet times, and possibilities, change. An even more compelling case against the inevitability of race can be found in considering medieval European geophysics and cosmology. How utterly unthinkable it must have been for a medieval European to consider the notion of a spherical Earth or a non-Earth-centered universe! Surely the beliefs that the Earth was flat and that it was the center of the universe were entrenched far more deeply in the medieval European consciousness than the inevitability of race is for people in the modern United States. In the latter case, scientists have already debunked the notion of biological race—what is left is residual belief and prejudice. This residual belief is strong, to be sure, but its strength cannot compare to that of many other mistaken beliefs in the past. So the assertion that race is too intractable to fight against and dispense with is not at all compelling when considered in a broader context. As I shall argue in Chapter 6, it is precisely the failure to look beyond the present time that hampers our ability to transcend belief in race.

With regard to responsibility for change, those who recognize incorrect and illogical systems of domination ought to argue and work against them. So it should be with race, which in the United States is a system of domination structured on white exclusivity and a totally baseless biological mythology. It is not enough to attempt merely to reorder the relations imposed by the racial structure, not when even proponents of the social realist formulation admit that the main criterion of social race—phenotypic classification—is "at best imprecise, and at worst completely arbitrary."

Race is precisely a problem that we must get beyond. Progress has moved us into an era where the traditional biological racial groups are, on the whole, no longer accepted by science. What reason, then, can possibly be offered for eschewing critical thought and accepting a social reality formulation of race? Particularly troubling is the assertion by Omi and Winant that posing race as a problem is somehow incorrect.[82] Rather, it is the failure to pose race as a problem, the acquiescence in the false consciousness of race, that is itself an abdication of intellectual responsibility. In what sense should the fact that it is "difficult to jettison widely held beliefs" mediate the scholarly search for truth? The first formulation of the modern notion of race in 1735 was incorrect, and the reproduction of that formulation today in the guise of the social reality conception of race is every bit as incorrect. Indeed, the intervening centuries make inexcusable any defense of the race concept, no matter what form it is presented in.

To their credit, Omi and Winant make explicit that their goal is to analyze the phenomenon of race, asserting that "the task for theory is to explain this situation."[83] Yet tied in with their explanation is the validation and naturalization of race: "[The explanatory task] is to avoid both the utopian framework which sees race as an illusion we can somehow 'get beyond,' and also the essentialist formulation which sees race as something objective and fixed, a biological datum. Thus we should think of race as an element of social structure rather than as an irregularity within it; we should see race as a dimension of human representation rather than an illusion."[84]

However, this approach merely naturalizes and reifies race. By constructing a false dilemma between color blindness and biological essentialism, Omi and Winant miss the opportunity to formulate an antiracial perspective that could incorporate both the recognition of the effects of race as well as arguments for its dissolution. An antiracial stance is capable of making the critical distinction between recognizing the work of the racial false consciousness and reifying that consciousness. It is true that race is currently an element of the American social structure, but it is at the same time an irregularity in the sense that it is a fallacious concept, and it ought to be challenged as such. Omi and Winant continually fail to distinguish between the myth of race and the fact that people believe in that myth. Thus, they call for race not to be seen as an illusion, when that is precisely what it is—an illusion that has sometimes engendered horrible consequences as a result of people's belief in it. By asserting specifically that race is not a problem, that it is not something Americans should get beyond, that it is not an illusion, and that it should be viewed as a natural part of the American social system, Omi and Winant merely reinscribe and naturalize the false notion of biological race.

Although the authors are indeed correct to note that at present a false consciousness of biological race operates upon American society, they are nevertheless wrong to assert that race is something Americans ought to live with and that it is incorrectly cast as a problem. Omi and Winant do more than describe the current state of the American racial paradigm, which by itself is certainly an unobjectionable and important endeavor. Namely, they endorse the idea of race as a useful, unproblematic, and natural part of the American social landscape. Interestingly, it would have been fully possible for Omi and Winant to explain racial construction without validating the basis of that construction. Had they undertaken to merely describe racial formation as opposed to describing and then validating it, their book would retain its force and congency without falling into the position of reproducing the myth of race. Their project to elucidate racial formation in the United States did not require them to legitimate the social construction of race. That they chose to do so is regrettable and mars an otherwise impressive work.

This is the fundamental flaw of Omi and Winant's paradoxical and formidable book, which is a metaphor for the race concept itself in the United States. They accept the inevitability of race and in so doing reinscribe it all the more deeply. In arguing that race is inevitable and wrongly characterized as a problem, they assert that "a more effective starting point is the recognition that despite its uncertainties and contradictions, the concept of race continues to play a fundamental role in structuring and representing the social world."[85] Yet how is acquiescence in the false consciousness of race to be seen as anything other than an abandonment of the ramparts of critical thought and scholarly responsibility? Race continues to play a fundamental role because it is an extremely strong and resilient myth. However, it is the responsibility of the scholar to point out that race is a myth and to criticize it as such, not to give it credence.

It is crucial to recognize racial categorization as a hegemonic enterprise. It has neither logical nor scientific foundation, yet it continues to operate as one of the primary methods of social ordering in the United States. That Omi and Winant recognize the American racial construct as hegemonic is evident in their citation of Antonio Gramsci. The authors note Gramsci's view "that in order to consolidate their hegemony, ruling groups must elaborate and maintain a popular system of ideas and practices—through education, the media, religion, folk wisdom, etc.—which [Gramsci] called 'common sense.' It is through its production and its adherence to this 'common sense,' this ideology (in the broadest sense of the term), that a society gives its consent to the way in which it is ruled."[86]

What is puzzling, however, is Omi and Winant's willingness nonetheless to accept such a false and imposed hegemonic arrangement. That American society has accepted certain lamentable conditions, from race to slavery to the repression of women, provides no excuse for intellectuals to follow suit like so many lemmings. Given their preference for not challenging "widely held beliefs," it is legitimate to ask where the two authors' logic would have placed them vis-à-vis the great issues of the past. The assertion that race is too intractable to challenge is strikingly similar to earlier arguments suggesting that general emancipation, women's suffrage, and public school integration were all pipe dreams not worth pursuing. Indeed, Americans owe the societal progress that has been made since the days of slavery to people who were willing to challenge, rather than accede to, hegemonic arrangements.

It isn't merely the hierarchical structure of the American racial paradigm that is hegemonic, however; the underlying hegemony is the very system of racial categorization itself that serves to structure society in such a way that people do not realize they are the objects of oppression. The arbitrary division of American society into blacks and whites as distinct and exclusive groups is oppressive regardless of hierarchy. Hypodescent and racism both depend on race as a foundation. The struggle against racism must continue, but we must at the same time understand that the foundation of racism, the race construct, must be rejected as well. The racial paradigm is hegemonic and as such ought to be resisted, not validated. Gramsci himself argues against accepting this kind of hegemonic received opinion, advising instead that "common sense is an ambiguous, contradictory and multiform concept, and . . . to refer to common sense as a confirmation of truth is a nonsense."[87] The commonsense, hegemonic, false consciousness of race is just such a nonsensical concept.

Writing elsewhere, Winant grapples rather obviously with the contradiction inherent in the idea of race as common sense:

> Indeed, if race is so much a part of "common sense"; if it is so involved in the production of person, culture, state, and nation; if racial identity is so recognizable, so palpable, so immediately obvious, then in practical terms at least, it becomes "real." . . . On the other hand, though, this "reality" is a rank illusion. It is patently inadequate, if not wholly false, to understand human experience, individual or collective, in racial terms. . . . Race is not only real, but also illusory. Not only is it common sense; it is common nonsense.[88]

Yet the contradiction and ultimate falseness of race inspire in Winant not continuing critical challenge but rather a strange and disappointing resignation: "All the evidence suggests that once created and institutionalized, once having evolved over many centuries, racial difference is a permanent, though flexible, attribute of human society."[89] But what evidence is this? It certainly is not the evidence provided by medieval European belief in a flat Earth, or in the Earth as the center of the universe. As I have already argued, these beliefs—which schoolchildren today consider utterly foolish—were far more ingrained than current belief in race. It cannot be the evidence provided by past belief in disease as the work of evil spirits, or in the supposed harmlessness of cigarette smoke. Nor can it be the evidence provided by millennia of belief in the natural superiority of men over women. In fact, what the evidence suggests is that even the most deeply and fiercely held false beliefs are subject to radical change over time through the power of enlightenment and rational thought.

If the only factors to consider in the battle against racial thinking were people's false belief in biological race and people's reification of that belief into a social reality view of race, it would be a difficult enough struggle. However, another consideration greatly complicates the goal of transcending race in the United States. This complicating factor is federal racial categorization and the extent to which such categorization serves as one of the best means at our disposal to track discrimination and discourage institutional racism.

One of the ironies of the federal government's positive involvement in civil rights in the latter half of the twentieth century is that one of the primary tools of civil rights enforcement has been a system of federal racial classification that has also worked to legitimize the idea of race as a meaningful category. To simply do away with federal racial classification overnight would cripple civil rights compliance monitoring and undo decades of progress in federal antidiscrimination efforts. Therefore, the antiracialist approach must also acknowledge and accept the practical responsibility of moving beyond race without undermining the very important work of civil rights compliance monitoring.

Whether considering the elimination of racial categorization or the addition of a multiracial category, it is critical to first have an informed understanding of federal racial classification. The importance of civil rights compliance monitoring, and the difficulty of devising an acceptable alternative to the current method of relying on racial statistics, was made especially clear by the White House announcement of January 19, 1998, unveiling a plan to increase annual federal civil rights spending from $516 million to $602 million in the 1999 budget.[90] This would represent nearly a 17 percent increase, amounting to $86 million. Federal racial categorization would be a fundamental factor in determining how a great deal of this money would be spent. The history of federal racial categorization, the extent of its spread throughout both the public and private sectors, and its application in civil rights compliance monitoring are among the subjects of Chapter 2.

Notes

1. Keith Shocklee, Eric Sadler, and Carl Ridenhour, "Fear of a Black Planet," on *Fear of a Black Planet* by Public Enemy, Def Jam Recordings, Columbia Records (CK 45413), 1990.

2. In medieval Europe many people believed that the Earth was flat, yet despite this mistaken appreciation of geophysics they developed a coherent civilization. Similarly, people in the United States have found ways to rationalize and live with the false consciousness of race. One must visualize oneself outside the American racial system in order to see how it perpetuates itself and how it masquerades as an already present empirical condition of the world.

3. This thought experiment is adapted from an earlier version originally published in my article "Race in the Face," *Interrace*, June-July 1994, 26.

4. That the important differences between people are cultural and not racial is illustrated by an encounter I had a few years ago with two colleagues. My Afrocentric friend began a statement with the words "We Africans . . ." but he was stopped cold by our colleague from Sierra Leone. She halted him in midsentence, telling him in no uncertain terms that he was an American, not an African, and that he'd do well to remember this fact in her presence. That experience continues to impress upon me the fact that the American idea of racial identity is not a universal one.

5. Marvin Harris, *Patterns of Race in the Americas* (Westport, Conn.: Greenwood Press, 1964), 56.

6. Marvin Harris and Conrad Kotak coined the term "hypo-descent" in "The Structural Significance of Brazilian Racial Categories," *Sociologia* 25 (1963): 207.

7. Harris, *Patterns of Race*, 56.

8. I want to be very clear in acknowledging that so-called racial mixture between whites and Asians, and whites and Native Americans, is indeed problematic. However, neither of these cases is as problematic as black/white racial mixture, either immediately or through succeeding generations.

9. The infamous Susie Guillory Phipps case of the 1980s consisted of a district court trial and several appeals involving a Louisiana woman whose birth certificate listed her as colored in virtue of her having had a single black ancestor in the late eighteenth century. Phipps argued that she was raised white, that she considered herself white, that she lived her life as a white person, and that her birth certificate should therefore be changed ac-

cordingly. The district court disagreed, two circuit courts of appeal upheld the decision, and neither the Louisiana nor U.S. Supreme Courts would review the case. See F. James Davis, *Who Is Black? One Nation's Definition* (University Park: Pennsylvania State University Press, 1991), 9–11.

10. Gunnar Myrdal, *An American Dilemma: The Negro Problem and Modern Democracy* (New York: Harper and Brothers, 1944), 113.

11. Harris, *Patterns of Race,* 56.

12. Cheryl I. Harris, "Whiteness As Property," *Harvard Law Review* 106, no. 8 (June 1993): 1714.

13. Stephen Satris, "'What Are They?'" in *American Mixed Race: The Culture of Microdiversity,* ed. Naomi Zack (Lanham, Md.: Rowman and Littlefield, 1995), 54.

14. These examples are adapted from Spencer, "Race in the Face," 26.

15. Race has at varying times and in various places referred to species, nationality, religion, and biological classification. Although a precise dating may be impossible, it appears that race in regard to humans began to acquire its protobiological meaning sometime between the systematization of American slavery via slave codes in the late seventeenth century and the publication of Carolus Linnaeus's *Systema Naturae* in 1735. See Harris, "Whiteness As Property," 1715–1745; Winthrop D. Jordan, *White over Black: American Attitudes Toward the Negro, 1550–1812* (New York: W. W. Norton, 1977), 44–98; and Stephen Molnar, *Human Variation: Races, Types, and Ethnic Groups,* 4th ed. (Upper Saddle River, N.J.: Prentice Hall, 1998), 4–6, in this regard.

16. Kwame Anthony Appiah and Amy Gutman, *Color Conscious: The Political Morality of Race* (Princeton: Princeton University Press, 1996), 114.

17. Peter A. Angeles, ed., *Dictionary of Philosophy* (New York: Barnes and Noble, 1981), s.v. "reification/reism."

18. I am indebted to Patricia Penn-Hilden for the latter analogy.

19. Some would add Hispanics to this list; however, since federal racial guidelines treat Hispanics as an ethnic, and not a racial, group, I shall follow that practice as well.

20. Harris, "Whiteness As Property," 1718.

21. Jordan, *White over Black,* 93–94.

22. Ibid., 95.

23. Ashley Montagu, *Man's Most Dangerous Myth: The Fallacy of Race,* 6th ed. (Walnut Creek, Calif.: AltaMira Press, 1997), 69.

24. Michel Foucault, *The Order of Things: An Archaeology of the Human Sciences* (New York: Vintage Books, 1973), 158.

25. Jordan, *White over Black,* 218.

26. Stephen Jay Gould, "The Geometer of Race," *Discover,* November 1994, 67.

27. Jordan, *White over Black,* 221.

28. It was Blumenbach who first applied the term *Caucasian* to humans as a scientific classification. He felt that the people of the Caucasus area were the most beautiful in the world.

29. Gould, "Geometer of Race," 69.

30. Jordan, *White over Black,* 223.

31. Foucault, *The Order of Things,* 160.

32. Audrey Smedley, *Race in North America: Origin and Evolution of a Worldview,* 2d ed. (Boulder: Westview Press, 1999), 165.

33. Myrdal, *American Dilemma,* 92.

34. To be sure, the Moors enslaved Christian Iberians captured during border skirmishes on their shared peninsula; however, sub-Saharan Africans purchased via the trans-Saharan caravan trade also ended up in those portions of Iberia under Moorish control.

35. Frank M. Snowden, *Before Color Prejudice: The Ancient View of Blacks* (Cambridge: Harvard University Press, 1983), 68.

36. Jordan, *White over Black*, 4–5.

37. Slavery was also different in English colonies in the Caribbean, where the ratio of Europeans to Africans as well as the ratio of men to women was markedly different from that found in English colonies on the North American mainland. Therefore, the point isn't that English slavery in itself was unique but rather that English slavery under certain conditions found in English North America led to a form of racial slavery different from other forms of slavery that developed in the Americas.

38. Harris, "Whiteness As Property," 1716.

39. Ethnocentrism has likely existed since the first time one human group came into contact with another. Distrust and hatred of others go far back into the mists of time, but the race concept and the particular hatreds derived from it are relatively new ideas on the timeline of human experience.

40. Michael Omi and Howard Winant, *Racial Formation in the United States: From the 1960s to the 1990s*, 2d ed. (New York: Routledge, 1994), 61.

41. Snowden, *Before Color Prejudice*, 63.

42. Jack D. Forbes, *Africans and Native Americans: The Language of Race and the Evolution of Red-Black Peoples* (Urbana and Chicago: University of Illinois Press, 1993), 99–100.

43. Foucault, *The Order of Things*, 162.

44. Robyn Wiegman, *American Anatomies: Theorizing Race and Gender* (Durham, N.C.: Duke University Press, 1995), 23.

45. Ibid., 30.

46. Samuel A. Cartwright, "Diseases and Peculiarities of the Negro Race," in *The Cause of the South: Selections from De Bow's Review, 1846–1867*, ed. Paul F. Paskoff and Daniel J. Wilson (Baton Rouge: Louisiana State University Press, 1982), 27.

47. Ibid., 29.

48. Smedley, *Race in North America*, 247.

49. Omi and Winant, *Racial Formation*, 15.

50. Herman Hoetink, *The Two Variants in Caribbean Race Relations* (Oxford: Oxford University Press, 1967), 88–89.

51. This change involved the assumed racial groups only. There remained, of course, prejudices against females, rooted in a biological essentialism similar to that being displaced in the case of racial groups.

52. Myrdal, *American Dilemma*, 110, 115.

53. Although some of these scientists may perhaps speak of race and racial groups, it is important to note that in many cases what they are describing is not at all equivalent to traditional notions of race in the United States. Concepts such as breeding populations and clines have displaced the crude notions of a three- or four-race system of biological classification.

54. Additionally, the other phenotypic features that supposedly represent Negroidness and Caucasoidness are uncorrelated with skin color. There are black people with pale skin, thin noses, and naturally nonkinky hair. There are blacks who are lighter in skin color than so-called whites. The reason such persons are categorized as black has to do with the way

the American race construct works as a system of exclusion designed to perpetuate the myth of white racial purity.

55. Molnar, *Human Variation,* 8.

56. Alan Goodman, "The Race Pit," *Anthropology Newsletter* 39, no. 5 (May 1998): 52.

57. Jared Diamond, "Race Without Color," *Discover,* November 1994, 86.

58. Molnar, *Human Variation,* 287.

59. I am indebted to George Armelagos for relating this joke.

60. Richard J. Herrnstein and Charles Murray, *The Bell Curve: Intelligence and Class Structure in American Life* (New York: The Free Press, 1994), 271.

61. Ibid.

62. Quoted in Herrnstein and Murray, *The Bell Curve,* 296.

63. Ibid., 296–297.

64. Black identification is more likely in the latter case, but certainly not impossible in the former. The mere use of the labels *Afro-American* or *black* reveals next to nothing about genetic mixture or phenotype. It is certainly possible in the American scenario for a self-identified Afro-American to appear more white than self-identified whites. As a case in point, Walter White, president of the National Association for the Advancement of Colored People (NAACP) from 1931 to 1935, was so light skinned that with his light-colored hair and blue eyes he was able to pass for white in the American South and write a first-hand account of lynching without being detected as a Negro (*Rope and Faggot: A Biography of Judge Lynch* [Salem, N.H.: Ayer Company, 1928]). Anthropologists estimated that White was no more than one sixty-fourth sub-Saharan African. The interesting thing about Walter White in the present context is that his second wife, though white, was darker in appearance than he was. They were taken to be an interracial couple—only he was assumed to be white and his wife black. Davis, *Who Is Black?* 7.

65. Diamond, "Race Without Color," 84.

66. Omi and Winant, *Racial Formation,* 60.

67. Appiah and Gutman, *Color Conscious,* 38.

68. Hoetink, *Two Variants,* 89.

69. I want to draw a distinction between acting in accord with the received opinion due to considerations of personal safety and actually internalizing the received opinion merely because it *is* the received opinion. Certainly one can imagine that standing in a public place in Salem, Massachusetts, in 1692 and declaring that witches did not exist would be ill advised from the standpoint of self-preservation. The idea of the social reality of race, however, is analogous to believing in a flat Earth or in witches merely because so many other people do. As such, it represents an abandonment of critical thought.

70. Omi and Winant, *Racial Formation,* 159.

71. Yehudi O. Webster, *The Racialization of America* (New York: St. Martin's Press, 1992), 82.

72. Appiah and Gutman, *Color Conscious,* 83.

73. Webster, *Racialization of America,* 76.

74. Abby L. Ferber, "Exploring the Social Construction of Race," in *American Mixed Race: The Culture of Microdiversity,* ed. Naomi Zack (Lanham, Md.: Rowman and Littlefield, 1995), 157.

75. Ibid., 160.

76. Ian F. Haney López, "The Social Construction of Race," in *Critical Race Theory: The Cutting Edge,* ed. Richard Delgado (Philadelphia: Temple University Press, 1995), 193.

77. Ferber, "Social Construction," 157.

78. Walter Benn Michaels, "Autobiography of an Ex–White Man: Why Race Is Not a Social Construction," *Transition* 7, no. 1 (1998): 131.

79. Omi and Winant, *Racial Formation*, 55.

80. Ibid.

81. Ibid.

82. It is difficult to conceive of Omi and Winant asserting that belief in a flat Earth was not a problem, and that because it was a widely held belief it should have been accepted even by people who knew better, but that is precisely the logical implication of their position on race as a social reality.

83. Omi and Winant, *Racial Formation*, 55.

84. Ibid.

85. Ibid.

86. Ibid., 67.

87. Antonio Gramsci, *An Antonio Gramsci Reader: Selected Writings, 1916–1935*, ed. David Forgacs (New York: Schocken Books, 1988), 346.

88. Howard Winant, "Racial Dualism at Century's End," in *The House That Race Built: Black Americans, U.S. Terrain*, ed. Wahneema Lubiano (New York: Pantheon, 1997), 89–90.

89. Ibid., 108.

90. Jonathan Peterson, "Stakes Raised in Civil Rights Fight," *Las Vegas Review-Journal*, January 19, 1998, A1.

2

Federal Racial Categorization

Omnis definitio in jure civili periculosa.

—*Georg W. F. Hegel*[1]

Overview

At the close of the twentieth century, the U.S. government finds itself in a paradox with no obvious solution. At issue is the problem of how to reduce the significance of race in American life while continuing to counter racial discrimination in an aggressive way. As I have argued in Chapter 1, a personal stance against racism does not require acceptance of the false concept of racial categorization; however, the specific means employed by the federal government to monitor and act against racism relies on precisely such a classification system. The government maintains statistics and requires reporting of racial data by federal and state agencies, as well as by certain private sector institutions, in order to facilitate the tracking of social and political inequalities by racial group. Disparate statistical representation in terms of employment, mortgage approvals, or access to health care, for instance, may be indicators of racial discrimination.

According to Suzann Evinger, a policy analyst in the Statistical Policy Office of the Office of Management and Budget (OMB)'s Office of Information and Regulatory Affairs, "Disparities in social and economic status, credit experience, educational attainment, health outcomes, and availability of health services, can reveal underlying civil rights problems."[2] Similarly, a statistical analysis report prepared for the National Center for Education Statistics notes that, "For example, the OCR [Office for Civil Rights] in the Department of Education uses racial and ethnic data to detect possible racial discrimination in ability grouping, discipline, athletics, financial aid, and programs for special populations."[3] Such problems and such responses persist regardless of the fact that race does not exist. These problems continue to plague American society because people continue to believe that race is real, that every person on the planet has specific markers that may be used to place her or him into one of three, four, or five distinct and exclusive racial groups.

Given that the government has an interest in tracking racial discrimination via statistics in this way, however, there must be a certain set of categories on which to build these statistics. In the mid-1990s, when OMB was considering revisions to the standards for the classification of federal data on race and ethnicity, the official document setting forth the existing policy was *Office of Management and Budget Statistical Policy Directive 15: Race and Ethnic Standards for Federal Statistics and Administrative Reporting* (OMB 15). The policy had been essentially unchanged since 1977, although the history of the document itself is rather complicated, as I shall describe in this chapter.[4] In accord with this document, until OMB's October 1997 revision, four racial categories were recognized in the United States for purposes of federal statistics and reporting: *American Indian* or *Alaskan Native, Asian* or *Pacific Islander, Black,* and *White.* In addition to allowing respondents to "mark all that apply," the revision separated the former Asian and Pacific Islander category into two separate categories, so that now there are five racial categories. Additionally, there are two ethnic categories: *Hispanic origin* and *not of Hispanic origin.* The reference group in this arrangement is the majority non-Hispanic white group, and the foregoing system of categorization is designed to facilitate the tracking of data on those major perceived minority groups that have been oppressed throughout the history of the United States by the government itself.[5] Although there are many other groupings by which people identify themselves, each of the non-white groups specified by the federal standards has a particular history of oppression at the hands of the U.S. government, and it is this oppression and the resulting racism and continuing stigma therefrom that is the rationale for these categories.

Historical oppression was and remains the primary logic behind the selection and maintenance of this particular set of racial categories for tracking and monitoring. Indeed, systematic, government-sanctioned oppression against particular groups of non-whites may reasonably be said to be one of the primary recurrent themes of U.S. history at least until the late twentieth century. In Lawrence Wright's words, "The white colonizers of North America conquered the indigenous people, imported African slaves, brought in Asians as laborers and then excluded them with prejudicial immigration laws, and appropriated Mexican land and the people who were living on it. In short, the nonwhite population of America has historically been subjugated and treated as second-class citizens by the white majority."[6]

The effects of this oppression on the descendants of those people who were its original targets remain in varying degrees to this day. Although overt, government-sponsored oppression such as the conquest and removal of Native peoples, the enslavement and Jim Crow segregation of Africans and their descendants, the restrictive immigration policies and wartime internment programs targeted against certain Asian peoples, and the failure to honor the treaties and land grants guaranteed to former Mexicans are no longer practiced by the U.S. government against select members of its own citizenry, it yet remains the case that those policies of oppression were so powerful and so destructive that they have left lasting legacies that Americans must acknowledge and address. Moreover, the racism and discrimination fostered by that oppression remain active in the United States, on both personal and institutional levels. The primary vehicle the U.S. government has utilized for addressing this historical oppression and its contemporary remnants is the enactment and enforcement of antidiscrimination laws, and the statistical tracking of racial discrimination.

The federal use of race in the statistical tracking of civil rights compliance has led to an extensive, interlocking network of laws and programs:

> Annual reports of workers by job category and by race and ethnicity must be filed by all employers of at least 100 persons, state and local governments, primary and secondary schools, and colleges and universities. The Equal Employment Opportunity Commission (EEOC) monitors all private employers, schools, and labor organizations under Title VII of the 1964 Civil Rights Act, while the Office of Federal Contract Compliance Programs in the Department of Labor monitors contractors doing business with the federal government. Reviewers compare employment patterns by racial and ethnic categories to find evidence of employment discrimination by race or ethnicity. Employer data have been collected annually this way for the past 25 years.[7]

Testifying before Congress in 1993, Reynolds Farley, a research scientist with the University of Michigan's Population Studies Center, listed several of the different federal policies tied to census racial statistics that the Census Bureau reviewed when planning the enumeration of 1990: (1) "implementing the Voting Rights Act, especially Justice Department approval of redistricting"; (2) "implementing Title VII of the Civil Rights Act of 1964 regarding discrimination in employment including data needs of the Equal Employment Opportunity Commission and the Federal Office of Contract Compliance"; (3) "implementing the Fair Housing Act of 1968 and related laws designed to eliminate discrimination in the housing market including the Community Reinvestment Act of 1977 and the Equal Credit Opportunity Act"; and (4) implementing "laws regarding federal programs for American Indians and the native peoples of Alaska."[8] According to Farley, these "legislative mandates for information about race, Spanish-origin and ancestry are closely linked to those groups once targeted for discrimination."[9]

These interconnected laws are built on racial statistics, and they affect people in visible and invisible ways, on personal and political levels. The racial checkboxes on employment forms, school registration documents, insurance applications, and the like are mandated by these laws, while congressional redistricting is subject to possible review based on the relative racial composition of the particular district in question.[10] Racial classifications that had at one time served as markers of exclusion from American society are now utilized in an attempt to counter discrimination and bring about inclusion. Herein, however, lie the roots of the present paradox. The integration of once officially shunned groups into American society has resulted in the statistical separation of those same groups so that continuing discrimination against them can be monitored and counteracted. Furthermore, reliance on racial statistics collected through the numerous check-boxes one encounters on forms and applications reinforces popular belief in race.

The antiracial advocate is therefore faced with a dilemma on the issue of federal racial statistics. On the one hand, there is no question that these statistics serve to reify the race concept in American life; on the other, they are one of the best means at hand for countering covert and institutional discrimination. Although this dilemma is a difficult one, I do not think that it is unresolvable. The danger lies in the extreme positions of either demanding the immediate cessation of all federal racial statistics-keeping, or asserting that because of civil rights compliance monitoring we should accept the permanence of racial categorization. Either of these two options is inadequate, but they are not the only choices. We can instead recognize that racial categorization is a fallacy we must transcend (and that federal racial categorization is an important part of that fallacy), but that at the same time the practical matter of continued racism demands our best efforts to uncover and counter it. Indeed, for the morally conscious racial skeptic, the only impediment to full rejection of all racial categorization is the fact that federal racial statistics are such an integral part of the civil rights compliance monitoring effort.

Clearly, summarily doing away with federal racial statistics would be a benefit only to racists and cannot be considered a serious option. What is needed instead is a two-pronged effort: (1) a continued erosion of the race concept through the voices and writings of academics, scientists, and other intellectuals in what would essentially be a public mass education campaign; and (2) a concerted effort to find alternative ways for the federal government to track discrimination without resorting to racial categorization. Until such an alternative can be found, however, the continued use of racial statistics in federal civil rights compliance monitoring is the lesser of two evils. Therefore, my arguments in favor of continuing federal racial categorization until such alternative means are available should not be read as a contradiction of my antiracial philosophy. Rather, these arguments represent a sincere attempt to deal—philosophically, morally, and practically— with the complex and knotty dilemma posed by the unreality of race and the reality of racism.

In considering the federal government's collection of racial statistics, it is critical to remember the key point: that these statistics are utilized for the express purpose of monitoring civil rights compliance. As I shall make clear in this chapter, federal racial categories were not designed with the intent, and do not now carry the intent, of validating the personal identity choice of any individual citizen. To complain that the federal race categories do not allow one to express one's individual, personal identity choice is to fail to understand the purpose of those categories. And it is this failure to understand the purposes and uses of the federal categories that has led to much of the controversy surrounding the multiracial category debate. That federally mandated racial categorization and statistics are ubiquitous in American life is a commonplace. What is less understood, however, is precisely what led to this overwhelming reliance on federal racial categorization. It is only when we are cognizant of why federal racial categorization was instituted, and of how it developed, that we can make intelligent decisions about altering these categories.

The History of Federal Racial Categorization

Before delving into the history of federal racial categorization, it will be helpful to take a moment to clarify precisely what history we are going to examine. Federal racial categorization involves the collection and reporting of consistent, transferable racial data for the positive policy purpose of civil rights compliance monitoring. OMB provides the following brief, but useful, overview of the federal race categories:

> The current standards were developed in cooperation with the Federal agencies to provide consistent and comparable data on race and ethnicity throughout the Federal government for an array of statistical and administrative programs. Development of the data standards stemmed in large measure from new responsibilities to enforce civil rights laws. Data were needed to monitor equal access to housing, education, employment opportunities, etc., for population groups that historically had experienced discrimination and differential treatment because of their race or ethnicity. The categories that were developed represent a political-social construct designed to be used in the collection of data on the race and ethnicity of major broad population groups in this country, and are not anthropologically or scientifically based. The standards are used not only in the decennial census (which provides the "denominator" for many measures), but also in household surveys, on administrative forms (e.g., school registration and mortgage lending applications), and in medical and other research. The standards provide a *minimum* set of categories for data on race and ethnicity. . . . Directive No. 15 does *not* tell an individual who he or she is, or specify how an individual should classify himself or herself.[11]

My focus in this book and especially in this chapter is on two components from the above description. My arguments will revolve around what the federal race categories are, and what they are not. That they are a specific means of monitoring civil rights compliance, and that they are expressly not a means for people to validate their personal identities, are two sides of the same dialectical coin.

One of the more common errors made in regard to federal racial classification is the assumption that such classification is at least several centuries old. Commentators will invoke the history of decennial censuses as proof that federal racial categorization is as old as the republic, but this is a mistake. Although we can look to early censuses for various kinds of data, including population totals by race, we cannot do much more than that. The very point of establishing a federal system of racial classification was to allow federal agencies at all levels to compare, combine, and otherwise integrate racial data so that a particular racial statistic could have meaning outside of the agency that collected it. The decennial census takes on a heightened focus when it draws near, but not even the modern census can by itself be said to constitute federal racial categorization. It is merely one part of the larger scope of federal racial classification and, even considering congressional reapportionment, is not by any means the most important part. Thus, when considering federal racial categorization, we must look toward OMB's categories, not the census.

It is possible to locate the origins of the federal race categories—or, more precisely, their prehistory—in 1957, with the Civil Rights Act of that year, which established the U.S. Commission on Civil Rights.[12] The purpose of the commission was "to assess the status of civil rights and the federal government's efforts to protect these rights."[13] At the time, U.S. statistical policy was directed by Bureau of the Budget Circular A-46, *Statistical Procedures*, dated March 28, 1952. Exhibit A of Circular A-46, "Standards for Statistical Surveys," contained a subparagraph titled "Standard definitions and classifications"; however, there were no definitions concerning racial classification. The circular addressed standard commodity and industrial classifications, and provided standard definitions of metropolitan areas, employment and production workers, and payroll reporting periods.[14]

The founding of the Commission on Civil Rights was an early move in an emerging paradigm shift in the interest of the government in collecting and maintaining statistics on non-whites. For the first time, albeit in the absence of standard federal classifications, data on minorities—and on Afro-Americans especially—was desired for the express purpose of tracking and documenting inequality based on race:

> Since the 1960s, data on race and ethnicity have been used extensively in civil rights monitoring and enforcement covering areas such as employment, voting rights, housing and mortgage lending, health care services, and educational opportunities. These legislatively-based priorities created the need among Federal agencies for compatible, nonduplicative data for the specific population groups that historically had suffered discrimination and differential treatment on the basis of their race or ethnicity.[15]

There was some feeling during this time that, in the spirit of integration, racial statistics ought to be done away with entirely; but such sentiment was relatively short lived in the face of the growing federal emphasis on monitoring civil rights progress. An illustration of the expanding zeitgeist of racial monitoring comes by way of the shifting attitude of the American Civil Liberties Union (ACLU), which "tried to get the question on race deleted from the 1960 census schedule."[16] In contrast, thirty-five years later, Chris Hansen, a senior staff counsel with the national office of the ACLU, gave the following account of his organization's use of racial categorization and statistics:

Of course we should continue to collect data on race and ethnicity. . . . The ACLU has used race data in school desegregation cases, most notably in *Brown vs. Board of Education*. Topeka kept no race data from 1956–1966. If it hadn't started keeping those data in the 60s, we would never have been able to establish that the schools there are still not desegregated. Even more recently . . . federal data on mortgage lending supplied by the Home Mortgage Disclosure Act (HMDA) have firmly established the existence of race discrimination in lending and helped identify those most culpable, many of whom are now being more intensively investigated for possible litigation. . . . Continued collection of race/ethnicity data is essential.[17]

In a similar case of reversing direction, William Peterson relates that "New Jersey did omit race and color from its birth and death certificates for the year 1962 (restoring them, however, one year later)."[18] In any case, with the passage of the Civil Rights Act of 1964 and the Voting Rights Act of 1965, the tide of racial categorization and statistics keeping would become increasingly overwhelming. Decades later, these two acts remain the primary impetus for governmental racial classification.

The Civil Rights Act of 1964 outlawed employment discrimination by declaring it unlawful for an employer "to fail or refuse to hire or to discharge any individual, or otherwise to discriminate against any individual with respect to his compensation, terms, conditions, or privileges of employment, because of such individual's race, color, religion, sex, or national origin."[19] Additionally, Title VIII of the same act mandated—explicitly—the collection of racial statistics by directing that:

The Secretary of Commerce shall promptly conduct a survey to compile registration and voting statistics in such geographic areas as may be recommended by the Commission on Civil Rights. Such a survey and compilation shall, to the extent recommended by the Commission on Civil Rights, only include a count of persons of voting age by race, color, and national origin, and determination of the extent to which such persons are registered to vote, and have voted in any statewide primary or general election in which the Members of the United States House of Representatives are nominated or elected, since January 1, 1960.[20]

However, in terms of governmental racial classification and record keeping, it is Title VI of the act that would prove to be one of the primary wellsprings of federally mandated racial statistics. Title VI of the Civil Rights Act of 1964 is not at all lengthy, and its most important element is but a single sentence: "No person in the United States shall, on the ground of race, color, or national origin, be excluded from participation in, be denied the benefits of, or be subjected to discrimination under any program or activity receiving Federal Financial Assistance."[21]

Considering, first, the size of the federal government apparatus in the United States, and second, the number of public and private agencies, institutions, employers, schools, financial institutions, and other organizations and individuals that receive some form of funding from the government, it becomes apparent that the actual reach of this act is extraordinary. The linkage of civil rights compliance with racial statistics as interpreted though Title VI set in motion a vast, interlocking web of federal regulations by all manner of agencies, mandating the use of racial statistics so as to comply with Title VI. As federal agencies developed new programs and revised their current operating procedures in light of Title VI, the question of how to demonstrate compliance effectively and economically had to be addressed:

> With the passage of Title VI, Congress required Federal agencies to "demolish the lingering barriers to full participation faced by minorities" in federally funded activities and programs. Consequently, each agency has primary and ultimate responsibility for enforcement of nondiscrimination in its Federal financial assistance programs. That responsibility encompasses reactive duties, such as investigation and handling of complaints of discrimination and imposition of sanctions, as well as proactive obligations to ensure continuing compliance with Title VI and adequate understanding of its rights and responsibilities.[22]

Racial statistics were an efficient and economical means for a federal agency to keep track of its own racial composition as well as that of the programs and activities receiving funding through association with it. Of great consequence was the fact that each agency was responsible for determining its own compliance monitoring means. The decentralization inherent in this arrangement left open the question of precisely what racial categories each agency would utilize, a factor that would take on major significance in the 1970s.

Another momentous piece of legislation, enacted the following year, reinforced further the exigency and utility of employing racial statistics for compliance purposes. The first three paragraphs of the Voting Rights Act of 1965 (sections 2–4) contain nine separate references admonishing against the denial or abridgement of the right to vote on account of race or color. This language does not in itself mandate the collection of racial statistics; it merely requires state and local voting authorities to not make distinctions based on race in regard to prospective voters. Section 6, however, provides an explicit reference to counting people by race. When discussing, in the case of voting rights violations, the possible appointment of examiners to maintain lists of persons eligible to vote in federal, state, and local elections, the act specifies that the attorney general should consider "among other factors, whether the ratio of nonwhite persons to white persons registered to vote within such subdivision appears to him to be reasonably attributable to violations of the fifteenth amendment or whether substantial evidence exists that bona fide efforts are being made within such subdivision to comply with the fifteenth amendment."[23]

Additionally, section 13 directs that such listing of voters by examiners

> shall be terminated . . . whenever the Attorney General notifies the Civil Service Commission, or whenever the District Court for the District of Columbia determines in an action for declaratory judgment brought by any political subdivision with respect to which the Director of the Census has determined that more than 50 per centum of the nonwhite persons of voting age residing therein are registered to vote, (1) that all persons listed by an examiner for such subdivision have been placed on the appropriate voting registration roll, and (2) that there is no longer reasonable cause to believe that persons will be deprived of or denied the right to vote on account of race or color in such subdivision.[24]

Compliance with the Voting Rights Act therefore required that persons registered to vote be counted by race in cases where violations were deemed possible, and in the documented event of such violations that persons of voting age be counted by race and verified by the Census Bureau.

The Civil Rights Act of 1964 and the Voting Rights Act of 1965 ushered in a new and dramatically different era, one of collecting racial statistics for positive policy purposes. The specific references in the two acts to counting persons by race and to making compliance judgments based on racial ratios could not help but have a substantial impact on policymakers and authors of new and revised federal, state, and local programs. While the acts simply required the absence of any discrimination based on race, the ultimate proof of compliance would seem to lie in producing statistics demonstrating a reasonable proportion of nonwhites to whites. These two important acts of legislation provided the groundwork for using racial statistics as the measure of compliance with civil rights laws.

On September 16, 1965, less than two months after the Voting Rights Act became effective, President Lyndon Johnson issued an executive order setting certain guidelines for federal contractors and subcontractors in which he directed that all government contracts include the provision that the contractor agree not to practice racial discrimination, and further, that:

> each contractor having a contract containing the provisions prescribed in Section 202 shall file, and shall cause each of his subcontractors to file, *Compliance Reports*

with the contracting agency or the Secretary of Labor as may be directed. *Compliance Reports* shall be filed within such times and shall contain such information as to the practices, policies, programs, and employment policies, programs, and *employment statistics* of the contractor and each subcontractor, and shall be in such form, as the Secretary of Labor may prescribe.[25] (emphasis added)

A strong precedent for compliance with civil rights policy had thus been set by the ever growing reliance on racial statistics.

At the same time that these legislative and executive initiatives were being issued, there was an unrelated occurrence that would eventually intersect with civil rights legislation and ultimately have a profound effect on federal racial categorization. On October 16, 1964, President Johnson issued Executive Order 11185, which established the Federal Interagency Committee on Education (FICE).[26] The commissioner of education, who was made chair of the committee, was to report to the secretary of the Department of Health, Education, and Welfare (HEW), whose responsibility it was to "identify the education needs and goals of the Nation and from time to time . . . recommend to the President policies for promoting the progress of education."[27]

In April 1973, the FICE Subcommittee on Minority Education completed a report, "Higher Education for Chicanos, Puerto Ricans, and American Indians,"[28] and presented it to Caspar Weinberger, secretary of Health, Education, and Welfare, who reportedly "showed particular interest in the portion of the report that deplored the lack of useful data on racial and ethnic groups. Further, he encouraged the implementation of the report's second recommendation to '. . . (1) coordinate development of common definitions for racial and ethnic groups'; and '(2) instruct the Federal agencies to collect racial and ethnic enrollment and other educational data on a compatible and nonduplicative basis.'"[29]

The above, oft-cited account is not the entire story, however. The description of events offered by a participant reveals the history in question to be somewhat more complicated. Grace Flores-Hughes, at the time a member of the HEW Office for Spanish Surnamed Americans, relates that she attended a spring 1973 meeting held to discuss the FICE higher education report, during which Native American and Hispanic representatives objected to the terminology used to describe their groups and then walked out of the meeting—refusing to consider the report until the relevant ethnic identifications were reworded to their satisfaction.[30] "After efforts to get Native and Hispanic Americans back to the table to discuss the report's findings failed, the OE (Office of Education) officials decided to form an interdepartmental task force to address the issue of racial/ethnic identification. The Task Force on Racial/Ethnic Categories was formed in 1973, and was comprised of white, black, Hispanic, Asian, and Native American civil servants."[31]

FICE organized its Ad Hoc Committee on Racial and Ethnic Definitions with the goal of developing a practical set of racial and ethnic designations that could be used effectively and consistently by government agencies. The twenty-five-member committee, composed of officials from "Federal agencies with major responsibilities for the collection or use of racial and ethnic data,"[32] sought to find racial and ethnic categories that could be "aggregated, disaggregated, or otherwise combined so that the data developed by one agency could be used in conjunction with the data developed by another agency."[33]

The necessity for standardized racial categories was an inevitable outgrowth of the fact that each federal agency was fully responsible for promulgating its own civil rights compliance policy. Working independently and having various goals and priorities, different agencies developed different categories for their own particular use. In order to see why racial categorization was fragmented across government agencies in this way, it will be useful to take account of federal statistical policy regarding race at the time. Federal statistical policy in general was still directed by the Bureau of the Budget's Circular A-46 *(Statistical Procedures)* of 1952. On August 8, 1969, the bureau amended Circular A-46 with Exhibit K ("Race and Color Designations in Federal Statistics").[34] The purpose of the amendment was to "set forth acceptable designations of race or color in statistical publications."[35] The amendment noted that race as used in federal statistics was "not a clear-cut biological definition" and, further, that reference to color had divided the U.S. population into whites and non-whites, resulting in statistical presentations relating to color having the same terminology as statistical presentations relating to race.[36]

Exhibit K did not actually designate racial categories, however, except in the broadest of terms. It was primarily concerned with data presentation, not collection. The only racial groups mentioned in the exhibit were "Negro" and "white," and these were not defined in any way. The main purpose of the exhibit was to announce that the designation "non-white" was no longer acceptable for use in federal statistics and to point out when other designations such as "Negro," "other races," and "all other races" were allowed. *White* and *Negro* were specifically mentioned as acceptable designations, as were the aforementioned collective descriptions; however, Exhibit K did not provide any further guidance as to acceptable racial designations. In terms of races other than Negro and white, agencies were free to make their own determinations as to which or how many individual racial categories to utilize, with the result that statistical data that might have potentially been useful to aggregate at levels higher than the agencies themselves were essentially noncompatible and therefore useless outside the collecting agency. It was in this environment that the FICE ad hoc committee set about developing standard racial categories for use across all government agencies.

The FICE ad hoc committee developed the following racial and ethnic definitions, which were endorsed by FICE on April 23, 1975:[37]

A. American Indian or Alaskan Native. A person having origins in any of the original peoples of North America.

    B.   Asian or Pacific Islander. A person having origins in any of the original peoples of the Far East, Southeast Asia, or the Pacific Islands. This area includes, for example, China, Japan, Korea, the Philippine Islands, and Samoa.

    C.   Black/Negro. A person having origins in any of the black racial groups of Africa.

    D.   Caucasian/White. A person having origins in any of the original peoples of Europe, North Africa, the Middle East, or the Indian sub-continent.

    E.   Hispanic. A person of Mexican, Puerto Rican, Cuban, Central or South American, or other Spanish culture or origin, regardless of race.[38]

Two ways of collecting data using these categories were suggested by the ad hoc committee, which declined to recommend one method over the other in the absence of a field test.[39] The first method was to list the five categories as mutually exclusive options:

_____Hispanic
_____American Indian or Alaskan Native
_____Asian or Pacific Islander
_____Black/Negro, not of Hispanic origin
_____Caucasian/White, not of Hispanic origin[40]

Committee members were concerned about the potential reliability of data on Hispanics, given the inclusion of this ethnic category among racial categories, and they specified that the combined format should only be used provided that white and black persons of Hispanic descent be identifiable as Hispanic.[41] Toward this end, and also to reduce the possibility of confusion on the part of respondents, the modifier "not of Hispanic origin" was attached to the black and white categories in this format.[42] Much nonsense has been written that has been critical of the Hispanic designation, when in fact it was part of an earnest effort to compile data on historically oppressed people.[43]

    The committee as well noted that the combined format was particularly suited to observer identification and was the preferred method of EEOC, the HEW Office for Civil Rights, and the Office of Federal Contract Compliance.[44] In employment settings in particular, observer identification is likely to be utilized for compliance reporting as opposed to the self-identification of employees.[45] The problematic mixing of racial and ethnic categories in the combined format was acknowledged; however, the committee justified it in part on the basis of the sentiment expressed by a Hispanic committee member who pointed out that "Hispanics see themselves as one group ethnically and culturally despite the racial variety within the group."[46]

The second method was a format that separated race and ethnicity, more applicable to the data needs of the census and more suitable for self-identification by respondents, according to the committee:[47]

1. What is your racial background?
_____American Indian or Alaskan Native
_____Asian or Pacific Islander
_____Black/Negro
_____Caucasian/White

2. Is your ethnic heritage Hispanic?
_____Yes   _____No[48]

The ad hoc committee also considered the use of an *Other* category, "principally for individuals of mixed racial backgrounds and those who want the option of specifically stating a unique identification."[49] In the end, however, the majority of the committee remained opposed to such a category except in very particular circumstances. The committee determined that an *Other* category could be appropriate only in cases of self-identification, only if the number of responses remained small, and only if the respondents specified the standard group with which they identified.[50] The *Other* category was not one of the categories ultimately endorsed by FICE, however. Significantly, then, something close to a multiracial category was considered, but not adopted, by the ad hoc committee. Even had it been adopted, however, respondents would still have been required to designate a major group for purposes of compliance monitoring. It is important to point this out, as it demonstrates that the primary purpose of the categories has always been to document discrimination and not to provide a means for validating self-identity. The *Other* category was ultimately rejected by the committee because it fell too far outside the clear and explicit goals of federal racial categorization.

On May 3, 1974, between the establishment of the FICE ad hoc committee and the committee's final report, OMB coincidentally issued revised Circular A-46, *Standards and Guidelines for Federal Statistics,* section 7(k) and Exhibit F ("Race and Color Designations in Federal Statistics"), which set forth policy on racial and ethnic categorization.[51] However, this exhibit was exactly the same as the revised Exhibit K of the previous iteration of Circular A-46.

The reissuing of this policy contrasted with the work being undertaken at the same time by the FICE ad hoc committee, and it served to reiterate why that work was so necessary. At the time of its reissuing in 1974, Exhibit F was already obsolete in the sense that the statistical policy that would soon supersede it, providing standard racial categories for use by all government agencies, was at that moment being developed by the FICE ad hoc committee. In fact, the longer and more detailed succeeding policy would incorporate the text of the 1974 Exhibit F under the section titled "Presentation of Race/Ethnic Data."[52] Only one decade after passage of the Civil Rights Act of 1964, racial categorization for statistical purposes was well on the way toward becoming codified and standardized across all governmental agencies, as evidenced by this excerpt from the September 1975 issue of *Statistical Reporter:*

> The Office for Civil Rights of the Department of Health, Education, and Welfare and the Equal Employment Opportunity Commission are committed to the use of the FICE categories and definitions in all compliance reports required of educational institutions during the 1975–76 school year. During this period the application of the new categories will be optional for other agencies. FICE plans to request a field test of the proposed categories by the Bureau of the Census. When the test has been completed, the Ad Hoc Committee of FICE which developed the categories will meet to review the results and recommend any necessary refinements of the terms and definitions. After completion of these steps, the chairman of FICE is expected to transmit updated categories to the Office of Management and Budget with the recommendation that they be promulgated as the standard for all Federal statistics on race or ethnicity.[53]

OMB, HEW, EEOC, and the General Accounting Office (GAO) agreed in spring 1975 to use the draft FICE categories for a minimum one-year trial period.[54] The agencies' experiences were then considered:

> At the end of the test period, OMB and GAO convened an *Ad Hoc* Committee on Racial/Ethnic Categories to review the experience of the agencies which had implemented the standard categories and definitions and to discuss any potential problems which might be encountered in extending the agreement to all Federal agencies. This Committee, which met in August 1976, included representatives of OMB, GAO, the Department of Justice, the Department of Labor, the Department of Health, Education, and Welfare, the Department of Housing and Urban Development, the Bureau of the Census, and the Equal Employment Opportunity Commission. Based upon the discussion in that meeting, the Office of Management and Budget prepared minor revisions to the FICE definitions and circulated the proposed final draft for agency comment. These revised categories and definitions became effective in September 1976 for all compliance recordkeeping and reporting required by the Federal agencies represented on the *Ad Hoc* Committee.[55]

OMB then revised Exhibit F to Circular A-46 (renamed "Race and Ethnic Standards for Federal Statistics and Administrative Reporting"), which became effective for all government agencies on May 12, 1977, and required that all existing data collections become consistent with the revised exhibit no later than January 1, 1980.[56]

The revised racial and ethnic categories specified by the circular are as follows:

1. American Indian or Alaskan Native. A person having origins in any of the original peoples of North America, and who maintains cultural identification through tribal affiliation or community recognition.
2. Asian or Pacific Islander. A person having origins in any of the original peoples of the Far East, Southeast Asia, the Indian subcontinent, or the Pacific Islands. This area includes, for example, China, India, Japan, Korea, the Philippine Islands, and Samoa.
3. Black. A person having origins in any of the black racial groups of Africa.
4. Hispanic. A person of Mexican, Puerto Rican, Cuban, Central or South American or other Spanish culture or origin, regardless of race.
5. White. A person having origins in any of the original peoples of Europe, North Africa, or the Middle East.[57]

The only differences between these categories and the earlier FICE categories were the stipulation for tribal affiliation attached to Native American/Alaskan Native identification (an option suggested originally by the FICE committee), the movement of persons from the Indian subcontinent from the White category to the Asian category, and the dropping of the Negro and Caucasian designations. The preference of OMB was for data on race and ethnicity (Hispanic versus non-Hispanic) to be collected separately; however, OMB allowed both the separate and combined formats developed by FICE to be used, leaving it up to individual agencies to determine which format best fit their specific needs. The exhibit specified that these categories were to be used "by all agencies in either the separate or combined format for civil rights compliance reporting and equal employment reporting for both the public and private sectors and for all levels of government."[58] Twenty years after the passage of the Civil Rights Act of 1957 and the establishment of the U.S. Commission on Civil Rights, both the collection of racial statistics and the specific racial categories to be used in such collection were now mandated by the federal government.

A 1992 GAO report encapsulates the history this way:

The enactment of the Civil Rights Act of 1964 (PL 88-352) created the need for the federal government to collect statistics on race for compliance and enforcement purposes in such areas as education and housing. There were no standard definitions or procedures for collecting such data in the early 1960s, but a need for both became apparent by the 1970s as a variety of public and private entities began using racial data collected by various federal agencies for policy and trend analysis. A desire for data on the status of an emerging multiracial Hispanic population created the need for data by ethnic group as well.[59]

In a very short time, however, changes in agency responsibility would alter the administration, though not the content, of the new statistical policy guidelines. The authority for the establishment of government statistical policy derives from section 103 ("Government Statistical Activities") of the Budget and Accounting Procedures Act of 1950: "The President, through the Director of the Bureau of the Budget, is authorized and directed to develop programs and to issue regulations and orders for the improved gathering, compiling, analyzing, publishing, and disseminating of statistical information for any purpose by the various agencies in the executive branch of the Government. Such regulations and orders shall be adhered to by such agencies."[60] When OMB was established in 1970, this authority was transferred to that agency's director.[61]

On October 7, 1977, President Jimmy Carter issued Executive Order 12013, which transferred the responsibility for statistical policy from OMB to the Department of Commerce.[62] The secretary of commerce then established the Office of Federal Statistical Policy and Standards (OFSPS), which performed the functions and responsibilities formerly carried out by the Statistical Policy Division of OMB.[63] In response to the executive order, the secretary of commerce directed the reissuing of OMB Circulars A-39, A-46, A-65, and A-91: "The standards associated with these circulars are hereby reissued and will be enforced by the Department of Commerce. . . . The Department will soon be issuing the Statistical Policy Handbook which includes the standards (now called "Statistical Policy Directives") discontinued as OMB circulars."[64]

The directive dealing with racial designations was the fifteenth in a series of nineteen statistical policy directives issued by the Department of Commerce, and marks the first use of the designation "Directive No. 15."[65] The title of the directive ("Race and Ethnic Standards for Federal Statistics and Administrative Reporting") was retained from the revised Exhibit F of OMB Circular A-46, which it replaced. However, it is important to recognize that this directive was issued by the *Department of Commerce*, a fact that is usually misreported by commentators. Indeed, the 1994 *Federal Register* that solicited comments for potential review of federal racial classification included historical background information that made no mention of the transfer of statistical policy authority to the Department of Commerce, leaving the impression that statistical policy with regard to racial designations has always been the purview of OMB.[66] OMB explains that the Department of Commerce's involvement in Directive No. 15 is omitted so as not to confuse people.[67] Although there is an understandable and practical logic to this explanation, given the already arcane nature of government directives, circulars, committees, and so on, my purpose here is to reconstruct the full and accurate history of federal racial categorization, and this particular detail is an important one.

Although the basic authority for determining statistical policy had been transferred to the Department of Commerce, OMB still maintained Federal Reports Act authority, as indicated in the *Statistical Policy Handbook:*[68] "Federal Data collection activities are subject to approval by the Office of Management and Budget . . . or the General Accounting Office. The Federal Reports Act, as implemented by OMB Circular A-40, permits the Director of OMB to disapprove any request from a Federal agency for collecting identical information from 10 or more respondents or a similar recordkeeping requirement."[69]

The section of the *Statistical Policy Handbook* that replaced OMB Circular A-46 was titled "Directive No. 15: Race and Ethnic Standards for Federal Statistics and Administrative Reporting."[70] In this directive, all references to the *Statistical Policy Division* of OMB that appeared in OMB Circular A-46 were changed to the *Office of Federal Statistical Policy and Standards*. The guideline for obtaining approval for variations in statistical reporting, however, was not altered: "Any other variation will have to be specifically authorized by OMB through the reports clearance process (see OMB Circular No. A-40)."[71]

Prior to OMB's 1997 revision, the most recent administrative change regarding statistical policy resulted from the Paperwork Reduction Act of 1980, which reestablished OMB as the promulgating agency for statistical policy. The Paperwork Reduction Act created OMB's Office of Information and Regulatory Affairs,[72] whose administrator was delegated with authority for all information policy covered by the act.[73] It also delegated to the director of OMB the authority to "develop and implement Federal information policies, principles, standards, and guidelines" and to "provide direction and oversee the review and approval" of a number of information management functions including "statistical activities."[74] Ironically, the authority for enforcing statistical policy, which still issued from section 103 of the Budget and Accounting Procedures Act of 1950, was transferred from the Department of Commerce back to OMB, where the policy on racial statistics had originated.

An ultimately unsuccessful change to racial statistical policy was considered in 1988, when OMB solicited public comment on a draft circular revising statistical activities, the last paragraph of the penultimate section of which added an additional racial category: "In establishing reporting systems and collecting data, agencies should permit individuals to identify themselves as 'other' if they believe they do not fall into any of the categories listed above."[75]

This proposal, essentially the same as the *Other* category proposed by the FICE Ad Hoc Committee on Racial and Ethnic Definitions some thirteen years earlier, was soundly rejected by a number of federal agencies having responsibility for monitoring racial discrimination. On July 15, 1988, in a four-page letter to OMB, the chairpersons of the Committees on Education and Labor; the Select Committee on Aging; the Post Office and Civil Service, Subcommittees on Census and Population and on Civil Service; Government Operations, Subcommittee on Human Resources and Intergovernmental Relations; Education and Labor, Subcommittee on Employment Opportunities; Finance and Urban Affairs, Subcommittee on International Finance, Trade, and Monetary Policy; and the Judiciary, Subcommittees on Civil and Constitutional Rights and on Criminal Justice rejected the proposed addition of an *Other* category by citing the deleterious effects such a change would have on the government's ability to monitor racial discrimination: "In light of these important concerns, we strongly recommend that the proposed changes not be implemented in their current form. We cannot overstate our concern and belief that little measurable improvement in the quality of Federal statistics or in service to the public will accrue from the implementation of the proposed changes."[76]

The final anomaly in the history of OMB 15 is that there seems never to have been an OMB regulation promulgating it, since OMB's references to the directive tend to refer rather to Department of Commerce Statistical Policy Directive 15. OMB 15's title—"Statistical Policy Directive 15" (or "Directive No. 15")—makes sense only in the context of Department of Commerce statistical policy directives issued in the late 1970s as a result of Executive Order 12013. When the Department of Commerce took over responsibility for statistical policy, it reissued OMB Circular A-46 as Department of Commerce Statistical Policy Directive 15. However, when OMB regained that authority several years later, it retained the title ("Statistical Policy Directive 15"), which has led to much historical confusion.

The material reprinted by OMB in the appendix to the 1994 *Federal Register* soliciting comments on potential revision of OMB 15 is actually the text of the revised Exhibit F of OMB Circular A-46, dated May 12, 1977, which was soon superseded by Department of Commerce Statistical Policy Directive 15.[77] It would appear that OMB never reissued Department of Commerce Statistical Policy Directive 15 as an OMB document, so there is no official reference to OMB Statistical Policy Directive 15. Several telephone calls to OMB all elicited the response that the May 12, 1977, document was the proper reference—despite the fact that it was rescinded, and that it was not titled "OMB Statistical Policy Directive 15."[78] This anomaly was finally cleared up when OMB 15 was superseded by the publication of the October 30, 1997, revised standards for the classification of federal data on race and ethnicity, which I examine in Chapter 5.

My purpose in documenting the historical minutiae of this statistical policy is to bring coherence and accuracy to what has generally been an anecdotal exercise. As this historical review has shown, it is not the case that OMB 15 had been in effect since 1977 or 1978, as is often asserted. Although the government's basic statistical policy had been the same ever since publication of revised Exhibit F of OMB Circular A-46 (1977)—indeed, it had been essentially the same for certain federal agencies since the report of the FICE Ad Hoc Committee on Racial and Ethnic Definitions (1975)—OMB 15 did not come into existence officially until the Paperwork Reduction Act of 1980 returned full responsibility for federal statistical policy back to OMB from the Department of Commerce.

One might object that the distinctions I am drawing here are insignificant, given that the basic statistical policy remained the same; however, it is important to insist on accuracy in these matters since errors regarding the title and enforcing authority of the statistical policy document at particular points in time are often mirrored in the form of errors concerning the coherence and logic of the categories themselves. Therefore, insistence on accuracy in technical and administrative matters relating to federal race policy and its history will serve to reinforce the need for accuracy in regard to consideration of the actual content of the policy as well. The history of federal racial categorization is a complex one that has never before been set down accurately and fully, and it is for the sake of establishing for the record the genesis and development of federal racial categorization that I invoke this level of detail. With this in mind, it will be useful now to address some of the more common criticisms of the federal categories themselves.

Criticisms of Federal Racial Categorization During the OMB 15 Review

The racial categories mandated by the federal government have been the subject of intense debate in recent years as their logic, applicability, and usefulness have come into question. The report of a February 1994 Committee on National Statistics (CNSTAT) workshop convened at the request of OMB for the purpose of beginning a review of federal racial categories summarizes the complaints this way: "Since its promulgation in 1977, Directive 15 has come under increasing scrutiny because of logical flaws in its categorization, the rapidly changing demographic profile of the United States, and clearer understanding of racial and ethnic identity as a social construct."[79]

I shall consider each of these complaints, as they represent the misgivings of many commentators who disagree with the federal categories. In conducting this analysis, I want specifically to keep in mind my comments in the previous section regarding the need for accuracy and attention to detail in understanding and criticizing federal racial classification. In light of those remarks, then, it is significant to note that the bibliography of the CNSTAT workshop report lists as the entry for the statistical policy directive the following: "U.S. Office of Management and Budget. '1978 Statistical Policy Directive No. 15: Race and Ethnic Standards for Federal Agencies and Administrative Reporting.' *Federal Register* 43: 19269–19270."[80]

The first thing we note is the fact that the citation cannot be to an OMB statistical policy directive since the *Federal Register* issue cited is the one announcing the transfer of statistical policy functions from OMB to the Department of Commerce, thus discontinuing OMB Circular A-46. Additionally, the title of the directive printed in that issue of *Federal Register* is "Race and Ethnic Standards for Federal *Statistics* and Administrative Reporting," not "Federal *Agencies*."[81] Finally, Appendix B of the workshop report is given as a reprint of OMB 15, with a note at the bottom of the first page of the appendix reading, "This appendix presents the complete text of Directive 15, issued May 12, 1977, by the U.S. Office of Management and Budget."[82] This is incorrect, however, as the version reprinted in the report's appendix makes reference to the Office of Federal Statistical Policy and Standards, which did not come into existence until control of statistical policy functions had passed from OMB to the Department of the Commerce, and so it cannot have been dated May 12, 1977. It is therefore instead the version published in the *Federal Register* of May 4, 1978.

I should state as well that these types of errors are common in many accounts of the history of federal racial statistical policy; the CNSTAT report merely provides a convenient example. Indeed, a 1992 report by GAO to the chairman of the House Committee on Government Operations makes a similar error, stating that OMB 15 "has been in effect since 1980"[83] but then reproducing the same May 4, 1978, Department of Commerce text.[84]

I point out these errors not to demonstrate editing flaws in the reports, for there would be no further purpose in that. Rather, I point them out in order to foreground the following discussion of the specific criticisms of federal racial classification mentioned above and to reiterate my intention of bringing accuracy and coherence to a history that is often repeated incorrectly over and over again. I shall in the process demonstrate that many of the criticisms are made without regard to or knowledge of the context, or the deliberative processes that went into the determination, of the federal racial categories. As such, many of them (including the criticisms voiced by multiracial advocates) are complaints made in a vacuum.

The most common criticism registered against federal racial statistical policy has to do with the logic and consistency of the categories. The CNSTAT report notes that:

> One of the prime criticisms of the current classification is that it lacks a consistent logic. Some of the categories are racial, some are geographic, some are cultural. Several participants commented that a primary concern of respondents, if not of federal agencies, is the perception of a fair treatment in the definition of categories. The categories now represent a combination of historical, legal, and sociological factors, but that is not explicitly acknowledged.[85]

Two complaints are embedded in the above passage—one having to do with consistency and the other having to do with explanation. The former complaint must be placed in the context of the origins of the statistical policy in order to address it accurately. Federal racial categorization is, after all, a statistical policy in support of monitoring antidiscrimination efforts, not a biological taxonomy. Indeed, language to the effect that "these classifications should not be interpreted as being scientific or anthropological in nature" appears as early as the revised Exhibit F of 1977, and such language has been retained in all subsequent iterations of the policy.[86] Although this disclaimer is sometimes taken as de facto proof of the policy's lack of structural integrity, such a view misses the point of the categories and of the policy itself. It is important to remember that the policy originated partly as a response to the need for comparable racial categories in order to meet the compliance requirements of civil rights laws. What is important here is not that the categories be scientifically logical (as I argued in Chapter 1, no racial categories have any scientific validity in any event), but rather that they accurately reflect the categorizations people make when they engage in racially discriminatory behavior.

When the FICE Ad Hoc Committee on Racial and Ethnic Definitions developed its categories, racism and discrimination were the operative concerns, not biology or genetics. The ad hoc committee was composed of "Federal Agencies with major responsibilities for the collection of racial and ethnic data."[87] It is reasonable to assume that they had such collection responsibilities because they were involved in the oversight of civil rights compliance, and the list of agencies represented bears this out. Among the agencies represented on the ad hoc committee were the Census Bureau, the Bureau of Labor Statistics, the Bureau of Indian Affairs, the Department of Housing and Urban Development, the HEW Office for Civil Rights, the Equal Opportunity Commission, the HEW Office for Spanish Surnamed Americans, the HEW Office of Asian American Affairs, and the U.S. Commission on Civil Rights, to name only some.[88]

The committee developed its definitions based on the differing relationships of the U.S. government to the minority groups in question. The logic of the categories rests on the differential treatment that is connected to the factors cited in the definitions themselves. It must be remembered that what the ad hoc committee was doing was standardizing the racial categories that most agencies were in fact using, albeit in inconsistent and nontransferable ways. According to one member of the FICE ad hoc committee, they "just wanted to bring coherence to what federal agencies were already doing."[89] Commentators frequently suggest that these categories were developed with little thought to potential problems they might later cause, yet in reality the FICE ad hoc committee worked long and hard in considering precisely those questions that are the subject of complaints today. As the FICE report itself notes, "The categories are the product of considerable discussion, disagreement, give-and-take, and compromise on the part of the Ad Hoc Committee members."[90] The resulting categories were the product of serious deliberation and engagement, and should be given credit as such even as they are criticized.

The American Indian/Alaskan Native category was developed with the aim of protecting the interests of Native Americans whose ancestors were the victims of federal Indian wars and removal policies. The committee did in fact give thought to including all indigenous peoples of the Americas in this category but decided not to because "the number of South American Indians in this country is small, and to include them might present data problems for agencies concerned with 'Federal Indians,' or those eligible for U.S. Government benefits."[91] Central and South American Indians were instead placed in the Hispanic category—creating the presumption that all such peoples are of Spanish culture, which is not the case and which has become increasingly problematic as Central and South American Indian immigration into the United States has continued to grow.

The CNSTAT report notes that "Directive 15's definition of an 'Asian race' category does not exist in Asian countries, nor does it correspond to an Asian identification in any other country."[92] Yet it hardly requires mentioning that no race term corresponds to any reality anywhere. The issue here is not the self-identity of the victim of racism, but rather the perceptions and actions of the racist. The Asian category has historical resonance as pertaining to certain people who have been oppressed legislatively in the United States and who still suffer from that history and the racism that is its legacy. This is the source of its legitimacy as a category for civil rights compliance monitoring. The racist American who discriminates against a Chinese American in the morning and a Korean American at noon is unlikely to know the national heritage of either but has in his own mind assigned them to a singular category. In terms of federal statistical policy, it matters less that an individual might consider herself Vietnamese American as opposed to Asian than that the practices of employers, institutions, and mortgage lenders who happen to discriminate against Chinese Americans, Japanese Americans, Korean Americans, and Vietnamese Americans, for example, be capable of being tracked for civil rights compliance with respect to the category *Asian*.[93] Clearly, this federal race category, as well as the others, poses a dilemma for racial skeptics, many of whom advocate the continued use of such categories even while recognizing their problematic status. The only justification for not eliminating the federal categories is their enormous value in facilitating civil rights compliance monitoring.

The Black category grew out of a need to delineate Afro-Americans, who of course have the legacies of American slavery, Jim Crow segregation, and continuing racism to contend with. The definition of a member of this group as a "person having origins in any of the black racial groups of Africa" is an example of the kind of compromise that went on within the ad hoc committee.[94] Some members wanted to include the word *Africa* in the category name. The eventual compromise was to include the reference to Africa in the definition, which also served to make it conceptually comparable to the other racial categories in that they all referred to groups originating in specific parts of the world.[95]

The Hispanic category was proposed by committee member Grace Flores-Hughes, who wanted to find a term that would indicate the Spanish origin of the particular people it described without including people whose ancestors did not suffer the same discrimination as this group at the hands of the U.S. government, such as Spanish-speaking Europeans, for instance. This is the perfectly logical reason why the Hispanic category denotes Mexican-Americans, for instance, but not Spaniards. The term *Latino* was rejected because of its literal association with the Latin language and the Roman Empire, which might lead to erroneously including Italians in the category.[96]

Finally, the primary difficulty with the White category revolved around persons from the Indian subcontinent:

> The question at issue was whether to include them in the minority category "Asian . . ." because they come from Asia and some are victims of discrimination in this country, or to include them in [the White] category because they are Caucasians, though frequently of darker skin that other Caucasians. The final decision favored the latter. While evidence of discrimination against Asian Indians exists, it appears to be concentrated in specific geographical and occupational areas.[97]

Persons having origins in the Indian subcontinent were eventually moved to the Asian category by the revised Exhibit F of OMB Circular A-46.

It should be noted that a minority of committee members working in civil rights areas made the argument that there should be no category denoting whites, but instead one group titled "Persons not included in the other four categories," which would consist of all those people who were not members of one of the four specific minority groups defined by the committee.[98] In retrospect, this was an appealing idea, as it would have eliminated some of the controversy today regarding the classification of groups whose members may feel they do not fit the established categories, such as some Middle Easterners. It would also have reinforced the primary purpose of the standard categories, which was compliance monitoring in regard to those groups the United States has a special obligation toward. This proposal was not, however, accepted by the majority of the ad hoc committee, and it remains a tempting artifact, an intriguing alternative.

In answer to the criticism frequently leveled at the federal race categories as regards their logic and consistency, the categories in fact have an internal logic that is entirely consistent with their primary purpose of delineating those minority groups that have suffered historical, government-sponsored oppression in the United States. According to the CNSTAT report: "Although the directive is clear about what it is not, it is silent on the basis of its chosen categorization. National origin, race, culture, and community recognition are all combined to create a complicated and inconsistent classification scheme. At the workshop, one frequently heard suggestion for improving the categorization would be to state more clearly the principles on which it is based."[99]

It should be clear by now that this criticism is in error, for the categories were designed specifically to define those particular populations that have suffered historical, long-lasting oppression at the hands of the U.S. government. Because each of these groups has had a different historical relationship to the federal government, it was necessary to describe them using differing criteria, as explained by former FICE ad hoc committee member Juanita Lott in her congressional testimony: "Yes, I think the reason we are measuring and categorizing the way we are is because of the kind of relationship the U.S. Government has had with different groups of people; that indeed the relationship with the American Indian population is specific, that there are treaties that go back beyond legislation."[100]

This approach is not inconsistent, however. Rather, it would be inconsistent to attempt to create a system of classification for these groups based on the mysticism of biological race. It would be inconsistent to ignore the differential treatment these groups received, as well as the differential ways they tend to be identified in American society. The federal categories at least correspond to historical, phenotypic, and cultural criteria that were used and still are used to discriminate against persons in those groups. In this regard, Amy Gutman's concept of *color consciousness* (color standing as a kind of shorthand for a person's package of physical characteristics), as opposed to race consciousness, is helpful.[101] In Gutman's account:

> Contingent color consciousness, or what we can simply call color consciousness for short, rejects race as an essential, natural division among human beings and also rejects the idea that there are morally relevant differences that correspond to racial divisions among human beings. Color consciousness entails an awareness of the way in which individuals have historically come to be identified by superficial phenotypical differences—such as skin color and facial features—that serve as the bases for invidious discriminations and other injustices associated with race. Were we to lack color consciousness of this contingent kind, we would be blind to a basic source of social injustice.[102]

It might indeed be desirable to have more explanation for the bases of the categories so that erroneous criticisms such as those contained in the CNSTAT report can be avoided. In future versions of federal race policy, a statement as to the reasons for the different types of categorization utilized might certainly be in order. I want to acknowledge again the philosophical difficulty facing the racial skeptic who advocates the continued use of the federal categories in the battle against institutional and covert racism. Such application of these categories should not be taken as an argument for extending their legitimacy beyond the federal milieu, however. Additionally, serious efforts must be made to find alternative means for accomplishing the important task of antidiscrimination monitoring.

As for the concern that the categories do not reflect the current demographic profile of the United States, this criticism is not to the point, although it is a very common misunderstanding. Presiding over congressional subcommittee hearings on the OMB 15 question in 1993, Representative Thomas Sawyer reflected that "in an effort to produce comparable, standardized data, the Government developed what could be described as categories of convenience. They convey an illusion of specificity that fails to capture the dynamic patterns of our population."[103] Similarly, Sawyer's counterpart in chairing the 1997 subcommittee hearings, Representative Stephen Horn, makes the same error. Noting that the ongoing review of the OMB 15 categories was a "vital issue for the enforcement of the civil rights laws of our nation," Horn then questioned "whether these categories are adequate to measure our society now and in the coming decade."[104]

Both Sawyer and Horn make the same mistake of assuming that the federal categories ought to capture every demographic possibility in the United States. People make this mistake in part because of the link between the federal race categories and the census. The entire federal government, including the Census Bureau, came under the requirement to use these categories as of May 12, 1977, when OMB issued the revised Exhibit F of Circular A-46. It is important to understand, however, that these categories represent only the minimum standard for *reporting* data. In no sense are federal agencies or any other parties limited to these categories in terms of *collecting* data.

The primary purpose of the categories is to provide data on several specific minority groups in the United States. Federal racial categories originated from an impulse to better identify those traditionally oppressed groups across all government agencies. The categories are not meant to be the only way agencies may collect and use demographic data, however. Government agencies may use finer distinctions in their categorizations as long as the data can be reaggregated into the basic categories for federal reporting purposes,[105] although only a few agencies, such as EEOC and the National Center for Health Statistics, have availed themselves of this option.[106]

Certainly the Census Bureau is an example of an agency that makes wide use of subcategorizations that can be reaggregated. Under the *Race* question, the 1990 census form listed fourteen choices in addition to a write-in option. Three of the choices were under the American Indian category, and a full nine choices were provided under the Asian/Pacific Islander category.[107] All the federal race categories can potentially be subdivided further. The Black category, for instance, could have a Caribbean-descent subdivision, which could be further divided along specific national or regional lines (British, French, and so on). If the need arises to break down the demography of the United States in as much detail as possible, it can be done with the proper data instrument; however, this is not usually the purpose when people are asked to list their race on a form.

What most commentators fail to understand is that the federal race categories and the census are two different entities with two different purposes. The purpose of the former is to facilitate the tracking of discrimination against several very specific subpopulations—not every possible subpopulation in the United States. The purpose of the latter, on the other hand, is to gather as much demographic information about the country's population as possible. The categories and the census are linked in that the Census Bureau must be able to report its data in the OMB format, but—and these are the two critical points—it can collect the data in as much demographic detail as it desires; and, while it must be able to report statistical information in the OMB format, it may also report it any number of other ways if the OMB format is not specifically required. The key for all data collection agencies and data collection instruments is that they must be capable of reporting information in accord with the federal race categories when called on to do so. Nothing stops the Census Bureau from issuing various statistical reports using all manner of subcategories, as long as it is still able to provide a report in the OMB format if necessary.

What Representatives Sawyer and Horn, the writers of the CNSTAT report, and most commentators fail to grasp is that racial check-boxes for discrimination monitoring purposes are distinct from the demographic purposes of the census. The check-boxes mandated by OMB are not designed with the latter purpose in mind, and they do not serve it. Demographic information on people of Middle Eastern descent can be obtained, for instance, if the census includes such a category, which it can do without changing the federal race categories since the Census Bureau would simply recode those responses as *White* for federal reporting purposes. This would be an appropriate census category if demographic information was desired on that particular population. However, adding a Middle Eastern category to the OMB designations, on the other hand, would be inappropriate since Middle Easterners cannot in any sense be said to have been the victims of systematic, historical discrimination by the U.S. government to the degree that Afro-Americans, Native Americans, Asians, and Hispanics have been.

So it is not the case that the OMB categories should reflect the full demographic diversity of the United States, for that is not their purpose. Rather, they very specifically apply only to certain minority groups. Persons who argue that the federal categories should be broadened to make them better match the overall diversity of the U.S. population are simply out of touch with the purposes and machinery of civil rights compliance monitoring. One could certainly raise the argument that the Census Bureau should be exempted from the requirement to report in the OMB format, but that is different from wrongly attempting to force the federal race categories to serve the purposes of the Census Bureau.

That the federal categories are driven by the needs of the government in its compliance monitoring effort, and not in its census effort, is very often lost in discussions. Like the Census Bureau, agencies and private-sector data collectors are free to further divide the categories into as many subgroups as their data needs require, providing they reaggregate the data prior to reporting for federal purposes. If a particular agency has a need for more detailed demographic data, it can design a collection instrument to meet that need. For example, the Small Business Administration might for its own needs elect to collect data on Asians by subdivisions of national ancestry, and it would be free to do so as long as whatever data it collected could be reported externally in the OMB format.

Private-sector institutions generally do not utilize subcategories, however, tending rather to use the federal categories as the default standard. This is perhaps because the addition of subcategories would add processing costs to the data collection and presentation effort, and the institutions would have to absorb the costs of reaggregating the data. These costs might involve increased staffing, redesign of forms, and the purchase of more advanced statistical software, for instance. Despite these factors, some private institutions have made use of finer distinctions in their data collection efforts.

Too often commentators appear to assume that these racial categories were meant to fit the self-identification preferences of every individual. It is civil rights laws, however, that mandate the federal use of racial statistics. As mentioned above, the title of Directive No. 15 is "Race and Ethnic Standards for Federal Statistics and Administrative Reporting." The federal statistics and administrative reporting alluded to are those concerned with civil rights compliance. So, although OMB has defined acceptable racial categories for federal reporting, it must be remembered that any such reporting is meant to be in support of antidiscrimination compliance monitoring; it is not intended to provide a minutely detailed demographic profile of the nation or to validate any particular individual's personal identity choice, the latter being a point to which I shall return in some detail when assessing the racial category changes sought by some multiracial advocates.

The final criticism from the CNSTAT report that I shall take up is the suggestion that the federal categories are inadequate vis-à-vis a "clearer understanding of racial and ethnic identity as a social construct." As I argued in Chapter 1, the acceptance of race as a social construct is fraught with problems, in effect representing the reformulation of biological race in a new guise. The point with regard to federal racial statistics is not whether race is real but whether people, agencies, and institutions commit acts of racial discrimination. In this sense, the alleged social construction of race is irrelevant both to the behavior of the racist as well as to the victimization of the racist's target.

And so, we are brought back to the paradox with which I began this chapter—that the effort to reduce the significance of race in American life has led to an emphasis on race in regard to civil rights compliance monitoring. On forms, applications, and virtually any piece of paper one forwards to any level of government bureaucracy there is a check-box for racial identification. These boxes serve a tremendously significant function in that they help in the compilation of statistics that uncover suspicious patterns in hiring, promotion, and service that may be attributable to racism. There is no doubt that levels of discrimination in hiring, contracting, promotions, schooling, and a host of other areas have declined significantly since civil rights compliance monitoring went into effect. This is not to say that the problem has been solved, for there continue to be areas that demand improvement; but it is undeniable that much progress has been made due in part to the use of federal racial statistics. The United States is in many respects far removed from 1964, and continuing frustrations with civil rights progress should not be cause to minimize the gains of the past.

Americans, however, are at a point where they must consider seriously the dilemma of relying to such a degree on federal race terminology. Despite the undeniably positive effects of using compliance monitoring to combat racism, the proliferation of racial check-boxes and racial statistics limits the ability ultimately to move away from the idea of race as a meaningful concept. Clearly, it is neither wise nor practical to simply dismantle the U.S. civil rights compliance structure at this point. What is needed instead is continued use of compliance monitoring, along with a commitment to finding alternative methods for tracking discrimination. The federal race categories have worked to cement the idea of race in U.S. society as much as they have worked to uncover patterns of racial discrimination. Any potential revisions to these categories must be considered with the utmost gravity and concern, both for the primary purpose of the categories in providing a statistical language for civil rights compliance monitoring and for the effects the categories have in solidifying the idea of race as a reality.

Early in this chapter, I asserted that two related concepts would guide my discussion in this chapter and in the book generally, and we would be well served to revisit them prior to moving on to explicit considerations of multiracial identity and a federal multiracial category. First, federal racial classification exists for the primary purpose of monitoring continuing discrimination against specific groups to whom the United States has particular, historical responsibilities. This is serious business in that it represents the best tool Americans have for reducing and eliminating covert and institutional discrimination. Second, in absolutely no sense is federal racial classification intended to provide a means for persons to validate their self-identity choices. Such considerations are simply outside the very particular scope of the federal race categories. With these facts in mind, we may now move to an examination of multiracial identity.

Notes

1. "In civil law, definition is always hazardous." In Georg W. F. Hegel, *Hegel's Philosophy of Right,* trans. T. M. Knox (Oxford: Oxford University Press, 1967), 14, 305.

2. Suzann Evinger, "How Shall We Measure Our Nation's Diversity?" *Chance* 8, no. 1 (Winter 1995): 8.

3. Department of Education, National Center for Education Statistics, *Racial and Ethnic Classifications Used by Public Schools,* NCES 96-092, by Nancy Carey and Elizabeth Farris, project officer Judi Carpenter (Washington, D.C., 1996), 14.

4. Although the basic text of the policy has remained unchanged, it is not correct to assert, as many commentators do, that OMB 15 had been in effect since 1977. There have been several changes involving which government agency has had responsibility for implementing the policy, and I shall detail those changes in this chapter.

5. It is important to note that although discrimination against whites can certainly be monitored via these categories, they were designed specifically to aid in monitoring discrimination against the major groups in the United States who have been the victims of government-sanctioned oppression.

6. Lawrence Wright, "One Drop of Blood," *New Yorker,* July 25, 1994, 55.

7. Evinger, "How Shall We Measure?" 8.

8. House Subcommittee on Census, Statistics, and Postal Personnel, Committee on Post Office and Civil Service, *Hearings on the Review of Federal Measurements of Race and Eth-*

nicity, testimony by Reynolds Farley on April 14, 1993, 103d Cong., 1st sess., April 14, June 30, July 29, and November 3, 1993, 56.

9. Ibid.

10. National Research Council, Committee on National Statistics, Panel on Census Requirements in the Year 2000 and Beyond, *Modernizing the U.S. Census,* ed. Barry Edmonston and Charles Schultze. (Washington, D.C.: National Academy Press, 1995), 250–253.

11. Executive Office of the President, Office of Management and Budget, "Recommendations from the Interagency Committee for the Review of the Racial and Ethnic Standards to the Office of Management and Budget Concerning Changes to the Standards for the Classification of Federal Data on Race and Ethnicity," by Sally Katzen, *Federal Register* 62, no. 131 (July 9, 1997): 36874.

12. *Civil Rights Act of 1957, U.S. Statutes at Large* 71 (1957): 634.

13. Evinger, "How Shall We Measure?" 7.

14. Executive Office of the President, Bureau of the Budget, "Exhibit A: Standards for Statistical Surveys," *Circular no. A-46: Statistical Procedures* (March 28, 1952): 4.

15. Executive Office of the President, Office of Management and Budget, "Standards for the Classification of Federal Data on Race and Ethnicity," by Sally Katzen, *Federal Register* 60, no. 166 (August 28, 1995): 44674.

16. William Peterson, "Politics and the Measurement of Ethnicity," in *The Politics of Numbers,* ed. William Alonso and Paul Starr (New York: Russell Sage Foundation, 1987), 195.

17. Chris Hansen, "Race/Ethnicity and Data Collection," *Poverty and Race* 4, no. 2 (March-April 1995): 17.

18. Peterson, "Politics," 195–196.

19. *Civil Rights Act of 1964, U.S. Statutes at Large* 78 (1964): 255.

20. Ibid., 266.

21. Ibid., 252.

22. Commission on Civil Rights, *Federal Title VI Enforcement to Ensure Nondiscrimination in Federally Assisted Programs* (Washington, D.C., June 1996), 14.

23. *Voting Rights Act of 1965, U.S. Statutes at Large* 79 (1965): 440.

24. Ibid., 444.

25. President, Executive Order, "Equal Employment Opportunity, Executive Order 11246," *Code of Federal Regulations, Title 3: The President, 1964 and 1965 Compilation* (1967): 340–341.

26. President, Executive Order, "To Facilitate Coordination of Federal Education Programs, Executive Order 11185," *Code of Federal Regulations, Title 3: The President, 1964 and 1965 Compilation* (1967): 260.

27. Ibid., 259.

28. Despite persistent research efforts I have been unable to locate a copy of this report. I have consulted government resources, the Educational Resources Information Center (ERIC), current FICE personnel, and several members of the 1974–1975 FICE Ad Hoc Committee on Racial and Ethnic Definitions, which was commissioned as a direct of result of the report. Available evidence and conversations with ad hoc committee members lead me to conclude that the report was never actually published.

29. Federal Interagency Committee on Education, *Report of the Ad Hoc Committee on Racial and Ethnic Definitions* (Washington, D.C., April 1975), 1.

30. Grace Flores-Hughes, telephone conversation with author, October 28, 1996.

31. Grace Flores-Hughes, "Why the Term 'Hispanic'?" *Hispanic,* September 1996, 64.

32. Federal Interagency Committee on Education, *Report of the Ad Hoc Committee,* 1.

33. Ibid., 7.

34. Executive Office of the President, Bureau of the Budget, "Exhibit K: Amendment to Circular no. A-46, Race and Color Designations in Federal Statistics," Transmittal Memorandum no. 8, August 8, 1969.

35. Ibid.

36. Ibid.

37. Federal Interagency Committee on Education, *Report of the Ad Hoc Committee,* 12.

38. Ibid., 12–13.

39. Ibid., 7.

40. Ibid.

41. Flores-Hughes, "Why the Term 'Hispanic'?" 64.

42. Grace Flores-Hughes, telephone conversation with author, October 30, 1996.

43. Indeed, I have been guilty of this myself. In my article "Notes from the Struggle Against Racial Categorization: Challenge or Collaboration?" *Interrace,* October-November 1994, 18–22, I criticize the various OMB 15 categories without appreciating their impact on civil rights compliance monitoring. My criticisms in that article of the Association of MultiEthnic Americans' proposed 1993 revision to OMB 15, however, were valid.

44. Federal Interagency Committee on Education, *Report of the Ad Hoc Committee,* 7–8.

45. National Research Council, Committee on National Statistics, *Spotlight on Heterogeneity: The Federal Standards for Racial and Ethnic Classification, Summary of a Workshop,* ed. Barry Edmonston, Joshua Goldstein, and Juanita T. Lott (Washington, D.C.: National Academy Press, 1996), 18.

46. Federal Interagency Committee on Education, *Report of the Ad Hoc Committee,* 8.

47. Ibid.

48. Ibid.

49. Ibid., 10.

50. Ibid., 10–11.

51. Executive Office of the President, Office of Management and Budget, "Exhibit F: Race and Color Designations in Federal Statistics," *Circular no. A-46: Standards and Guidelines for Federal Statistics* (May 3, 1974).

52. Ibid., 4.

53. O. Jean Brandes, "Racial/Ethnic Categories for Educational Statistics," *Statistical Reporter* 76, no. 3 (September 1975): 51.

54. Katherine K. Wallman and John Hodgdon, "Race and Ethnic Standards for Federal Statistics and Administrative Reporting," *Statistical Reporter* 77, no. 10 (July 1977): 450.

55. Ibid.

56. Executive Office of the President, Office of Management and Budget, "Exhibit F (Revised May 12, 1977): Race and Ethnic Standards for Federal Statistics and Administrative Reporting," *Circular no. A–46: Standards and Guidelines for Federal Statistics* (May 3, 1974): 3–4. This marks the first use of the title "Race and Ethnic Standards for Federal Statistics and Administrative Reporting."

57. Ibid., 1.

58. Ibid., 3.

59. General Accounting Office, General Government Division, *Federal Data Collection: Agencies' Use of Consistent Race and Ethnic Definitions,* GAO/GGD-93-95, by L. Nye Stevens (Washington, D.C., December 1992), 2.

60. *Budget and Accounting Procedures Act of 1950, U.S. Statutes at Large* 64 (1950–1951): 834.

61. Department of Commerce, Office of Federal Statistical Policy and Standards, *Statistical Policy Handbook* (Washington, D.C., 1978), 65.

62. President, Executive Order, "Relating to the Transfer of Certain Statistical Policy Functions, Executive Order 12013," *Federal Register* 42, no. 197 (October 12, 1977): 54931–54933.

63. Department of Commerce, *Statistical Policy Handbook,* v.

64. Department of Commerce, Bureau of the Census, "Transfer of Responsibility for Certain Statistical Standards from OMB to Commerce," by Juanita M. Kreps, *Federal Register* 43, no. 87 (May 4, 1978): 19260.

65. Ibid., 19269.

66. Executive Office of the President, Office of Management and Budget, "Standards for the Classification of Federal Data on Race and Ethnicity," by Sally Katzen, *Federal Register* 59, no. 110 (June 9, 1994): 29831–29832.

67. Suzann Evinger, telephone conversation with author, September 1996.

68. Department of Commerce, *Statistical Policy Handbook,* 65.

69. Ibid., 4.

70. Ibid., 37.

71. Ibid., 38.

72. *Paperwork Reduction Act of 1980, U.S. Statutes at Large* 94 (1980): 2814.

73. Ibid., 2815.

74. Ibid.

75. Executive Office of the President, Office of Management and Budget, "Guidelines for Federal Statistical Activities," by Wendy L. Gramm, *Federal Register* 53, no. 12 (January 20, 1988): 1552.

76. House Subcommittee on Census, Statistics, and Postal Personnel, Committee on Post Office and Civil Service, *Hearings on the Review of Federal Measurements of Race and Ethnicity,* testimony by Sally Katzen on July 29, 1993, 103d Cong., 1st sess., April 14, June 30, July 29, and November 3, 1993, 224–225.

77. Executive Office of the President, "Standards for Classification," 29834.

78. Executive Office of the President, Office of Management and Budget, Letter to the Heads of Executive Departments and Establishments, "Subject: Rescission of Office of Management and Budget Circulars nos. A-39, A-46, A-65, and A-91," signed by James T. McIntyre Jr., April 13, 1978.

79. National Research Council, *Spotlight on Heterogeneity,* 1.

80. Ibid., 59.

81. Department of Commerce, "Transfer of Responsibility," 19269.

82. National Research Council, *Spotlight on Heterogeneity,* 65.

83. General Accounting Office, *Federal Data Collection,* 2.

84. Ibid., 10–11.

85. National Research Council, *Spotlight on Heterogeneity,* 37.

86. Executive Office of the President, "Exhibit F (Revised May 12, 1977)," 1. Indeed, the 1969 Exhibit K of Circular A-46 stated that race as used in federal statistics was "not a

clear-cut biological definition." Executive Office of the President, "Exhibit K, Amendment to Circular no. A–46."

87. Federal Interagency Committee on Education, *Report of the Ad Hoc Committee*, 1.

88. Ibid., iv.

89. Juanita T. Lott, telephone conversation with author, October 25, 1996.

90. Federal Interagency Committee on Education, *Report of the Ad Hoc Committee*, v.

91. Ibid., 3.

92. National Research Council, *Spotlight on Heterogeneity*, 32.

93. One might certainly argue that the more recent immigrant groups did not suffer the severity of discrimination directed by the U.S. government at Chinese Americans and Japanese Americans in past eras, for instance; but the racist is more concerned with discriminating based on the myth of race than he is with actual nationalities, and this is what must be tracked statistically.

94. Federal Interagency Committee on Education, *Report of the Ad Hoc Committee*, 4.

95. Ibid.

96. Flores-Hughes, "Why the Term 'Hispanic'?" 64.

97. Federal Interagency Committee on Education, *Report of the Ad Hoc Committee*, 4–5.

98. Ibid., 5

99. National Research Council, *Spotlight on Heterogeneity*, 36.

100. House Subcommittee on Census, Statistics, and Postal Personnel, Committee on Post Office and Civil Service, *Hearings on the Review of Federal Measurements of Race and Ethnicity*, testimony by Juanita T. Lott on April 14, 1993, 103d Cong., 1st sess., April 14, June 30, July 29, and November 3, 1993, 69.

101. Kwame Anthony Appiah and Amy Gutman, *Color Conscious: The Political Morality of Race* (Princeton: Princeton University Press, 1996), 110. Unlike Michael Omi and Howard Winant in *Racial Formation in the United States: From the 1960s to the 1990s*, 2d ed. (New York: Routledge, 1994), Gutman does see race as a problematic element in American society.

102. Appiah and Gutman, *Color Conscious*, 163–164.

103. House Subcommittee on Census, Statistics, and Postal Personnel, Committee on Post Office and Civil Service, *Hearings on the Review of Federal Measurements of Race and Ethnicity*, testimony by Thomas Sawyer on July 29, 1993, 103d Cong., 1st sess., April 14, June 30, July 29, and November 3, 1993, 197.

104. House Subcommittee on Government Management, Information, and Technology, Committee on Government Reform and Oversight, *Hearings on Federal Measures of Race and Ethnicity and the Implications for the 2000 Census*, testimony by Stephen Horn on July 25, 1997, 105th Cong., 1st sess., April 23, May 22, and July 25, 1997, 507.

105. Executive Office of the President, "Exhibit F (Revised May 12, 1977)," 3.

106. National Research Council, *Spotlight on Heterogeneity*, 11.

107. National Research Council, *Modernizing the U.S. Census*, 198.

3

Multiracial Identity

Question: By what characteristics do multiracial people define themselves as a group or a distinct category?

Answer: The essential attribute of a multiracial category is that those persons have parents of two or more racial categories.

—Susan Graham, executive director, Project RACE[1]

If identities are not metaphysical, timeless categories of being, if they point not to ontologies but to historical specificities and contingencies; if their mapping of bodies and subjectivities are forms of and not simply resistances to practices of domination—then a politics based on identity must carefully negotiate the risk of reinscribing the logic of the system it hopes to defeat.

—Robyn Wiegman[2]

Philosophical and Ideological Considerations

The first point that must be made about the notion of multiracialism is that it is in no sense new. In America, the concept is at least as old as the first attempts of British colonials to legislate against "interracial marriages, in order to prevent 'that abominable mixture and spurious issue.'"[3] Additionally, there have long been people who have refused to identify themselves according to the dictates of the American racial paradigm.[4] What we are witnessing at the dawn of the new millennium, however, is the beginning of a more public debate over race and identity that is paralleled by a slowly expanding scholarly discourse on multiraciality. Part of this new activity is a multiracial identity movement that has as one of its principal goals the modification of the federal race categories to include a multiracial category as denoting a distinct racial group.

The two main thrusts of the multiracial identity movement argue for accuracy and for self-esteem. The contention is that multiracial identification is more accurate for its adherents than monoracial identification.[5] Those who argue for accuracy to support their positions tend to claim that inadequate self-identification and self-esteem on the part of individuals who identify as multiracial or who have a multiracial identity imposed on them by others (i.e., children who are taught by their parents that they are multiracial) may lead to psychological pathology and dysfunction. They contend that for such individuals to develop proper self-esteem, their multiracial identification must be fully sanctioned.

I shall address arguments relating to accuracy in the course of this chapter, demonstrating that they are incompatible—indeed, inconsistent—points of reference for the multiracial category movement as a whole.[6] In other words, in the context of the movement, the argument for accuracy becomes embroiled in serious logical contradictions when analyzed in any depth. The failure of the movement to acknowledge the impossibility of arguing for a multiracial category from the perspective of racial accuracy is a serious deficiency when the movement's ideology is subject to real critical analysis.

Multiracial identity is predicated on the idea that race exists and that the offspring of persons from two different racial groups is a multiracial individual. According to Maria Root, editor of two well-known anthologies on multiracial identity (*Racially Mixed People in America* and *The Multiracial Experience: Racial Borders As the New Frontier*), "*Multiracial* refers to people who are of two or more racial heritages. It is the most inclusive term to refer to people across all racial mixes. Thus it also includes biracial people."[7] As Root's definition illustrates, a basic and undeniable principle of multiraciality is the acceptance of biological race. In the course of this chapter I shall point out the logical inconsistency inherent in this cornerstone of multiracial ideology. Asserting that multiracial individuals exist without simultaneously validating the reality of biological racial groups is a contradiction. That this is so would seem to follow common sense, yet one of the main tenets of the multiracial movement remains its assertion that a federal multiracial category would work somehow to destabilize the American racial paradigm.

Carlos Fernández, former president and current legal counsel of the Association of MultiEthnic Americans (AMEA), the major multiracial lobbying organization in the United States, claims that multiracial people asserting themselves "will also have the effect of breaking down the 'race' question."[8] G. Reginald Daniel describes multiracialism as having the "potential for undermining the very basis of racism, which is its categories,"[9] while Teresa Williams offers that "no other social reality than that of racially mixed people questions the one-dimensional racial structure upon which America has founded and built its national identity."[10] Laurie Shrage, in considering whether a mixed-race signifier might work in such a way, suggests the possibility that "the visibility of mixed-race, or multiply or ambiguously raced, persons might challenge a racial system that otherwise maintains the fictions of racial and ethnic purity and distinctness—fictions that are ever powerful despite the fact that the biological accounts supporting these distinctions have been overwhelmingly discredited."[11]

If, however, one is critical of race, it then becomes apparent that there is an inherent contradiction in the idea of multiraciality; for if race is a myth, then multirace must of necessity be a myth as well. Yet how is one to self-identify, to assert an identity, when the only language seemingly available is infused with the terminology of racialism? The answer lies in challenging rather than acceding to the hegemony of race and in rejecting the premise that personal identity need be race based to begin with.

In this regard, Linda Alcoff makes an important and often overlooked point when she reminds us that we should "consider what role this preference for purity and racial separateness has had on dominant formulations of identity and subjectivity and what the effects might be if this preference was no longer operative."[12] My reading of Alcoff's point is that what Americans take to be natural identities are overdetermined by a racial hegemony that ought to be challenged. The concepts of race and racial identity are neither natural nor necessary, but one must make the effort to get outside the system of racial classification in order to see that this is so. One of my arguments throughout this chapter will be that advocates of multiracialism never challenge, destabilize, or move outside the American racial paradigm, but instead always operate comfortably within its confines.

One strategy used by some multiracial advocates to obscure the necessary connection between biological race and multirace is the positing of race as a social instead of a biological reality. As I argued in Chapter 1, however, even the assertion of race as a so-called social reality is no more than the evocation of biological race in a disguised form. Moreover, even granting for a moment the notion of race as a social reality, it is not clear why the offspring of parents from different socially constructed or socially recognized racial groups should be considered multiracial. The very point of the social construction view is its alleged distance from biological race; yet this distancing is surely illusory if the offspring of parents from different socially defined racial groups can be seen as multiracial precisely because they are the *biological* children of their parents. In other words, if, in the social reality view, matters of biology have no relevance in categorizing the parents, then matters of biology should have no relevance in categorizing the offspring. If the social reality view of race is upheld, then the biological mating of persons from different socially defined races should have no bearing on what should be the socially defined race of the resulting child. However, it is precisely because race, despite the cautious substitution of social language for biological language, is still conceived of as a biological reality that the social construction subterfuge is inadequate.

An example of this kind of cautious but ineffective attempt to steer away from overt biological language is seen in the glossary of Root's anthology *The Multiracial Experience,* in which she offers: "*Biracial* refers to a person whose parents are of two different socially designated racial groups, for example, *black* mother, *white* father. In a less commonly used, but perfectly accurate meaning, biracial can also refer to someone who has parents of the same socially designated race, when one or both parents are biracial or there is racial mixing in the family history that is important to the individual."[13]

Here, Root attempts to sever any connection with biological race by making explicit reference to "socially designated racial groups." The apparent move away from biological race does not eliminate the logical problems inherent in this enterprise, however, but merely hides them temporarily. Dressing the mythology of biological race in the garb of socially designated race is a transparent artifice that does nothing to resolve the fact that the socially designated racial categories are precisely the same as the biological classifications upon which they are based. Moreover, by invoking the social reality framework in this way, additional complications arise that ensure the unsoundness of the multiracial argument.

It will be instructive to utilize Root's example and consider a couple consisting of a socially designated black woman and a socially designated white man. Let us suppose further that this couple adopts a socially designated Asian daughter. Are we to consider this Asian child biracial because her parents are members of "two different socially designated racial groups"? To do so would be consistent with Root's definition, but it would also be absurd. Rather, most would object that the child is not biracial because (1) she is Asian, and (2) she is not the biological child of these adoptive parents. In other words, it is not being the legal child of such parents that makes one biracial, but rather it is being the *biological* child of such parents that does.

Yet if this objection is made—and it surely would be, even by multiracial activists—it becomes clear that biology rather than social designation drives multiracial ideology and that wording such as "parents of different socially designated races" is merely a camouflage for biological race. If biological race were not the true framework of multiraciality, then having parents of "two different socially designated racial groups" would not be the definition of *biracial,* for there would be no racial significance to the parent-child biological relationship. Root's definition demonstrates that the evocation of the racial social reality is merely a euphemistic recoding of both biological race and hypodescent in more acceptable language.

Elsewhere, however, Root appeals to yet a different means of grounding multiracial identity, invoking a notion of personal choice by claiming that "a major difference between African Americans and multiracially identified African Americans is not a fundamental difference in racial heritage but rather that the latter group identify themselves as multicultural, multiracial, feel a kinship with more than one group, or more comfortably move between racial groups on a social basis."[14] On this logic, however, one would be every bit as justified in arguing for a new racial category based on class or political affiliation as for one based on feelings of kinship in which racial heritage is not a major factor.

If a fundamental difference in racial heritage between Afro-Americans who identify as black and Afro-Americans who identify as multiracial is not regarded as a major distinction between them, then Root's previous definition of *multiracial* as referring to "people who are of two or more racial heritages" immediately becomes suspect. In other words, if *multiracial* is defined as "people who are of two or more racial heritages," then it simply cannot be that a fundamental difference in racial heritage between black-identifying Afro-Americans and multiracially identifying Afro-Americans is not a major distinction between them. Indeed, in terms of Root's definition it would have to be the primary difference between them.

What is here demonstrated is a fundamental failure of multiracial ideology to exhibit logical consistency when subjected to the slightest scrutiny. Multiracialism is unquestionably based on a foundation of biological race; yet, when convenient, biological race is masked by talk of socially constructed race. When the latter proves inconvenient as well, multiracial advocates deploy a notion of personal choice, apparently—but not actually—detached from the biological racial foundation that makes even conceiving of multiracialism possible.

The social reality view of U.S. racial categorization holds that Americans place people in certain racial categories because they read key phenotypic cues as signifiers of particular racial groups, even though there is no scientific basis for these classifications. According to the social construction view espoused, for instance, by Michael Omi and Howard Winant (see Chapter 1), this kind of racial categorization is legitimate regardless of its biological falseness because it is alleged to be a social reality. In this arrangement, an external judgment becomes the center of an individual's racial identity irrespective of that person's own wishes. The statement could therefore be made that person X is black because people of X's phenotype are seen as black in the United States, whether one believes in biological race or not. Thus, at least on the surface, societal criteria appear to be the driving force of the social designation view of race.[15]

Yet advocates of multiracial identity who utilize the framework of socially designated race in order to avoid overt appeal to the underlying biological foundation inconsistently accept social designations of race for differently raced parents but not for their children, as evidenced by Root's definition above. On the one hand multiracial advocates accept as legitimate the different categorizations of two members of an interracial couple based on social designation (in a vain attempt to obscure the biological foundation of multiracialism), while on the other hand they argue specifically that such social designation not be used for categorizing the children. However, it is inconsistent to suggest that parents be classified racially based on social designation, and to then insist that the same criteria used to categorize the parents not be used to categorize their children.

If, for instance, the mother in Root's example above is considered black because of some socially defined criteria of blackness, consistent logic would hold that (depending on phenotype and current understandings of race in America) the child should be considered black for the same reason.[16] This is the logical consequence of utilizing the socially designated racial framework, yet multiracial advocates assert that social designation should not be used to classify the child, while simultaneously—and inconsistently—supporting classifying the parents racially based on societal criteria. This is the eternal contradiction of multiracial advocacy. It is an undeniable and inescapable logical inconsistency to erect multiracial identity on the foundation of socially constructed race, which, to reiterate my earlier point, is itself no more than the euphemistic reinscription of biological race.

Appealing to the social reality frame of reference does not make multiracial identity any more tenable, since properly employing such a view commits one to using that framework consistently, for parents of different socially designated racial groups as well as for their children. If social designation of phenotype is enough to categorize the parents racially, consistency demands that social designation of phenotype be enough to categorize the children racially as well. Thus, Root's explicit framing of race as a social, as opposed to a biological, category is inconsistent with her special pleading for biracial identity on the basis of biological mating. Root's multiracial argument is therefore contradictory to the system of social designation within which she has chosen to frame race.

Far from working against biological racial categorization, multiracialism is absolutely dependent upon it as a precondition of its own affirmation. Biological race is a necessary, though not a sufficient, condition for multiracialism. In other words, whereas multiracialism depends on the prior acceptance of biological race, biological race by itself does not necessitate the existence of multiracialism. In the simplest sense, then, multiracial identity cannot even be conceived of without first embracing some notion of distinct and exclusive biological racial groups. If, after all, a person X is to be understood as resulting from mixture, there must first be two different entities that are subsequently mixed together in order to bring X about. Samira Kawash makes this very point by explaining that "in trying to supplant the idea of racial or cultural identities with a more complex notion of hybridity, it is easy to forget that the very notion of hybridity is already predicated on conditions named by the essentializing division it seeks to counter, that is, the color line."[17] In the case of supposed multiracial identity, those conditions are parents or ancestors of different biological racial groups, assertions of race as a social category notwithstanding. Writing in a similar vein, Katya Azoulay argues that "recent appeals for new classifications such as 'multiracial' do not undermine race thinking; they can, however, obscure the history of racial and sexual violence for those whose multiracial genealogy was involuntary."[18]

Multiracialism is an unsound principle no matter what position one takes on biological race. Even if biological race had been real at some time in the distant past, and if races had at that time been distinct and exclusive categories, there has been so much population intermixture in the past several thousand years, in the past five hundred years especially, as to render preposterous the notion that any distinct and exclusive biological racial groups still exist. At this point in human history it must be admitted either that race does not and never has existed; or that if it once existed all people are now multiracial, and that as a practical matter the term *multiracial* is meaningless.

Yet the inconsistency of multiracial advocacy, over and above the false mythology of racial categorization upon which it depends, is not acknowledged. Even while ostensibly problematizing all notions of race, Naomi Zack, one of the better-known scholars writing about multiracial issues, reflects this logical problem when she contends that "the reality of mixed race needs to be written and talked out before the illusion of race itself can be dispelled."[19] One wonders what alchemy allows an illusion to produce a reality, however; for if race is an illusion, as Zack correctly asserts, then there is no mixed-race reality . . . only mixed-race confusion.[20]

This inconsistency is illustrated by the conflicting statements of Carlos Fernández. Fernández, testifying before Congress, declared that "many if not most ethnically-identified African Americans are 'multiracial,' so, incidentally, are most 'Hispanics,'"[21] while he asserted elsewhere that "the census must be based on 'truth and facts. And if a person has one black parent and a white parent, that's a fact.'"[22] Yet Fernández offers up a contradictory set of facts, for if most Afro-Americans are multiracial, as he stated before Congress, then it should be neither possible nor necessary for a black parent to be categorized differently than the child of "one black parent and a white parent," since this would contradict his assertion that most blacks are already multiracial.

Further confusion arises from the second part of Root's definition of biracial as referring to "someone who has parents of the same socially designated race, when one or both parents are biracial." Given Root's own distinction between biracial or multiracial people on the one hand and members of socially designated racial groups on the other, which, after all, is the raison d'être of the multiracial identity movement, it is impossible for someone to have a parent who is at one and the same time biracial and a member of a "socially designated race." It might be supposed that Root is referring to the grandparents being biracial rather than the parents, but this offers no solution either; for if one or both grandparents were biracial they could not produce a parent who was a member of a "socially designated race," since this person would ostensibly be biracial or multiracial as well.

I want to be quite clear in pointing out the logical problem in which Root becomes enmeshed via her biracial definition. If, in accord with Root's definition, we posit a hypothetical biracial person who has parents of the same socially designated race (both black, for example), and we further suppose that one of the parents is biracial (having black/white ancestry), then Root must explain how this parent can at the same time be both biracial and black. This is not as easy it might seem, for Root's own definition has trapped her into on the one hand attempting to draw a distinction between biracial people and persons of socially designated races and on the other allowing that a person can be both a member of a socially designated race and biracial at the same time. If both alternatives are possible, then *biracial* and *multiracial* stand as redundant and meaningless predicates.

Root's attempt, via the language of social designation, to camouflage multiracialism's dependence on a foundation of biological race results in precisely the same contradiction as that raised by hypodescent. Her definition results necessarily in the conclusion that since black people can be biracial (or biracial people black), there is a cardinal inconsistency in labeling them black (or biracial), whether we are dealing with biological or social designations. In the case of Afro-Americans, at least, the terms become interchangeable, and the distinction meaningless. At any rate, it is clear that there is a fundamental logical contradiction for multiracial philosophy at the level of first principles due to the impossibility of constructing a viable multiracial argument on the meritless foundation of race, whether in biological or social alter ego form.

Finally, the last clause of Root's definition relates to an aspect of multiracial identity politics that I shall revisit in my discussion of the multiracial category initiative in Chapter 4—self-identification. Root seems to leave multiracial classification as a personal choice when she states that multiracial identification is accurate when "there is racial mixing in the family history that is important to the individual." Yet accuracy demands that if there is race mixing in the family history, descendants would be multiracial whether they wanted to be or not. It is a common feature of multiracial ideology for impassioned arguments to be made on behalf of accuracy (i.e., that accuracy requires not classifying multiracials into the standard categories) but for accuracy to be ignored when it proves inconvenient, as in the case of Afro-Americans who have European and Native American ancestry farther back in their family histories. As Cecile Lawrence asks, "Where is the black hole into which the non-'black' ancestors of these people get sucked?"[23]

The idea that one's being multiracial depends on whether ancestral race mixing is important to the individual adds yet another wrinkle to an already confused ideology, for how is the multiraciality of the person who has ancestral racial mixing that is important to that person different—qua multiraciality—from that of the person who has ancestral racial mixing that is not personally important? Each individual in this scenario has ancestral racial mixing and should, if accuracy is really a concern, have the same racial classification regardless of personal preference.

Illustrative of this ambiguity is the phenomenon that in the multiracial movement a distinction is drawn between persons one might call immediately mixed and those who have race mixing farther back in their family histories. According to multiracial ideology, people with parents of two different racial groups are considered first-generation multiracials.[24] I shall return to this distinction in a more detailed way in Chapter 4 when I take up formal multiracial category initiatives. Again, as with so much of multiracial ideology, the Afro-American example will be key to illustrating this distinction, and ultimately in turning it on its head; for of course, if one of the parents of a first-generation multiracial individual is an Afro-American, the question must be raised as to why this parent is not already considered multiracial. Indeed, if accuracy is of any interest at all, the child of an Afro-American should be considered at least a sixth-or seventh-generation multiracial person regardless of the race of the other parent. It would seem that for ideological purposes, however, the multiracial movement's concern for accuracy is at best situational.

However, the implications and logical extensions of the statements people make are subject to the test of consistency, regardless of ideology. If race and multirace were for the briefest instant taken to exist, it would surely be a matter of fact and certainly not a matter of personal choice that person X is either multiracial or not—regardless of whether the racial mixing is important to the individual and regardless of whether it took place at conception or several centuries earlier in the family history. Nonetheless, advocates of a federal multiracial category inconsistently deploy a selective hypodescent as well as selective arguments insisting on accuracy when convenient. Rather than acknowledging the highly heterogeneous Afro-American population as entirely multiracial, advocates of a federal multiracial category distance themselves from the Afro-American group in order to distinguish themselves from it.

The arbitrariness involved in considering so-called first-generation persons multiracial while ignoring the European ancestry of most Afro-Americans is voiced by University of California at Los Angeles graduate student Thembi Lise McWhite: "If someone called me black, I would not correct them and tell them that I was not, because I see very little difference between my white mother and someone else's white ancestor, yet we have no problem calling that other person black. I think this whole racial labeling thing is very ambiguous. What's the difference between me, and my just as bright/light girlfriends with two 'black' parents?"[25]

It should be said as well that the superficial and inconsistent appeal to accuracy that is integral to the multiracial argument is most likely not devious but is rather the natural consequence of attempting to operationalize such a self-contradictory ideology. The necessity of binding multiracialism to race, whether biological or social, is a guarantee of invalidity, confusion, and inconsistency. New York University graduate student Deborah Thomas makes this very error when she states that "because American society adamantly upholds the false concept of racial purity and continues to see racial issues solely in terms of black and white (no pun intended), mixed-race Americans are still not officially represented on demographic information surveys. Put more simply, we have no block to check."[26] Although correctly terming racial purity a false concept, Thomas still attempts to give it validity; but race is nothing without purity. Once it is admitted that there are no pure races, no consistent categorization is possible. In this sense the only possible way to conceptualize racial issues *is* "solely in terms of black and white."[27] Arguing against racial purity while arguing for a multiracial category is self-defeating, since if one takes Thomas's position that racial purity is a false concept, one must then admit that there are no races, and no people who are monoracial or multiracial, because the words are meaningless.

Taking a stance similar to that of Thomas, Maria Root also makes an argument that unravels itself when examined critically:

> Whereas a child of 5 learns to classify an object by two categories or features simultaneously, for example, a blue *and* green ball, most Americans are overwhelmed by—or resistant to—the possibility that someone is both black *and* white, African American and Asian American. The average American's limited ability to think about race results in a limited ability to converse about race. Our racial vocabulary provides border markers that are rigid reflections upon our history of race relations and racial classification. Without the experience of recognizing race in all its manifestations and shades, we can not shift its meaning, deconstruct it, or combine it.[28]

Yet it must be said here that it is Root who cannot escape the grip of race, as, far from deconstructing it, she is working completely within the paradigm. It is precisely the false notion of biological race that makes it possible for her to conceive of "black *and* white." By positing the existence of "black *and* white" she is already fully complicit with the system she is unsuccessfully attempting to modify. Although appearing to protest the rigidity of American racial categorization, she nonetheless utilizes the category *black* in a monoracial and unproblematic sense while ignoring the fact that most Afro-Americans have European ancestry.

The multiracial argument requires the existence of those false racial categories, especially the black category that serves so well to obscure the multiple heritages of Afro-Americans, in order to differentiate so-called multiracials as a distinct category of people. David Goldberg correctly positions the multiracial argument within the dominant racial paradigm by asserting that "at best, then, the condition of mixed-race formation constitutes an ambivalent challenge to the racial condition from within the fabric of the racializing project."[29] Root's analogy of the colored ball, while simple and appealing, is ultimately ineffective because people are not black and white, nor blue and green. They are far too complex, with too much population mixture in their histories, to be categorized in so facile a manner.

Historical and Sociological Considerations

One of my goals in this book is to point out the inconsistency of multiracial proponents when in cases of so-called black/white intermixture they invoke a selective hypodescent in order to distinguish a child possessing African and European ancestry from a parent or ancestors having the same ancestry. In utilizing this tactic they and other commentators write and speak as though race mixing and mixed-race identity were new concepts in America, when nothing could be farther from the truth. They ignore the addition of European and Native American genetic material to the Afro-American population through the centuries, as well as the massive and continuous internal miscegenation that has taken place. To deny the centuries of population mixture in an Afro-American's genealogy by categorizing her as simply black, while at the same time categorizing as multiracial a child she might have with a white man, is to engage not only in a selective hypodescent but in the suspension of critical thought as well. As an example of this phenomenon, at a conference on multiracial identity, a researcher studying the attitudes of mixed-race students referred to those students, amazingly, as the first cohort of multiracial college students.[30] Whether this tendency represents selective amnesia or a true lack of historical knowledge, the result is the replication of a mythological Afro-American racial homogeneity and the consequent fallacious image of multiraciality as a new phenomenon.

Of course, British colonists in North America had been dealing legislatively with the issue of racial mixture since as early as the mid–seventeenth century and nonlegislatively for several decades prior to that, no doubt. These and many other important facts have been excised from the modern multiracial debate, however. Hence, much of that debate has taken place in a wholly uncontextualized form. For the sake of introducing some needed historical context, I will here provide a sense of the prominent place the mixed-race idea has occupied in the American experience. Without recapitulating the full history of African and European population mixture in colonial and national America, which Joel Williamson has laid out admirably, I will undertake a brief examination of American attitudes regarding the multiracial idea in times past.[31]

Most earlier works on the subject of multiracialism have situated the notion in *marginal person* theories of psychological identity confusion in the context of a monoracial construct, whereas more recent theories seek to cast it as a normal identity choice located explicitly within the same American racial paradigm. The older view saw the attempt to move outside strict racial lines as a guarantee of sustaining psychological damage. The newer version (which I shall consider in more detail later in this section), on the other hand, posits psychological danger in failing to move outside standard racial boundaries. Interestingly, as we shall see, there is less difference between these two schools of thought than one might suppose. What they share is an acceptance of biological race and the view that particular neuroses are natural for people who see themselves as members of two different racial groups.

We may turn to Gunnar Myrdal for a generalized view of the earlier form of physiological stereotyping directed at people seen as black/white mixes:

> There are many popular beliefs deprecating the mulatto: that they are more criminally disposed even than Negroes in general; that they tend to be sterile; that they—

having parents of two distinct races—are not harmoniously proportioned, but have
a trait of one parent side by side with a trait of the other parent, paired in such a way
that the two cannot function together properly; that they are more susceptible to tu-
berculosis; that, because Negroes have relatively long, narrow heads, Negro women,
with narrow pelvises, and their mulatto offspring are endangered when they bear
children of white men whose heads are rounder, and so on.[32]

Although these fallacies could have been disproved easily by prolonged observation, they tended to linger as a particularly hardy blend of folk belief and pseu-
doscience. Many scientists and medical professionals of the late nineteenth and
early twentieth centuries simply accepted them as part of their background understandings of race. Because these scientists considered whites and blacks to be
antipodal varieties of humans (perhaps even the results of polygenesis, or separate creation in the biblical sense), and because whites considered themselves far
superior to blacks, the scientists posited the existence of differing racial *essences*
or *geniuses*. Naomi Zack describes this construction as a case of scientists positing "a unique essence or 'genius' for each race that was present in all its members:
in cultural and biological rank, the white race was highest, the black race lowest;
the essence of the black race was infinitely transmittable from one generation of
direct genealogical descent to the next, but the essence of the white race could
only be preserved if the essence of the black race were not present with it in the
same individual."[33]

In his excellent study of American attitudes toward mulattoes and miscegenation between the Civil War and World War I, John Mencke argues that a loose
blending of polygenist thought, the Lamarkian idea of acquired characteristics,
and Darwinism resulted in the ascription of a superior European civilization to
the best and most advanced kind of racial essence, and the corollary ascription of
Negro backwardness to millennia of cultural and mental idleness in the tropical
African environment. In light of these two disparate essences, offspring resulting
from racial mixture were seen simultaneously as being intermediate between the
two groups, as well as being inferior to both. Mencke found that:

> The mulatto was generally perceived to be more intelligent than the black, as well as
> physically more attractive because of the predominance of white rather than black
> physical characteristics. In these terms, the mulatto was clearly superior to blacks. At
> the same time, it was widely believed that the mulatto was constitutionally weak,
> prone to debilitating diseases, like tuberculosis, and like all hybrids, basically infer-
> tile—facts which indicated certain basic inferiorities to both of the parent races.[34]

Although the hybrid degeneracy thesis faded over time, the psychological aspect of the marginality school of thought has been more damaging and longer
lasting. According to Paul Spickard, "Throughout most of postemancipation history, all this mythology was fastened with special force on the mulatto male. Pop-

ular fiction and movies for decades gave a compelling picture of the tragic mulatto, a character torn to the point of derangement between his desire to be White and the certainty that society regarded him as Black."[35]

This psychological angst has not been reserved exclusively for the male mulatto. In more recent decades, films such as *Pinky* (1949) and *Imitation of Life* (1934, 1959) have given a wide reading to the notion that mulatto women were inevitably torn between the races, destined to a tragic end unless they acknowledged and willingly accepted a Negro identity. Indeed, although they may seem to be different stories, both *Imitation of Life* and *Pinky* are essentially two sides of the same narrative coin. In the former film, the white-appearing mixed-race woman deserts the black race in order to pass as white, ultimately killing her mother figure and, metaphorically, the race as well. In the latter, the white-appearing mixed-race woman chooses instead to serve her "true" race, thus gratifying her mother figure's wishes and sacrificing only her own personal happiness in the process.

In the more remote past, well before the appearance of such films, American writers pursued a similar path. Frances Harper's *Iola Leroy, or Shadows Uplifted* (to invoke one of the more prominent examples) offered didactic messages advising mulatto women that their loyalties, lest there be any confusion, lay properly with the black race. The mulatto woman especially became a symbolic focal point—embodying issues of rape by slave masters, psychological repression and projection, sexual taboos, and the problematics of racial identity. The unchanging lesson for mulatto women and men in all these works is that the mulatto must either accept a Negro identity or suffer the neurosis and tragedy of never being able to reside safely in the white world.[36]

Mencke has identified three distinct mulatto themes in the literary works of Afro-American writers during the period of his study: (1) "the 'tragic mulatto,' a stereotyped image with a long literary history, designed to evoke the sympathy of the reader"; (2) "a stout-hearted hero or heroine who epitomizes middle-class virtues and who sees his/her role as a leader of the Negro race, despite the possibility, in many cases, of passing for white"; and (3) "a more complex individual who is sensitive to his position between the two races and who is more likely to opt for passing into the white world."[37]

Although Mencke categorizes only the first type as a tragic mulatto figure, it is possible to see all three profiles as variations on the tragic mulatto theme. The first case is the most overtly melodramatic; the mulatto is depicted as psychologically obsessed with the need to pass as white, often leading to disastrous consequences. Perhaps the best-known example of this type of characterization (although from a later period, and not created by an Afro-American) is the female mulatto character in Fannie Hurst's *Imitation of Life*, whose desperate need to be white causes untold pain to herself and to others. The second case is the opposite of the first in that self-denial, the obligation to help uplift the black race (often expressed in condescending and patronizing tones), and the celebration of middle-class virtues form the central message. In *Iola Leroy,* the title character and her immediate family typify this interpretation. Although satisfied with their decision to identify as black, these characters nonetheless sacrifice some measure of the wealth, love, and happiness they could easily have possessed if they had passed as white. The nobility of their collective character is related directly to the personal sacrifices they make in being true to their race.

Finally, the third case is the most subtle and nuanced. Here, there is less melodramatic flair and deeper examination of the meanings, attractions, and consequences of identifying with either race. Although the protagonist often chooses ultimately to pass as white, the reader is made to understand that the decision is neither uninformed nor rashly emotional. The unnamed narrator of James Weldon Johnson's *The Autobiography of an Ex-Colored Man* best represents this third, and most complex, literary interpretation of the mulatto. Rather than the overly dramatic pain of the first type, or the self-sacrifice of the second, this figure is haunted by a nagging guilt for having left the black race. Thus, all of these figures are tragic in that their personal identity choices lead inevitably to some form of sacrifice or unhappiness. It is not insignificant that most Afro-American writers of such stories were mulattoes themselves.

White writers also dealt with the topic of the mulatto, sometimes employing the first type of tragic mulatto figure in a decidedly more sinister vein, as representing a threat to white civilization via racial amalgamation.[38] These characters embodied the menace of invisible blackness while carrying the "savage" racial essence of the African just under their skins. Although these mulattoes might look white, they never really could be, and the necessary denial of their entry into the white race required the strictest vigilance.

I want to be clear in pointing out, however, that not all white writers who created mulatto characters used them to support such an ideology. Werner Sollors reports that on the whole it is difficult to draw firm conclusions about mulatto characterizations based on the race of the writer: "If one correlated the various 'typical' plot lines that have been offered as constituting *the* Tragic Mulatto, one would be surprised by the differences between one and the next version of the stereotype. And if one looks at the broad spectrum of literary production well into the twentieth century, the richness and variety of characters is remarkable. It is not a variety that easily divides by the author's racial background."[39]

These literary interpretations did not represent reality, but they did represent a certain perception on some level on the part of both whites and Afro-Americans regarding race, race mixture, and mulattoes. Significantly, the overwhelming majority of such texts—by both white and Afro-American authors—even where they were sympathetic to the mulatto figure, did not endorse further miscegenation. Atavistic children, suicides, deaths, and insanity were devices used commonly to mark the undesirability of continued race mixing. Although often positing and appreciating a peculiar psychic dilemma that was exclusive to the mulatto, Afro-American and white writers alike ultimately suggested, usually for very different reasons, that mulattoes needed to acknowledge and accept their lot with their darker sisters and brothers. Hence, for the mulatto, seeking to deny one's blackness was both traitorous and pathological. A person was either black or white, not both.

The tragic mulatto figure was surely more prevalent in literature than in actual life, and in fact there was a growing unification of mulattoes and darker Negroes during this time period. This phenomenon was characterized by Joel Williamson as the "Browning of America," referring to the gradual movement of mulattoes away from feelings of identification with whites (or distinctness from blacks) and toward a social and political solidarity with darker Afro-Americans.[40] The image of "browning" is also evoked as a reference to the relative decline of very light and very dark Negroes, as internal miscegenation worked to make both extremes more rare. This movement was the result of a shift that occurred primarily between 1850 and 1915, originating with pre–Civil War tensions that caused Southern whites to legislate away many of the legal privileges that had allowed free mulattoes a higher status than free blacks. The undifferentiated racism accompanying the onset of Redemption and Jim Crow segregation also worked to push the vast majority of mulattoes into the black camp. Both Williamson and Mencke suggest that by the second decade of the twentieth century whites and blacks both accepted mulattoes as members of the Negro group, standing at the top of it perhaps, but members of it nonetheless.

Writing in the early 1930s, Horace Mann Bond, himself a very light mulatto, made the point that except for occasional isolated groups, mulattoes had by then generally decided to either pass permanently as white or to identify as Negro:

> Time was when there were blue-vein societies and other organizations of like ilk among Negroes in this country, but they seem largely to have disintegrated, owing to two happy chances of fortune. The first has been that those who were so much like the dominant group as to demand and desire full fellowship to the extent of seclusion from the subordinate group have in great part folded their tents and crept quietly into the ranks of the whites, with no more flurry about it. The other fortunate thing has been the unyielding refusal of the dominant group to accept any of its hybrid progeny, if known as such, no matter how highly infused with the superior strain, into its domestic councils.[41]

In Bond's opinion, strict enforcement of hypodescent by the dominant group was a positive good for the Negro in that it allowed him to "focus his energies and that of all his potential leaders upon the immediate task of racial survival. There is here no widespread wasting of energies or efforts on the creation and maintenance of an intermediate group."[42]

As mulattoes took their places in the Negro race, they caught the attention of a group of intellectuals who were on their way toward helping the relatively new discipline of sociology achieve legitimacy. Somewhat more open-minded and less prejudiced than their predecessors, who had made the nineteenth century (especially the late nineteenth century) the acme of overt, anti-Negro racism, these scholars attempted to shake off the more extreme folk beliefs that had shaped racial thought up to the dawn of the twentieth century. They took an especially serious interest in the question of why mulattoes seemed to dominate so overwhelmingly the leadership positions within the Negro community.

Not all prejudice was set aside by any means, but some of the more overt fallacies (such as hybrid degeneracy, for instance) were discarded by these intellectuals. This was still a period of transition in the browning of America, however, and these sociologists sometimes demolished, and sometimes reified, the old folk beliefs. In particular, they continued to insist on positing an intense dissatisfaction on the part of mulattoes identifying as Negro, even though mulattoes had been settling gradually into this role since the 1850s. Perhaps it is not unreasonable to suggest that some amount of psychological projection was at the heart of at least a portion of these analyses. Writing about the mulatto in 1937, Everett Stonequist typifies this attitude:

> He is not the dejected, spiritless outcast; neither is he the inhibited conformist. He is more likely to be restless and race-conscious, aggressive and radical, ambitious and creative. The lower status to which he is assigned naturally creates discontented and rebellious feelings. From an earlier, spontaneous identification with the white man, he has, under the rebuffs of a categorical race prejudice, turned about and identified himself with the Negro race. In the process of so doing, he suffers a profound inner conflict. After all, does not the blood of the white man flow in his veins? Does he not share the higher culture in common with the white American? Is he not legally and morally an American citizen? And yet he finds himself condemned to a lower caste in the American system! So the mulatto is likely to think to himself. Living in two such social worlds, between which there is antagonism and prejudice, he experiences in himself the same conflict. In his own consciousness the play and the strife of the two group attitudes take place, and the manner in which he responds forms one of the most interesting chapters in the history of the Negro.[43]

Regarding race and race mixture, the most important of this new breed of sociologists was Edward Byron Reuter. I mention Reuter here because his book *The Mulatto in the United States: Including a Study of the Rôle of Mixed-Blood Races Throughout the World,* published in 1918, was the first systematic and relatively objective (for the time) study of race mixing in America. According to Mencke, "Reuter's book was the first full-scale, academic treatment of the mulatto in America," involving "a depth and sophistication of research and analysis not found in earlier studies of the subject."[44] Joel Williamson called *The Mulatto in the United States* "the only wholly relevant book" on the subject.[45] In terms of modern multiracial scholarship, however, references to Reuter's work have slipped from view. Even when his importance is acknowledged by later writers, they are often nonetheless strangely silent on the details of his thought. With the notable exception of Mencke, who devotes a generous six pages to him, Reuter's work on race mixture is usually relegated to the odd footnote here and there.

For instance, in Maria Root's first anthology on multiracialism *(Racially Mixed People in America)* there is but one reference to Reuter, and in her more massive second anthology *(The Multiracial Experience)* he is not mentioned at all. None of the contributors to Naomi Zack's two anthologies *(American Mixed Race* and *Race/Sex)* choose to mention Reuter, and in her own monograph *(Race and Mixed Race)* he merits only a single paragraph.[46] It is imperative, however, to understand Reuter if one wants to approach the contemporary multiracial debate with any semblance of historical context.

It would be best to begin with a frank examination of Reuter's racial views. With absolute bluntness Reuter assured his readers that the "lower culture of the Negro peoples is of course a simple observational fact and is to be accepted as such. To question it is to deny the obvious."[47] He was quite clear about the relative cultural merits of the Negro and white races, which he posited as representing "the antipodal degrees of human culture: at the one extreme are the standards of West Africa; at the other, those of Western Europe."[48] Nor did Reuter seem to think that there was any bias inherent in this arrangement, feeling certain enough of it to write that "no Negro questioned the superior ability of the white, and probably there is no Negro today who does not subconsciously believe the white man superior."[49]

Having established this hierarchical racial dichotomy, it was a simple matter for Eurocentric and sexist bias to conceive an ardent desire for white men on the part of Negro women. In Reuter's view, "the intermixture of the races everywhere has gone on to the extent of the white man's wishes. The Negro woman has never objected to, and has generally courted, the relationship. It was never at any time a matter of compulsion; on the contrary it was a matter of being honored by a man of a superior race. Speaking generally, the amount of intermixture is limited only by the self-respect of the white man and the compelling strength of the community sentiment."[50] To complete this exercise in psychological projection, Reuter asserted that the resulting mulatto offspring possessed a natural inclination to seek the obviously superior culture of white America: "There is no intention here to criticize the mulattoes or other men of mixed blood; quite the contrary. To recognize their desire to be white, their ambition to associate themselves through marriage or otherwise with the white race, is but to recognize their ability to appreciate the superior culture of the white group."[51]

In Reuter's view, however, it was imperative that the door to whiteness remain closed even to white-appearing mulattoes, so that the basis of white superiority could be therefore maintained. He felt quite strongly that "to admit the ambition of the mulattoes to be white and to accept them into the white race on terms of individual merit, means ultimately a mongrelization of the population and a cultural level somewhere between that represented by the standards of the two groups."[52]

I want to focus on this idea of cultural mongrelization, because it is evidence of an important logical flaw in Reuter's work that has relevance to my critique of multiracial ideology. Reuter went to some effort in attempting to distance himself from questions of biological essentialism, arguing that the race concept as he used it referred to social rather than biological groups. To this end he claimed that "practically all the present day races are the products of intermixture in varying degrees of previously more or less well established types, and the adaptation of the hybridized stock to the special environment. For the purpose in hand we are not concerned with race as a physical concept but with race as a social unity which arises by and through social development."[53]

Yet in his cultural mongrelization arguments against accepting mulattoes into white society, Reuter clearly implied the existence of some kind of biological component to cultural standards; for otherwise there is no reason to assume that cultural leveling would occur simply because of miscegenation. In other words, if a number of hypothetical mulattoes possessed the phenotype to pass as white, there would be no reason to suppose that these individuals would cause any presumed white cultural standards to fall. If they were to marry into white society, there is no basis other than a racially essentialist one for predicting a cultural decline. That Reuter nonetheless argued that such a decline would ensue indicates, despite his claim of understanding race as a "social unity," that he placed more emphasis on biology than on enculturation.

Interestingly, this is very similar to the social reality argument (see Chapter 1) that claims to be based on something other than biological race but that is in fact no more than a reinscription of that very idea. It is similar as well to the difficulty encountered by Maria Root in her attempt to posit race as a social rather than biological construct. Therefore, when Reuter argued that he had in effect removed considerations of biological race from his work, he was certainly incorrect. Nevertheless, he saw his conclusions in *The Mulatto in the United States* as having "had to do with the mulatto as a social group rather than as a biological type. Mixture of blood, however important or unimportant it may be in itself, has not been the subject of inquiry and there is no assumption concerning its good or ill effects."[54]

Yet racial essentialism and the "mixture of blood" were precisely the centerpieces of Reuter's argument. Far from showing that biology had no place in his theories, Reuter in fact presented a tortured set of arguments for mulatto superiority over blacks that were nothing if not explicit appeals to biological race:

> But from the Negro side the mulattoes are descended from the best of the race.
> . . . The choicest females of the black group became the mothers of a race of half-
> breeds. The female offspring of these mixed unions became chosen in turn to serve
> the pleasure of the superior group. By this process of repeated selection of the
> choicer girls of the black and mulatto groups to become the mothers of a new gen-
> eration of mixed-blood individuals there has been a constant force making for the

production of a choicer and choicer type of female. So far as a correlation maintains between physical perfection and mental superiority and in so far as such superiority is a heritable thing, the mulattoes, from one side of their ancestry at least, have tended to produce a superior type.[55]

Weaving together elements of Eurocentrism, sexism, Darwinism, and a kind of epistemic physiognomy, Reuter concluded that "the mulattoes, because of this process of sexual selection, are somewhat superior to the black Negroes."[56] Indeed, he went so far as to say that "in the American mulatto the evolution of a superior race may be seen in process."[57] A remnant of this idea remains alive today in the suggestion that black/white mixed-race children are more attractive than "monoracial" black children. Lisa Jones relates one of many typical such assertions along this line: "'How could we not love them,' boasted one white mother active in the census movement of her biracial children, 'they're so cute.'"[58]

The preceding review of Reuter's basic ideas will provide the context for a brief comparison of them with those of the modern generation of multiracial activists. A most interesting fact is the degree to which contemporary multiracial activists have appropriated certain of Reuter's ideas, although likely without realizing it. Just as multiracial advocates declare that multiracial people are the solution to today's racial turmoil, so too did Reuter (although for very different reasons) suggest as much for his time: "Incomplete as are the data, and tentative as the conclusions must consequently be, enough has been said to reveal the fact that the mulatto is the key to the racial situation. . . . In its acute and troublesome form, the 'race problem' is the problem of the mulatto."[59]

It is instructive to compare the foregoing to the congressional testimony of Carlos Fernández seventy-five years later:

We also believe that a positive awareness of interracial and multicultural identity is an essential step toward resolving America's, and also the world's, profound difficulty with the issues of race and interethnic relations. We are convinced that our [multiracial] community is uniquely situated to confront these issues because of the special experiences and understanding we acquire in the intimacy of our families and our personalities.[60]

Although Reuter and the modern multiracial activists cannot be said to share the same normative vision of the multiracial person's place in regard to the other races, the fact that the mixed-race individual is for each the key to the race problem is striking.[61] Indeed, throughout much of Reuter's work, there is a structural similarity to the ideas of contemporary multiracial activists and of those who support them. Both Reuter and today's activists can be seen as adherents of hypodescent, for instance. Reuter was a strict advocate of hypodescent. For him, no matter how white a mulatto might appear, that person could still never really be white. And, as I have already argued, multiracial advocates are fervent supporters of selective hypodescent in regard to the 30 million Afro-Americans in the United States. Without the artificial classification of Afro-Americans as monoracially black, multiracial advocates would be unable to posit the existence of multiracial children as a result of black/white sexual activity. So, whereas for Reuter the mulatto could never really be white, for multiracial advocates the same person is not really black. We find a striking structural similarity in the thinking of Edward Reuter and modern multiracial activists, but with a shift in polarity such that the recommendations as to what identity mixed-race people ought to claim are often reversed.

Past and present mixed-race ideologies both operate in the context of a monoracial biological reality. Biological race was as much a reality for Reuter as it is for multiracial advocates today. Without biological race, the positions of both are impossible. The primary difference between the two is that the former ideology was designed to persuade mulattoes to see themselves as black, whereas the latter strives to disrupt that connection by establishing the concept of a separate multiracial identity. In both cases, however, mixed-race identity can only be constituted against already existing, biologically pure racial groups.

Another significant similarity between Reuter and the contemporary multiracial movement is the extent to which mixed-race people are manipulated for political ends. Reuter himself was such a manipulator, as he strove to use his intellect and his status to argue that mulattoes should not seek to separate themselves from their darker sisters and brothers but should instead accept their places at the head of Negro society. However, he envisioned a socially subordinate Negro society along the path outlined by Booker T. Washington. Part of this vision depended on an extensive mystification of Negro oppression during and after slavery. For instance, in Reuter's view, one of the greatest evils of Reconstruction was "the almost complete destruction of the mutually sympathetic feelings which so generally had characterized the relations of the races during the slave period."[62] Therefore, he was critical of the equal rights rhetoric of W. E. B. Du Bois and other activist mulattoes who had founded or joined "radical movements" such as the NAACP:

> The bitter, abusive tone of so much present-day Negro literature does not voice the attitude of the Negro; the real Negro is remarkably free from bitterness. . . . They [the rank and file] accept the social situation and their place therein more as a matter of fact than as a hardship. The abstract rights for which certain individuals and groups within the race contend interest them very little or not at all. . . . There has been a pretty general acceptance by the more intelligent Negroes in all sections of the country of the Southern point of view.[63]

Reuter lavished special applause on those Southern mulattoes whom he felt had accepted their second-class citizenship, and he derided as self-interested agitators Northern mulattoes who were fighting for equal rights. He sought through his work to encourage uncommitted mulattoes to travel south to become the elite leaders of a permanently subordinate society, assuring them that "by going South, the educated Negro is allowed to forget that he is denied privileges granted to others, that the race is looked upon as inferior and treated as alien. These are things which concern the individual very little. Aside from the professional agitator, they distress the Negro not at all."[64]

There is a remarkable structural similarity here between the arguments of Reuter and Charles Byrd, a modern multiracial activist who offers: "We have to not confuse the black political elite with the general black population, which does not as rigidly oppose a separate category as do the so-called leaders. In fact, the average black isn't nearly as concerned about suppressing a mixed-race identifier or about, say, reparations for slavery as are the Mfumes, Conyers and Jacksons of the world."[65] Although Reuter is clearly the more objectionable of the two, both attempt to argue for a particular mixed-race position by suggesting the existence of a fissure between "the average black" and black leaders.

This aspect of Reuter's thought is important because it is an example of the attempted manipulation of mixed-race people. The important thing to understand here is that Reuter's bid to manipulate mulattoes was for the sake of suppressing Negro rights and for supporting continued dominance by whites via the notion of white racial purity. Given his beliefs about cultural mongrelization, Reuter's attempt to maintain white purity by advocating the exclusion of mulattoes was not surprising. Here, then, was nothing less than the deployment of sociology for the political purpose of maintaining the disenfranchisement of Negroes where such policies were already in place, and of discouraging further equal rights activism.

The significance of this earlier form of exploitation will become apparent when in Chapter 5 I highlight the support that certain political factions extend toward a federal multiracial category. Briefly, modern politicians and political activists who are uninterested in antidiscrimination efforts welcome the idea of a federal multiracial category as a means of diluting and disrupting the civil rights compliance monitoring effort. To the extent that a separate multiracial category would undermine the historical continuity of statistical records and make it more difficult to track covert and institutional discrimination, such a category receives support from politicians otherwise uninterested in working for the benefit of non-white constituents. In both the contemporary case and the case of Reuter's work, outside forces demonstrate an interest in manipulating the self-identification of mixed-race people. Reuter's goal was to support white dominance by having mulattoes identify as leaders of a permanently inferior caste, whereas today otherwise unconcerned political actors appropriate the multiracial cause for reasons of their own.

Finally, Reuter put forth a marginality thesis based on the mulatto's presumed frustration with experiencing an eternally unrequited striving for whiteness while being linked inextricably to the so-called pure Negro group:

Between these two groups, one admiring and the other despising, stand the mixed-bloods. In their own estimation, they are neither the one nor the other. They despise the lower race with a bitterness born of their degrading association with it, and which is all the more galling because it needs must be concealed. They everywhere endeavor to escape it and to conceal and forget their relationship to it. They are uncertain of their own worth; conscious of their superiority to the native they are nowhere sure of their equality with the superior group. They envy the white, aspire to equality with them, and are embittered when the realization of such ambition is denied them. They are a dissatisfied and an unhappy group.[66]

Reuter became an influential figure in the emerging field of sociology, serving as president of the American Sociological Society (1933); secretary-treasurer (1936–1938) and president (1939) of the Sociological Research Association; fellow of the American Association for the Advancement of Science; and consulting editor of the McGraw-Hill Sociology series (1928–1946).[67] He wrote or coauthored nine books and more than forty articles and book chapters (as well as many reviews).[68] Though mixed-race studies were not Reuter's only professional focus, the end result of his work in this field was the legitimization of the classic tragic mulatto thesis by its validation in the new discipline of sociology, a shift that allowed the tragic mulatto to move from the world of literature to the world of academia and textbooks:

> The desire of the mixed-blood man is always and everywhere to be a white man; to be classed with and become a part of the superior race. The ideal—the center of gravity—of the hybrid group is outside itself. The ideal of beauty, of success, of all that is good and desirable is typified by the superior race. The ambition of the man of mixed-blood is to be identified with the superior group; to share its life, its work, and its civilization. . . . Everywhere, were it possible, the mixed-blood group would break with their darker relatives, hide their relationship to them, and, through marital relations, obliterate from their offspring the physical characteristics which mark them as members of a backward and despised race.[69]

Reuter's influence was far-reaching. His mentor and the founder of the "Chicago school of sociology," Robert Park, echoed Reuter's assertions of mulatto difference, although in decidedly more muted tones. Note, however, the bias and the lapses into folk belief into which even a respected scholar such as Park could so easily fall:

> The mulatto and the mixed blood are often sensitive and self-conscious to an extraordinary degree. They do not have, on the other hand, the *insouciance* and *naïveté* which makes the Negro invariably so ingratiating and agreeable a companion. Mulattoes, also, are keenly aware of the defects of the Negro, but because their status is so intimately bound up with his, they are not able to view these defects with the

same objectivity and tolerance as the white man does. One of the consequences of his more intense self-consciousness is that the mulatto lives at a higher tension than the Negro. He is more intelligent because, for one thing, he is more stimulated, and, for another, takes himself more seriously.[70]

Perhaps Reuter's overall assessment of the mixed-race individual can best be summarized briefly: "Psychologically, the mulatto is an unstable type."[71] Over time, however, Reuter moderated the tone, if not the content, of his pronouncements regarding mulatto psychology. In a short work entitled "The Personality of Mixed Bloods," published as a book chapter in 1931 but written a few years earlier, Reuter utilized less of the overtly pathological language he had used previously in favor of an approach that was somewhat more muted. Nonetheless, still asserting that the mulatto was "an unadjusted person," he wrote that:

It is only when the resulting conflict is resolved by the mixed blood's accommodation to the socially-defined place—membership in, and leadership of, the backward group—only when he identifies himself with it, participates in life on that basis, and finds the satisfaction of his wishes in that group organization that he escapes the conflict resulting from his divided heritage. It is only through an identification of himself with the social group to which the social definitions consign him that he can find a tolerable life and develop a wholesome personality.[72]

What must not be forgotten, though, is that Reuter's hypodescent-driven prescription for the psychological well-being of mulattoes was deployed in support of an ideology of white purity and white supremacy, within the context of biological race. When contemporary multiracial activists rail against traditional tragic mulatto characterizations, they are fighting the remnants of portions of Reuter's work, even while they resurrect and appropriate other aspects of his thought. Although tragic mulatto literature long predated him, it was Reuter who gave scholarly validity and academic substance to those pathological myths. Any serious discussion of establishing a federal multiracial category must take into account the historical significance of Edward Reuter and his work. In particular, advocating the establishment of such a category without acknowledging past constructions of race and mixed race, or previous attempts to manipulate mulattoes, would be a fundamental error.

In contradistinction to Reuter, much modern work on multiracial identity attempts to offer a framework for positive multiracial identity development by supporting the same idea of essentialist biological racial groups. Within the context of distinct and exclusive racial groups, multiracial persons are cast as being different from any of the basic groups. The difficulty with this approach, however, is that it is merely the reverse side of the marginality thesis, reinscribing it by suggesting that the failure to provide positive multiracial identity intervention results in stereotypically neurotic behavior. Dorcas Bowles deploys this new pathology by asserting that the "failure to identify with one parent means that identification with that parent cannot be integrated as part of the bi-racial child's self-identity. This leads to feelings of shame, emotional isolation and depression."[73]

Ruth McRoy and Edith Freeman suggest a similar natural pathology for persons who are seen as mixed race by declaring:

> For children to view their mixed-racial background positively, the family must nurture both parts of the background by providing the child with both black and white role models and by exposing the child to black as well as white peers in the community and in school. In this process, the child is able to acquire more realistic attitudes and perceptions about his or her racial background. Mixed-race adolescents who are unable to reconcile their mixed cultural background into a personal and socially acceptable coalescence will not resolve this developmental stage. Thus, the individual may exhibit neurotic behavior.[74]

In addition to conflating race and culture, McRoy and Freeman validate essentialist ideas of normative racial identity in their self-appointed roles as psychological doomsayers. Their view that so-called mixed-race people must draw upon the essentialist cores of their constituent races in order to be healthy psychologically serves to strengthen rather than destabilize racial categorization. Further, the authors suggest by implication that all people considered to be mixed race prior to the modern age of counseling must indeed have been neurotic, tragic mulattos, given that such persons did not have the advantage of this kind of psychological intervention.

In regard to assertions that psychological health can only be ensured by adopting a monoracial identity, I have written elsewhere: "All this business of either conforming to rigid identity types or being labeled confused is a pipe dream of psychologists desperately in search of a theory."[75] The same holds true for assertions that tragic neurosis is the inevitable result of the failure to adopt a multiracial identity. Given the above review of the older marginality thesis, it is clear that for these newer theorists the pathology remains, but the polarity has been switched. Elaine Pinderhughes, writing about mixed-race children, echoes the above researchers by providing the same sort of near-schizophrenic analysis: "If the child fails to acquire the emotional flexibility required to negotiate [these] processes . . . and/or does not have available supports and models—both parental and environmental—a conflicted, ambivalent, confused, and negative sense of identity will emerge."[76]

What is objectionable about these newer psychosocial models is not the notion that children should be given access to all parts of their heritages. It would likely be valuable for all children to learn about their various heritages, as valuable for one child to learn about her Irish and German heritages as for another child to learn about his Afro-American and Jewish heritages.[77] The critical objection to the foregoing psychological and sociological theses is that they begin with the presumption of racial groups as natural entities, never problematizing or challenging such frameworks in the course of their studies. Thus, the value of such research is automatically constrained by the limits of its own design. By accepting the race construct as normative, these researchers fail to consider the possibility that not everyone is as frantically affected by race as their studies presume. They also fail to consider that some persons may reject race while still acknowledging the *cultural* differences of their parents as well as the racism of much of society. Instead, these sorts of studies validate the marginality and tragic mulatto hypotheses of the past, resurrecting them as the natural outcome of a failure to provide explicit multiracial identity instruction to children. By working uncritically within the bounds of racial mythology, these researchers circumscribe the value of their own work, in essence finding results that are overdetermined by their own subjective presumptions.

Work such as that of Dorcas, McRoy and Freeman, and Pinderhughes reinforces the popular stereotype of black/white mixed-race individuals as persons who do not fit into either the white or the black racial groups, and who as a result are rejected by both. This presumption, however, is not borne out by research of a more critical nature. The confused identity assumption is a long-standing myth that has been taken up by these newer psychologists and sociologists, who never question the presumptions of race they build into their own studies. What fuels these psychosocial theories is the fact that their objects of study do not fit into the commonly accepted, bifurcated racial arrangement, as Anne Wilson points out in her observation that "when people say that mixed race children have 'identity problems,' what they usually mean is that mixed race children have problems fitting themselves into socially defined categories; more specifically, that the children have difficulty discovering where they belong in relation to the black and to the white group."[78]

Wilson notes further that the "'betwixt and between' image of mixed race people is a stereotype and one which has not, so far, been supported by empirical research."[79] Many people resolve this alleged dilemma by simply rejecting the idea that they must fit into either one or the other group, or by rejecting race in its entirety. For such people, as Barbara Tizard and Ann Phoenix point out, what makes sense is to be comfortable with oneself, regardless of external attempts to impose identity.[80]

Wilson draws a similar conclusion in considering normative racial identity and children who identify as mixed race. In her judgment, "If the main findings of the study had to be summarized in a single sentence it would be that mixed race children do not necessarily conform to the stereotype of the social misfits caught between the social worlds of black and white. Not all mixed race children are torn between the ethnic loyalties of their parents and not all spend their lives trying to make themselves acceptable to *one* ethnic group."[81] As Wilson puts it, "The definition of *mis*identification depends entirely on one's prior assumptions about what constitutes a socially and psychologically viable racial identity."[82] Researchers who fail to remove the blinders of racial essentialism merely replicate their own foreordained expectations, whereas those who are able to step outside the false consciousness of race gain a far greater perspective, as demonstrated by Tizard and Phoenix, who in their research found that the "great majority of the sample did not experience the feelings of social isolation and rejection by both black and white groups which the marginality theorists described as 'their fate.'"[83]

Racial misidentification and confusion for so-called mixed-race persons are certain only in the context of distinct, pure, and exclusive racial groups—groups that do not exist. Moreover, if races today really were distinct and exclusive categories, there could be no *in-between* people, and multiracial advocates would have to assent to the principle of hypodescent to justify the American monoracial paradigm. Yet multiracial advocates situationally reject hypodescent while accepting racial categorization in general. More specifically, they reject hypodescent for the child of a white and a black parent, for instance, while inconsistently accepting hypodescent for the black parent. Alternatively, as mentioned previously, even if races were at one time existent, population mixture over the past few thousand years has ensured that all humans are already multiracial. In the former case multiracialism is impossible, whereas in the latter it is redundant.

This is not merely a question of semantics. I am arguing here that people are accountable for the philosophical positions they take and for the implications of those positions. When viewed from a critical perspective, multiracialism only appears to destabilize racial categorization. It is true that the notion of multiraciality seems to cast doubt on the possibility of racial categorization by problematizing the distinct and exclusive status of racial groups. However, this is only an apparent destabilization, since the very idea of multiracialism depends entirely on the existence of distinct and exclusive races that are subsequently mixed together. Multiracial identity cannot be advocated while being presented simultaneously as a way to destabilize racial categorization, since multiracial identity relies upon racial categorization as its underlying rationale. By debunking racial categories, multiracial advocates would be negating the precondition of their own purported identity. Therefore, the multiracial argument for the destabilization of race—if taken to its logical consequences—is a reductio ad absurdum, since multiraciality is only conceivable in the context of distinct and exclusive racial groups.

To be sure, the establishment of a federal multiracial category would not serve to destabilize the American monoracial paradigm, which can very easily accommodate yet another non-white category along the black/white hierarchical continuum, since the basic dynamic would remain unchanged. Attention to this practical aspect is crucial, for additional categories that stand above black in the hierarchy pose no threat to the current power structure as long as they are non-white categories. Katya Azoulay offers one reason for concern in arguing that a federal multiracial category "does not signify an end to race thinking but is suggestive of a diminishing affirmative attitude toward blackness. The resurrection of a middle category seems to be threatening just at a time when renewed attention is being paid to the link between problems of structural inequality and racism."[84]

Further Inconsistencies in the Multiracial Idea

Who, then, is multiracial? Or a better question might be, Who is *not* multiracial? The answer, in the context of the present argument, is that either everyone is multiracial or no one is. Since there are no biological racial groups, there can be no biological multiracial group, unless by "multiracial" one intends simply to delineate all of humankind. Taking the example of Afro-Americans, multiracialism is immediately a redundant principle, since if one holds to a belief in biological race, then Afro-Americans are all multiracial.[85] If biological races exist, then the first English/African offspring in North America would have been multiracial, and all present descendants of such persons would be multiracial as well. It is inconceivable, though, to suppose that many Afro-Americans, if any at all—through nearly 400 years of intermarriage, rape, casual sex, concubinage, and especially internal miscegenation—could count only unmixed Africans as ancestors.[86]

The reason for this is that a single individual entering the family bloodline adds potentially an entire genetic portfolio to that branch of the family tree. This is true whether such a person is a legal spouse, a casual sex partner, or a rapist. What people normally consider to be their family trees are generally truncated, arbitrary, and incomplete views at best, omitting unknown or embarrassing branches. The actual regression backward from the individual is not a straight line but an exponential curve: two parents, four grandparents, eight great-grandparents, sixteen great-great-grandparents, and so on. Any ancestor of one of the sixteen great-great-grandparents is an ancestor of the individual as well. The traditional view of a family genealogy as an ever expanding tree growing upward from a single ancestral base is inaccurate. This perspective does not account for the histories of persons entering the family line as spouses or sexual partners, except to sometimes announce their appearance as if from nowhere, as if without histories of their own.[87] For this reason, a family tree is more properly conceived of as a banyan tree, with individual trunks dropping down from each of the branches. Each person born on a particular branch receives a genetic inheritance not only from the main trunk but also from the individual trunks of persons who entered the family line on that branch.

In the case of Afro-Americans, the mixture of West African and European (and often Native American) genetic material continues to this day, even without the active involvement of whites, as F. James Davis describes:

> It is important to note that the mixing of genes is continuous within a group defined by the one-drop rule, even if sexual contact with the out-group declines or ceases.

That is, miscegenation occurs when there is sexual contact between unmixed African blacks and mulattoes, and between mulattoes and other mulattoes, not just when there is mixing between whites and African blacks or whites and mulattoes. In all four of these instances, genes from populations derived from Europe and sub-Saharan Africa are being mixed. In mulatto-mulatto unions, genes are mixed whether the ancestry of one individual is mainly white and the other mainly black, or the ratios are more nearly even. This genetic mixing is not publicly defined as such, and the marriages concerned are certainly not thought of as intermarriages. Yet very often these unions involve much more miscegenation than occurs between whites and near-white "blacks."[88]

The American racial paradigm, fueled by the principle of hypodescent, is structured so as to ignore the white component in offspring when intermixture is involved. Alternatively, the phenomenon of racial passing serves as evidence that whites whose families have been in the United States for several generations can never be certain that their family lines contain no African component.[89] In an extremely conservative estimate, approximately 90,000 Afro-Americans began passing as white between 1880 and 1925.[90] It must also be remembered that the most successful acts of passing will never be uncovered. Yet these complexities—intermixture and passing—do not intrude on general conceptions of race in the United States, solidifying them through hypodescent in the former case and ignoring the effects in the latter case.

A well-known example of such genealogical oversimplification is Alex Haley's 1974 novel *Roots: The Saga of an American Family,* which served as an inspiration for millions of Afro-Americans to search for their African heritage. Indeed, one can attribute the general explosion of American popular interest in genealogy directly to Haley's book and the ensuing television miniseries (which set records for viewership). Haley's search to find information about his African ancestor, Kunta Kinte, and the village from which he came is a heartwarming story known to many Americans. Yet the line of descent from Alex Haley back to Kunta Kinte is popularly seen as the only line, when in fact it is but one of many.

Of Alex Haley's many ancestors, Kunta Kinte was only one, and a male one at that. The fact that Kunta Kinte was remembered specifically by Haley's elders as "the African" is the reason for the focus on him in the book, but it would be a mistake to assume that the Kinte-Haley line is the only line, or even the only important one.[91] The point of *Roots* was that Haley had found the missing link to his past, when in fact he had found only one such link. For instance, Kinte's daughter was raped by her owner, Tom Lea (who was of English descent), and bore a child who was an ancestor of Haley's; yet the idea that Haley's roots extend to Britain is apparently not of interest, nor relevant to his racial designation.[92] David Moore calculates that of Haley's 256 six-times great-grandparents, 88 were non-African; among them were Irish, English, and Cherokee people.[93] There are therefore 255 alternative lines of descent from Alex Haley back to a six-times great-grandparent, more than a third of whom are non-African. In Moore's view, "As a matter of pure theory or strict bloodline genealogy, Alex Haley could have identified any of these non-African ancestors as his root, but as a matter of practice and American social mandate, that is hard to imagine."[94]

The point of this example is not to fragment Alex Haley into various specific percentages of racial heritage but rather to demonstrate the illogical nature of race and multirace, either as biological or social categorizations. There is no grouping, whether racial, ethnic, or national, that can capture the diversity of heritage of Alex Haley. To assert that Haley was black is to ignore utterly the fact that one-third of his known ancestors came from someplace other than Africa. To label him multiracial is to make no distinction between him and the average (supposedly monoracial) Afro-American in that regard. What made Alex Haley black is neither biology nor heritage—it is hypodescent. Kwame Anthony Appiah makes a crucial point about accuracy and identity when he argues that "history may have made us what we are, but the choice of a slice of the past in a period before your birth as your own history is always exactly that: a choice."[95] In the United States, these kinds of choices are overdetermined by the American racial paradigm.

The example of Alex Haley makes clear that if multiracial identification is to be claimed as a legitimate category of racial classification, then there is no justifiable rationale for failing to classify America's 30 million Afro-Americans as multiracial. In terms of genetics, they have a significant European heritage, established at the very least by the well-documented history of population mixing that occurred in America during the slave era and by the ensuing internal miscegenation. If multiraciality is to be understood as the result of so-called race mixing, then Afro-Americans qualify as multiracial. On what ground could they possibly be disqualified? The wide array of phenotypic features present in the Afro-American population are a testament to the generations of African, Native American, and European intermixing that have occurred in the United States over the past 400 years. When people consider Afro-Americans a monoracial group, whether as partners in ostensibly interracial marriages or as parents of multiracial children, they ignore the fact that Afro-Americans have been racially mixed for centuries. Lyn Lewis, chair of the University of Detroit–Mercy Sociology Department, criticizes the arbitrariness of multiracial ideology on this very point, saying that it "assumes that racial mixing started last year and therefore we need to do something about it. . . . The question can be raised, who can say he or she is not multiracial? It creates a category that basically everyone fits into."[96]

After all is said and done, however, we are still left with the human face of multiracial identity politics. Despite the contradictory implications of multiracial advocacy, it has its adherents, just as does the monoracial identity politics upon which it is based. This is not surprising, since monoracial and multiracial advocates are operating within the same paradigm, with the only difference being that whereas monoracialists want to keep the system of racial classification just as it is, multiracial advocates are attempting to modify it slightly. It is important to see that the purpose of multiracialism is not to overthrow the American racial paradigm but merely to alter it so as to include another non-white category within the present framework. The existing paradigm is needed because the assertion of multiracial identity requires the paradigm's monoracial classifications in order to provide the categories against which so-called multiracial people may distinguish themselves as a separate group.

The stimulus for multiracial advocacy is dissatisfaction with the constraints and contradictions of the American racial paradigm. In the context of the debate over OMB Directive 15 (see Chapter 2), persons who identified themselves as multiracial, or parents who identified their children as such, were frustrated by the fact that participating in the system required accepting a monoracial identity at some level.[97] If the multiracial impulse were actually a radical as opposed to a collaborative ideology, it would not build on racial categorization in order to construct itself. Rather, like antiracialism, it would seek to demonstrate the absurdity of all racial categorization. Instead, however, the multiracial movement's explicit goal is merely the addition of a single new category to the existing American racial paradigm. It is important to keep this point in mind when considering arguments presented on behalf of multiracial identity politics.

People are beginning to sense the contradiction of accepting a monoracial identification for themselves while simultaneously placing their parents (or more remote ancestors) in different racial categories. At this point of frustration, people have at least three choices. They may (1) accept monoracial classification (usually in the lower status group), (2) claim an intermediate identity within the racial paradigm, or (3) reject the paradigm itself. The second choice, the route taken by multiracial advocates, is in the simplest sense an attempt to fit in, with the cost of fitting in being acceptance of biological racial categorization and hypodescent.

One recognizes and may even sympathize with such frustration, but ultimately it is the responsibility of intellectuals to unmask the inconsistencies and contradictions of racial and multiracial ideologies regardless of how much emotional investment well-intentioned people have put into wishing they were true. Ramona Douglass, president of AMEA, gives voice to the sentiment behind much multiracial advocacy in stating that "although there were organizations for the separate parts of my heritage, nothing addressed my needs as a multiracial person. . . . Everyone seeks their own, whatever that means. I wanted a sense of community."[98] It is, however, the tyranny and hegemony of the racial construct that forces people to accept being thus pigeonholed in order to find community.

In this regard there is a double inconsistency in the multiracial position, for while ignoring the obvious and well-documented European ancestry of Afro-Americans, the movement simultaneously strives to combine into a single racial group numbers of people who have no evident commonality even under current understandings of race in America. In a sense it is a case of constructing a negative identity, as black/white, Asian/Hispanic, and Native American/white individuals, for instance, are placed in the same multiracial category—all because of what they supposedly are *not,* namely, monoracial. In the view of Candace Mills, editor and publisher of *Interrace* magazine, this is a wrongheaded way to categorize people, since it "has no meaning. It doesn't mean that all multiracial people have any shared experience. All it does is validate all the other racial categories as pure."[99]

The lack of real commonality in a multiracial category is illustrated by the work of Rebecca King and Kimberly DaCosta, who studied the differences between hapas (people of Asian/European heritage) and Afro-Americans who identify as multiracial, and determined that the respective goals of these two groups are quite different. In the view of King and DaCosta, "The different histories of the Japanese American and African American communities shape the nature of group participation of hapas and mixed-race African Americans. Hapas, rejected by the Japanese American community, form groups focused on getting that community to include them. Mixed-race African Americans, included in the common understandings of blackness but with an accompanying silencing of other parts of their heritage, form groups focused on validating that experience."[100] Additionally, as will emerge in Chapter 4, Hispanic and Native American organizations do not favor a federal multiracial category, which is significant given that these two populations possess a great deal of intermixture, and each with a dynamic that is different than either the hapa or Afro-American groups.

Little imagination is required to envision a time when multiracial identification becomes too ambiguous, too inaccurate; when people strive to identify by their specific mixtures rather than by the blanket category *multiracial,* which, after all, is not so much an affirmation of what people are as it is of what they are not. Why should the black/white individual be categorized along with the Asian/Native American individual? In this case what drives their placement in the same category is the monoracial construct, not their own individual heritages and identities.

From the point of view of accuracy, the multiracial label is no more precise than the label *other,* which multiracial advocates find so offensive. A multiracial classification does no more to describe the individual, and may indeed do somewhat less, than one of the standard categories, for it subsumes entire groups of extremely diverse people under a single, limiting, and explicitly nondescriptive label. In this sense the multiracial designation preserves the primacy of monoracial categorization, since for its adherents it is enough merely to be identified as possessing some unspecified mixture of the standard racial categories.

Thus, on another level, the same frustration that drives the multiracial movement in its rejection of monoracial classification must eventually recur, since Hispanic/Asian and Native American/white persons, for instance, would be placed together in the same category without regard to their own specific, individual heritages. If, according to the multiracialists' argument, a black/white per-

son should not be placed in the black category due to the inaccuracy of that categorization, then the same person should not be placed in the multiracial category since it is just as inaccurate. If multiracial advocates argue that black/white
persons are denied the fullness of their identity when placed in the black category, then those same advocates must also argue that black/white and
Asian/white persons would be denied the fullness of their respective identities if
placed in a multiracial category. Indeed, one could argue that Japanese/white, Ko-
rean/white, and Chinese/white persons would all be denied the fullness of their
respective identities if placed together in such a category.

It would be another matter if persons possessing different mixtures were not
all placed in the same category—if, for instance, Native American/white persons
had a separate category, if Hispanic/Asian persons had a separate one as well, and
so on. Then at least the contradiction of placing disparate people into a single
category because they do not qualify as members of one of the primary categories would be avoided. The basic fallacy of biological racial categorization
would, however, of course still apply to these categories. And, too, even this formulation would be complicated by questions such as why a black/white person
who is seven-eighths black should be placed in the same multiracial category as a
black/white person who is seven-eighths white.

Related closely to the above criticism—its reverse side, so to speak—is the fact
that the members of a single multiracial category are defined not by what they
are, but by what they are not. It might be objected that the members of this category would in fact be defined by what they are, that being *multiracial,* but such
an objection misses the point as well as the subtlety of the racial hegemony. An
individual categorized as multiracial is defined precisely as a person who is not a
member of any single racial category, but who is rather a mixture of two or more.
It is critical to understand the conceptual difference between this categorization
and that of the standard categories. In the latter case there are specific criteria, biologically false though they are, that prescribe membership in the group. In the
former case there are no specific criteria that one could apply to oneself. Rather,
the main criterion for membership is the fact that one is not a member of a
monoracial category. As such, there is no more justification for the purported
multiracial individual to feel more accurately categorized in the multiracial category alongside diverse people of widely varying phenotypes, heritages, cultures,
and ancestries than in one of the monoracial categories. In either case the person
is allocated to a category without regard for the individual specificities of that
person's own heritage. Viewed in this way, *multiracial* and the disdained *other* are
completely interchangeable terms, since each designates its members by virtue of
what they are not, rather than by what they are.

What must not be forgotten, however, is that this entire debate results from the
belief in the hegemonic fictitiousness of biological race. The extent to which people allow the race concept to have primacy in ordering their lives is staggering.
Teresa Williams goes so far as to assert that, in the United States, "one's assign-

ment into a sociopolitically defined single racial group is necessary in order to be a socially recognized, functional member of society."[101] This claim in turn leads Williams to posit differential "social-psychological processing strategies" for biracial persons.[102] It is profound and frightening that so many people, especially scholars, will invest so much of their personal identity in the racial myth as opposed to unmasking it.

Audrey Smedley seeks to draw attention to this problem by pointing out that "nothing is more indicative of the plight, and the pathology, of using race/biology as the main form of identity than the efforts on the part of some people to establish a 'mixed-race' category in the census and thus in American society."[103] Smedley sees multiracial angst as dependent on a prior belief in the monoracial construct, a belief that leads these persons to feel that they therefore have "no identity at all."[104] In Smedley's account:

> Some advocates of a new "mixed-race" category have argued that they need this new identity in order to recognize the "culture" of their white parent. In American ideology, a black parent presumably has "black" culture, and the white parent has "white" culture, with the unstated understanding that these are incompatible ways of life. Aside from the fact that this idea is nonsense, it continues to feed the psychic stress of a few individuals who have the feeling that they do not know who they are.[105]

Biological racial classification is of course a fallacy. Rather than rejecting it as false, however, multiracial identity politics has as its goal the modification of this fallacious system of classification to include a multiracial category. Herein lies a large portion of the inconsistency and contradiction of multiracial advocacy, for no coherent politics of personal or group identity can arise from the ashes of the bankrupt concept of biological race. This chapter has been concerned with the historical and philosophical implications of multiracial identity politics. There are also practical matters connected with the potential adoption of a multiracial category by the U.S. government. In the next chapter I shall undertake a close examination of formal proposals to add a multiracial category to federal racial classifications.

Notes

1. House Subcommittee on Census, Statistics, and Postal Personnel, Committee on Post Office and Civil Service, *Hearings on the Review of Federal Measurements of Race and Ethnicity*, testimony by Susan Graham on June 30, 1993, 103d Cong., 1st sess., April 14, June 30, July 29, and November 3, 1993, 119. (Response to written question of Representative Thomas Sawyer).

2. Robyn Wiegman, *American Anatomies: Theorizing Race and Gender* (Durham, N.C.: Duke University Press, 1995), 5–6.

3. Kenneth M. Stampp, *The Peculiar Institution: Slavery in the Ante-Bellum South* (New York: Vintage Books, 1956), 23. See also Winthrop D. Jordan, *White over Black: American Attitudes Toward the Negro, 1550–1812* (New York: W. W. Norton, 1977), 164.

4. Antiracialism is one way of rejecting the paradigm. In this chapter I shall consider whether multiracialism represents a similar rejection of the paradigm or whether it is instead complicit with it.

5. Of particular interest in this regard is the argument for multiracial accuracy in the context of public health, which I shall take up in some detail in Chapter 4.

6. The argument for self-esteem is considered in Chapter 4.

7. Maria P. P. Root, ed., *The Multiracial Experience: Racial Borders As the New Frontier*, (Thousand Oaks, Calif.: Sage Publications, 1996), xi.

8. Carlos Fernández, online posting, Interracial Individuals Discussion List, February 5, 1996 [ii@gnu.ai.mit.edu]. The Interracial Individuals Discussion List (II-LIST) is an electronic mailing list dedicated to multiracial issues.

9. Quoted in Lawrence Wright, "One Drop of Blood," *New Yorker*, July 25, 1994, 48.

10. Teresa K. Williams, "Race As Process: Reassessing the 'What Are You?' Encounters of Biracial Individuals," in *The Multiracial Experience: Racial Borders As the New Frontier*, ed. Maria P. P. Root (Thousand Oaks, Calif.: Sage Publications, 1996), 193.

11. Laurie Shrage, "Passing Beyond the Other Race or Sex," in *Race/Sex: Their Sameness, Difference, and Interplay*, ed. Naomi Zack (New York: Routledge, 1997), 184.

12. Linda Alcoff, "Mestizo Identity," in *American Mixed Race: The Culture of Microdiversity*, ed. Naomi Zack (Lanham, Md.: Rowman and Littlefield, 1995), 261.

13. Root, *Multiracial Experience*, ix.

14. Maria P. P. Root, "Mixed-Race Women," in *Race/Sex: Their Sameness, Difference, and Interplay*, ed. Naomi Zack (New York: Routledge, 1997), 167.

15. I am here utilizing for the purpose of argument the justification given by adherents of the social reality view, since Root is using this view as the framework for her racial definitions. The social reality position is of course merely a reinscription of biological race.

16. There is no doubt that under the American racial paradigm, such a child would in most cases be considered black.

17. Samira Kawash, *Dislocating the Color Line: Identity, Hybridity, and Singularity in African-American Literature* (Stanford: Stanford University Press, 1997), 5.

18. Katya G. Azoulay, *Black, Jewish, and Interracial: It's Not the Color of Your Skin, but the Race of Your Kin, and Other Myths of Identity* (Durham, N.C.: Duke University Press, 1997), 5.

19. Naomi Zack, ed., *American Mixed Race: The Culture of Microdiversity* (Lanham, Md.: Rowman and Littlefield, 1995), x.

20. Zack's words here call to mind that immortal rationalization from the Vietnam War: "It became necessary to destroy the town to save it." Quoted in Neil Sheehan, *A Bright Shining Lie: John Paul Vann and America in Vietnam* (New York: Random House, 1988), 719.

21. House Subcommittee on Census, Statistics, and Postal Personnel, Committee on Post Office and Civil Service, *Hearings on the Review of Federal Measurements of Race and Ethnicity*, testimony by Carlos Fernández on June 30, 1993, 103d Cong., 1st sess., April 14, June 30, July 29, and November 3, 1993, 133.

22. Quoted in Dexter Waugh, "Census Bureau to Review Mixed Category," *San Francisco Chronicle*, April 21, 1991, B5.

23. Cecile A. Lawrence, "Racelessness," in *American Mixed Race: The Culture of Microdiversity*, ed. Naomi Zack (Lanham, Md.: Rowman and Littlefield, 1995), 26.

24. A vernacular term, *mixies,* is used in a self-conscious and friendly way by some people who consider themselves multiracial to refer to themselves and others. In casual conversation, first-generation mixed-race individuals might be referred to as *first-gen mixies.* Alternatively, in the case of people with such mixtures earlier in their family histories, whether or not they are multiracial depends on whether the mixture is important to them—on whether they wish to recognize it—which makes a mockery of any arguments for accuracy.

25. Thembi Lise McWhite, online posting, Interracial Individuals Discussion List, May 14, 1996 [ii-list@hcs.harvard.edu].

26. Deborah A. Thomas, "Black, White, or Other?" *Essence,* July 1993, 118.

27. While stating that the only possible way to *conceptualize* race is to view it in terms of pure, distinct, and exclusive categories, I want to be clear in asserting that such a conceptualization remains a biological falsity.

28. Root, *Multiracial Experience,* xxii–xxiii.

29. David T. Goldberg, "Made in the USA," in *American Mixed Race: The Culture of Microdiversity,* ed. Naomi Zack (Lanham, Md.: Rowman and Littlefield, 1995), 254.

30. Nicholas Jones, "Mixed-Race Identity Formation: Hearing from Young Mixed-Race Adults" (paper presented at the Colorlines in the Twenty-First Century conference, Chicago, September 26, 1998).

31. Joel Williamson, *New People: Miscegenation and Mulattoes in the United States* (New York: The Free Press, 1980).

32. Gunnar Myrdal, *An American Dilemma: The Negro Problem and Modern Democracy* (New York: Harper and Brothers, 1944), 107.

33. Naomi Zack, "Race and Philosophic Meaning," in *Race/Sex: Their Sameness, Difference, and Interplay,* ed. Naomi Zack (New York: Routledge, 1997), 30.

34. John G. Mencke, *Mulattoes and Race Mixture: American Attitudes and Images, 1865–1918* (Ann Arbor, Mich.: UMI Research Press, 1979), 38.

35. Paul R. Spickard, *Mixed Blood: Intermarriage and Ethnic Identity in Twentieth-Century America* (Madison: University of Wisconsin Press, 1989), 254.

36. Mencke's detailed study of American literature incorporating mulatto figures between 1865 and 1918 in *Mulattoes and Race Mixture* is especially helpful here.

37. Mencke, *Mulattoes and Race Mixture,* 144.

38. Ibid., esp. chap. 5.

39. Werner Sollors, *Neither Black Nor White Yet Both: Thematic Explorations of Interracial Literature* (Oxford: Oxford University Press, 1997), 238.

40. Williamson, *New People,* chap. 3.

41. Horace Mann Bond, "Two Racial Islands in Alabama," *American Journal of Sociology* 36 (1930-1931): 554.

42. Ibid.

43. Everett V. Stonequist, *The Marginal Man: A Study in Personality and Culture Conflict* (New York: Charles Scribner's Sons, 1937; reprint, New York: Russell and Russell, 1961), 24–25.

44. Mencke, *Mulattoes and Race Mixture,* 78.

45. Williamson, *New People,* xi.

46. Naomi Zack, *Race and Mixed Race* (Philadelphia: Temple University Press, 1993), 117–118.

47. Edward B. Reuter, "The Superiority of the Mulatto," *American Journal of Sociology* 23, no. 1 (July 1917): 87–88.

48. Ibid., 83.

49. Ibid., 101.

50. Edward B. Reuter, *The Mulatto in the United States: Including a Study of the Rôle of Mixed-Blood Races Throughout the World* (Boston: Richard G. Badger, 1918; reprint, New York: Negro Universities Press, 1969), 162–163.

51. Ibid., 317–318.

52. Ibid., 104.

53. Ibid., 14 n. 7.

54. Ibid., 375.

55. Reuter, "Superiority of the Mulatto," 99.

56. Ibid., 100.

57. Ibid., 106.

58. Lisa Jones, *Bulletproof Diva: Tales of Race, Sex, and Hair* (New York: Doubleday, 1994), 58–59.

59. Reuter, *Mulatto in the United States*, 87–88.

60. House Subcommittee, testimony by Carlos Fernández, 128.

61. In fact, chapter 4 of Reuter's *The Mulatto in the United States* is titled "The Mulatto: The Key to the Race Problem."

62. Reuter, *Mulatto in the United States*, 350.

63. Ibid., 369–370.

64. Ibid., 387–388.

65. Charles Byrd, "Census 2000 Protest: *Check American Indian!*" *Interracial Voice,* January 7, 1998 <http://www.webcom.com/~intvoice/editor.html>.

66. Reuter, *Mulatto in the United States*, 103.

67. Edward B. Reuter, *The American Race Problem*, rev. ed. (New York: Thomas Y. Crowell, 1970), xvi. The original edition was published in 1927.

68. Donald G. Reuter, "Bibliography of Edward Byron Reuter, 1880–1946," *American Journal of Sociology* 52, no. 2 (1946): 106–111.

69. Reuter, *Mulatto in the United States*, 315–316.

70. Robert E. Park, "Mentality of Racial Hybrids," *American Journal of Sociology* 36 (1930-1931): 545.

71. Reuter, *Mulatto in the United States*, 102.

72. Edward B. Reuter, *Race Mixture: Studies in Intermarriage and Miscegenation* (New York: McGraw-Hill, 1931; reprint, New York: Johnson Reprint Corporation, 1970), 216.

73. Dorcas D. Bowles, "Bi-Racial Identity: Children Born to African-American and White Couples," *Clinical Social Work Journal* 21, no. 4 (Winter 1993): 427.

74. Ruth G. McRoy and Edith Freeman, "Racial-Identity Issues Among Mixed-Race Children," *Social Work in Education* 8, no. 3 (Spring 1986): 166.

75. Rainier Spencer, "Race and Mixed-Race: A Personal Tour," in *As We Are Now: Mixblood Essays on Race and Identity,* ed. William S. Penn (Berkeley: University of California Press, 1997), 129.

76. Elaine Pinderhughes, "Biracial Identity: Asset or Handicap?" in *Racial and Ethnic Identity: Psychological Development and Creative Expression,* ed. Herbert W. Harris, Howard C. Blue, and Ezra E. H. Griffith (New York: Routledge, 1995), 83.

77. I recognize that in the broad sense of America's Eurocentric cultural framework the former child has less learning to do. However, I am pointing explicitly to a much deeper historical and cultural exploration that would result in an Irish or German acuity beyond simple acknowledgement of ancestry—one more along the lines of the Afro-American or Jewish case in general.

78. Anne Wilson, *Mixed Race Children: A Study of Identity* (Boston: Allen and Unwin, 1987), 21.

79. Ibid., 195.

80. Barbara Tizard and Ann Phoenix, *Black, White, or Mixed Race? Race and Racism in the Lives of Young People of Mixed Parentage* (London: Routledge, 1993), chap. 5. While arguing against the assertion that the black/white mixed-race child must adopt a black identity in order to be healthy psychologically, the authors essentially show that children are much more reflective and resilient than pathology theorists give them credit for. The larger lesson is that, whether advancing the older or newer versions of the marginality thesis, such theorists are simply wrong.

81. Wilson, *Mixed Race Children*, 176.

82. Ibid., 78.

83. Tizard and Phoenix, *Black, White, or Mixed Race?* 86.

84. Azoulay, *Black, Jewish, and Interracial*, 99.

85. Excepting perhaps recent immigrants, of course. By *Afro-American* I generally mean those Americans whose African ancestors were brought to the Americas as a result of the Atlantic slave trade.

86. This statement presumes for the sake of argument that all African slaves who reached British North America either via the Caribbean or directly from Africa were themselves unproblematically unmixed, when, in fact, this can hardly be the case.

87. Also, the traditional family tree does not generally account for the histories of females, as it continues to trace only male family members. As such it is only half a family tree at best.

88. F. James Davis, *Who Is Black? One Nation's Definition* (University Park: Pennsylvania State University Press, 1991), 22–23.

89. Even in the case of recent immigrant families, if a member of the family has children with someone who has deeper ancestral ties in the United States, those children—through the newcomer to the family—may well have Afro-American ancestors who successfully passed undetected as white.

90. Davis, *Who Is Black?* 56.

91. Alex Haley, *Roots: The Saga of an American Family* (Garden City, N.Y.: Doubleday, 1974), 665.

92. Ibid., 428.

93. David C. Moore, "Routes: Alex Haley's *Roots* and the Rhetoric of Genealogy," *Transition*, n.s., 64 (1995): 15.

94. Ibid.

95. Kwame Anthony Appiah, *In My Father's House: Africa in the Philosophy of Culture* (Oxford: Oxford University Press, 1992), 32.

96. Quoted in Marc C. Tilles, "'Multiracial' Can Only Mean Further Racial Division," *Michigan Chronicle*, June 14-20, 1995, 1A.

97. What is significant here is the expressed wish to participate in the system. Refusing to accept the paradigm, on the other hand, neutralizes these frustrations without contradiction.

98. Quoted in Janita Poe, "Multiracial People Want a Single Name That Fits," *Chicago Tribune,* May 3, 1993, sec. 1, 1.

99. Quoted in Gary Younge, "Multiracial Citizens Divided on Idea of Separate Census Classification," *Washington Post,* July 19, 1996, A3.

100. Rebecca C. King and Kimberly M. DaCosta, "Changing Face, Changing Race: The Remaking of Race in the Japanese American and African American Communities," in *The Multiracial Experience: Racial Borders As the New Frontier,* ed. Maria P. P. Root (Thousand Oaks, Calif.: Sage Publications, 1996), 240.

101. Williams, "Race As Process," 193.

102. Ibid., 194.

103. Audrey Smedley, *Race in North America: Origin and Evolution of a Worldview,* 2d ed. (Boulder: Westview Press, 1999), 331–332.

104. Ibid., 332.

105. Ibid.

4

The Multiracial Category Initiative

If we have multiethnic categories, are they going to be telling us something? . . . With the multiracial/multiethnic categories being comprised of so many different combinations, what would the data tell us? What is the commonality among individuals in these categories?

—Steven Carbo, Mexican American Legal Defense and Educational Fund[1]

Overview

The multiracial ideology outlined in Chapter 3 has given rise to a growing movement, generally referred to by its constituents as the multiracial movement, that seeks to modify, though not challenge, the American racial paradigm. The movement is made up of various groups and organizations ranging from college support groups to regional associations to a national umbrella organization, the Association of MultiEthnic Americans (AMEA). Efforts sponsored by some in this movement—specifically AMEA and another national organization, Project RACE (Reclassify All Children Equally)—have been designed to change the designations used to categorize people racially on school, hospital, employment, government, and other forms. Although the two organizations have at varying times taken different strategic positions, at one point they shared the goal of revising OMB Directive No. 15 by adding an explicit multiracial designation to the existing official U.S. racial categories and to the census. Whether separately or jointly, however, these organizations have lobbied the U.S. government consistently on behalf of their respective causes.

The basic position of these two organizations (although there is significant ideological variation between them, as I shall describe) can be articulated by the following three points: (1) that some sort of basic right to have one's heritage acknowledged is being abridged by the absence of a federal multiracial category, (2) that the lack of a federal multiracial category is a specific health hazard, and (3) that a federal multiracial category will facilitate the dismantling of the American racial construct. These three issues represent the basic concerns of multiracial advocates in their efforts to amend federal racial classification. The first two will loom large in this chapter's analysis of the multiracial category initiative. I addressed the third issue in Chapter 3, arguing that a federal multiracial category could not dismantle race in America, the very thing that would make it possible. In Chapter 6, I will pursue this a bit farther and suggest that although in an abstract sense the multiracial idea can invalidate both race and then of necessity itself, an instantiated federal category would have precisely the opposite effect.

Before proceeding, I should mention three features of the multiracial category initiative. First, there was no singular multiracial category proposal, as several variations were proposed by the two major advocacy organizations in the 1990s. Second, all these were superceded by a 1997 proposal from Project RACE that was endorsed by AMEA and that did not specify a separate multiracial designation. However, because this later proposal (which I shall take up in Chapter 5) was not as desired by the two organizations as the earlier proposals, a thorough examination of these earlier proposals is in order. Project RACE most likely proposed the later version based on the certainty that OMB would reject the preferred options. Indeed, after making the proposal, Project RACE reversed itself and rejected it shortly thereafter. For these reasons, it will be imperative to examine all proposals, especially the earlier ones.

Third, these efforts by AMEA and Project RACE were not the first time a multiracial initiative was considered by OMB. As mentioned in Chapter 2, there was a proposal in 1988 to add the category *Other* to OMB 15. This effort "was supported by many multi-racial and multi-ethnic groups and some educational institutions," but it failed due to overwhelming opposition from "Federal agencies such as the Civil Rights Division of the Department of Justice, the Department of Health and Human Services, the EEOC, and the Office of Personnel Management, and from large corporations."[2] The failure of the 1988 proposal is illustrative of the fact that the agencies that use the federal racial categories for their intended purpose, and for whom the categories were specifically developed, are for the most part satisfied with them.[3] These agencies continue to be satisfied; and indeed, they have been joined by more voices.

Federal racial classification has attracted the hostility primarily of individuals and private organizations who object to the choices available on forms or who do not desire to categorize themselves or their members monoracially. As a result of such criticism and with an eye toward the upcoming 2000 census, Representative Thomas Sawyer, chairman of the Subcommittee on Census, Statistics, and Postal Personnel of the House Committee on Post Office and Civil Service, conducted four hearings on the subject in 1993.[4] During the third hearing, on July 29, 1993, Sally Katzen, administrator of OMB's Office of Information and Regulatory Affairs, announced that the agency would conduct a comprehensive review of federal racial classification.[5] In February 1994, at the request of OMB, the Committee on National Statistics (CNSTAT) conducted a workshop designed to "stimulate informed discussion by a wide variety of data users on the current standards."[6] The following month, OMB established and held the first meeting of the Interagency Committee for the Review of the Racial and Ethnic Standards. Also in 1994, OMB conducted public hearings in Boston, Denver, San Francisco, and Honolulu; developed a research agenda; and conducted literature reviews as part of the OMB 15 review process.[7]

The first three of the 1994 public hearings were announced in the *Federal Register* of June 9, 1994, which also solicited written comments from the public on a number of potential changes to OMB 15. Along with the proposal to add a multiracial category, there were other suggested changes. These included adding the category *Other,* providing an open-ended question on race and ethnicity, changing the names of several categories, moving Hawaiians from the Asian and Pacific Islander category to the Native American/Alaskan Native category, making Hispanic a racial as opposed to an ethnic designation, and adding a Middle Easterner category.[8] The public hearings and request for comments ultimately led to the oral testimony of 94 witnesses and the opinions of nearly 800 letter writers.[9] The results of both sources were published in the *Federal Register* of August 28, 1995, which provided a breakdown and analysis of six major issues based on the public's views. In addition, the committee set the research agenda through 1996 and described the general principles that would guide the review and decisionmaking process regarding changes to federal race categories. The August 28 *Federal Register* also solicited public remarks on its contents. Finally, the notice listed upcoming milestones of the continuing review:

Fall 1995: OMB analyzes *Federal Register* notice comments; receives results of May 1995 CPS [Current Population Survey] Supplement; and continues to consult on options with affected groups.

March 1996: Census Bureau conducts National Content Test (NCT) in preparation for 2000 Census.

June 1996: Census Bureau conducts Race and Ethnic Targeted Test (RAETT) in preparation for 2000 Census.

November 1996 through January 1997: Bureau of the Census provides test results from National Content Test and Race and Ethnicity Targeted Test.

Spring 1997: OMB publishes *Federal Register* notice on research results and proposed decision on changes, if any, to Directive No. 15.

Mid-1997: OMB publishes final decision regarding any changes to Directive No. 15 in a *Federal Register* notice.[10]

This comprehensive review of federal racial categorization was to last at least four years, through mid-1997, and cost millions of dollars. Following the 1994 congressional elections, however, the incoming Republicans implemented a reorganization of some House committees. As a result of that reorganization, the

Committee on Government Reform and Oversight assumed the responsibilities of the Committee on Post Office and Civil Service. The former committee's Subcommittee on Government Management, Information, and Technology held new hearings on federal racial classification, the first on April 23, 1997.[11] Additional hearings were scheduled for May 22 and July 25, 1997, and OMB extended the review period, with the final decision moved ahead from mid-1997 to October 1997.[12]

The multiracial category initiative, while certainly not the sole question to be considered by this massive evaluation, was nonetheless the main concern and the driving force of the review. Given the gravity of this issue, it is critical to understand the relationship between two very important elements of the debate. In particular, it must be remembered that although arguments are often made in reference to federal racial classification and the census, these are in fact two separate but connected entities. More properly, in terms of federal reporting requirements, the census categories depend on the OMB categories, and not vice versa. In other words, changes made to the federal race categories would alter the census, whereas changes made to the census would not affect the federal categories and would in fact have to be strictly within the latter's guidelines.

The Census Bureau has a variance permitting it to use the category *Other,* but it must adhere in every way otherwise to the federal reporting requirements directed by OMB. This does not mean that the Census Bureau cannot offer more than the standard categories for respondents to check, however, for it has the same authorization as any entity governed by the federal standards to provide more detailed categories (see Chapter 2). It must, however, reaggregate those additional responses into the standard categories for federal reporting purposes. Therefore, one could imagine the Census Bureau offering any number of categories and then reaggregating those responses for federal reporting purposes. Alternatively, the bureau could offer reports containing non-reaggregated statistics if the OMB format was not specifically required. The option to pursue these alternatives requires no specific authorization that the Census Bureau does not already possess.

One must be prepared to separate multiracial advocates' arguments into those that concern federal racial categorization and those that concern the census, when such a distinction is warranted. Unfortunately, however, many of these arguments fail to take this distinction into account, and people end up assuming that a change to the census, for instance, would affect racial check-boxes on school forms when in fact it would not. The Census Bureau might decide to pursue a more detailed data collection effort that could still be reaggregated into the standard categories without OMB making any changes to federal racial classification guidelines. The census form is a focal point for multiracial advocates, but, like an affirmative action form or the racial check-boxes on an insurance application, it is no more than an independent data collection instrument subject to the needs of its originator (the Census Bureau) and to the guidance of OMB. It is important to remain aware of these distinctions.

In addition to the federal review, on February 25, 1997, Representative Thomas Petri, a former member of the by now defunct Subcommittee on Census, Statistics, and Postal Personnel of the House Committee on Post Office and Civil Service, introduced H.R. 830, a bill to amend the Paperwork Reduction Act, which would require the addition of multiracial and multiethnic categories to federal racial and ethnic classifications.[13] H.R. 830 was a reintroduction of the same bill Petri had introduced with no success in the previous Congress.[14] Petri also testified in favor of a multiracial category before the House Subcommittee on Government Management, Information, and Technology on April 23 and July 25, 1997.[15]

Multiracial Category Proposals, 1993–1995

AMEA and Project RACE each submitted several multiracial category proposals to OMB between 1993 and 1997, and although those proposals sometimes shared common ground, it would be a mistake to see the two organizations as sharing the same ideological viewpoint. In particular, the dissimilar proposals they each offered in 1993 give a sense of the organizations' divergent agendas.

In her congressional testimony of June 30, 1993, Project RACE executive director Susan Graham outlined the changes her organization was proposing to OMB 15. Essentially, Graham's proposal involved the addition of a multiracial category for persons "whose parents have origins in two or more of the [existing] racial and ethnic categories."[16] The new classification was to stand alongside the standard categories in either the separate or combined formats. The Project RACE multiracial category was to be a stand-alone, separate classification with no further breakdown of the respondents' heritage or ancestry. Graham described this proposal during the February 1994 CNSTAT workshop, in which she was a participant:

> The Project RACE proposal for a revised directive differs from that of some other organizations. We propose the addition of the classification multiracial to the five basic racial and ethnic categories without further breakdown. In other words, multiracial children would only check multiracial and not be forced to list the race and ethnicity of their mothers and fathers. . . . Schools, employers, lenders, and others do not care about the breakdown. It is unnecessary for compliance purposes and only serves to satisfy curiosity.[17]

In effect, this proposal sought to create a new racial classification with the same status as the traditional classifications. This is significant in that, as described in Chapter 2, the standard categories were designed specifically to identify those groups that have suffered officially sanctioned oppression at the hands of the U.S. government.[18] I want to stress that the federal race categories were not designed to capture every conceivable way people might choose to identify themselves, for that would be an impossible task. Theoretically, self-identification could yield dozens if not hundreds of potential categories, highlighting the fact that federal racial categorization was not developed, and cannot possibly be utilized, to satisfy each person's self-identification desires. Paul Williams, general deputy assistant secretary for fair housing and equal opportunity of the Department of Housing and Urban Development, pointed out the inherent imprecision of the proposed multiracial category. In his view, "the use of the category even with a precise definition will not lessen the concerns we have for the infinite combination of racial classifications an individual could create under both a multiracial category or self-identification."[19]

The federal categories were not designed to be exhaustive in terms of individual identity but rather were designed specifically to delineate those major perceived groups that have at one time suffered oppression by the U.S. government, along with one group that has not suffered such oppression—the white group. In this context, the addition of a multiracial category is inappropriate and devalues the suffering of many millions of people, suffering that is the reason that these federal categories came into existence in the first place. Arthur Fletcher, chair of the U.S. Commission on Civil Rights, expressed such thoughts to Representative Sawyer's congressional subcommittee:

> Civil rights laws that prohibit discrimination on the basis of race, color, and national origin were enacted to protect all Americans, but policies that implement them must reflect the fact that certain groups, and any person who is considered by others to be a member of those groups, have suffered disproportionately from discrimination and barriers to equal opportunity. In terms of conducting and assessing enforcement programs, affirmative and equal opportunity programs, and the equity of federally funded programs, Federal agencies need information on racial and ethnic populations that reflects how individuals are likely to be classified and, thus, how they may be treated by other members of society. For the overwhelming majority of the American population, we believe these two perspectives are congruent, even when people are required to report only one race.[20]

An important potential effect on civil rights compliance monitoring is illustrated by the fact that Graham's proposal specifically required that self-identification be the sole means of collecting data. If respondents refused to self-identify, their data would either "default to one of the six categories" (the mechanism for such defaulting remaining unspecified) or be reaggregated proportionately across all the categories.[21] The significance here is that in many employment settings, workers are often suspicious of the motives of those who inquire about their race. Moreover, discriminatory actions stem from bigots' perceptions of race rather than from self-categorizations. It is phenotype that drives discrimination, regardless of the personal identity politics of the targets. For these reasons, employers and federal agencies concerned with monitoring civil rights compliance in the employment milieu rely on observer identification. The Project RACE proposal to summarily eliminate observer identification implies a troubling lack of concern for the primary purpose of federal racial categorization.

The weakening of civil rights compliance monitoring for the sake of self-esteem issues is a serious concern. Steven Carbo, staff attorney for the Mexican American Legal Defense and Educational Fund, in discussing the multiracial category initiative, cautions against changes to federal racial categorization that threaten antidiscrimination efforts:

> We continue to live in a society that identifies people by the color of their skin, by their physical appearance, or by their surname. People are not identified by the "percentage" of their racial or ethnic heritage. Discrimination continues to be based on what you look like, how you speak, and what name you were born with. Our society's ability to discourage such discrimination is based in part on the effective implementation of our civil rights laws. In this respect, the collection of race and ethnic data in the census is fundamental. Any changes to the data collection of race and ethnicity must be strictly scrutinized to ensure that the integrity of our civil rights laws [is] not compromised.[22]

Finally, the Project RACE proposal specified that multiracial responses be further broken down only if a variance was granted by the Office of Federal Statistical Policy and Standards—an office that had ceased to exist some thirteen years earlier, when, as detailed in Chapter 2, responsibility for federal statistical policy was transferred from the Department of Commerce back to OMB pursuant to the Paperwork Reduction Act of 1980.[23] At any rate, Project RACE intended that only a high-level variance authorize the multiracial category to be broken down into constituent races and ethnicities.

Given Project RACE's frequent deployment of medical concerns in identifying multiracial individuals, it is interesting that Graham would endorse a plan making it more difficult for data collectors to obtain an accurate assessment of what the organization claims is medically relevant information about people's ancestries. It is not enough to suggest a variance for medical forms, as relevant information might come from employment, school, or any other source of population statistics. In this sense the Project RACE stipulation against a further breakdown of multiracial responses into constituent subcategories seems related more to ensuring the separateness of the category itself than to expressing true concern for the accuracy of what might be medically relevant information. According to the Project RACE proposal, in the case of such a variance, "data shall be assigned by fractions into the appropriate other five racial and ethnic categories."[24]

Graham's assertion during the CNSTAT workshop that further breakdown was "unnecessary for compliance purposes" is simply erroneous. For example, in the case of an employer who discriminates against employees based on bigoted interpretations of their phenotypes, a multiracial category with no further breakdown would be worthless, indeed even harmful, to compliance monitoring efforts. In such a case, the stand-alone multiracial category would serve to mask the racist employer's discriminatory behavior, an assessment that is supported by Fletcher: "The Commission believes that a multiracial category would hamper the investigation of discrimination charges (including individual, systemic, and pattern and practice cases), the enforcement of affirmative action requirements (e.g., E.O. 11246) and the implementation of various Federal set-aside programs."[25]

The potentially destructive effect of a multiracial category on civil rights compliance monitoring is significant, notwithstanding the attempts of multiracial advocates to de-emphasize this threat. As evidenced by the testimony of Tony Gallegos, chair of the Equal Employment Opportunity Commission (EEOC), huge data sets of compliance-related information based on the standard categories and tailored to the needs of the agencies that utilize them already exist:

> The commission has a 15-year series of race/ethnic data specifically based on the race/ethnic categories defined in OMB Directive No. 15 in all sectors of employment. These sectors include not only private and federal government employment, but also state and local government, elementary and secondary public school districts, higher education and referral unions. To date, EEOC has experienced little or no difficulty in terms of data accuracy or public acceptance of the current race/ethnic categories in our data collection efforts. In evaluating recommendations for adding categories such as "Middle Easterner" or "multi-racial," it may appear that these more precise or "subject friendly" categories make sense for programs like the Census that asks individuals to self-identify their race and ethnic group. However, such categories may not prove useful for EEOC or other federal agencies utilizing EEO surveys that rely on the employer's observation and visual identification which reflects the community's perception of race.[26]

For the sake of emphasizing the important fact that discrimination stems from observer identification rather than self-identification, another example from Project RACE will be instructive here. Graham, arguing for the necessity of a multiracial category for purposes of monitoring discrimination against purported multiracial individuals, asks, "How can we determine the rejection rate in housing for multiracial people and interracial families if banks, savings associations, credit unions, and mortgage companies are not required to gather racial data for this segment of the population?"[27] Her question makes precisely the opposite point, however, for the following two reasons.

First, discrimination against people specifically because they consider themselves multiracial must be distinguished from discrimination against people because their phenotypes suggest the presence of a particular ancestry. In other words, it is highly unlikely that an act of discrimination against a person who identifies as multiracial is an act of bigotry based specifically on multiraciality;

such discrimination would most likely be based instead on whatever ancestry the bigot perceives in the multiracial person. That a person who identifies as multiracial is a victim of racism is no argument that she was so victimized *because* she is multiracial, as opposed to her having been victimized because her oppressor detected some particular ancestry in her. Indeed, even when the racist is aware of the victim's mixed heritage, it remains an open question whether he discriminates because he hates the mixture itself or because he hates what he perceives as one of the constituent parts of the mixture.

Two real-life examples are particularly illustrative of this point. In March 1994, Wedowee, Alabama, made national headlines when high school principal Hulond Humphries banned interracial dating at the upcoming Randolph County High School prom. Earlier in the year, Humphries had called one of his students, Revonda Bowen, a "mistake" because her father is white and her mother black.[28] Although one might argue that Humphries's actions were an example of racism directed against multiracial people, this would be an error. Humphries had a record of discriminating against Afro-American students, including "encouraging black and white students to ride separate buses to the county vocational school," and administering discipline, to include corporal punishment, inconsistently and disproportionately to Afro-American students.[29] Humphries's record, and his comments regarding Bowen, are indicative of anti-Afro-American bigotry. His condemnation of race mixture stemmed not from any conception of mixed-race persons as members of a distinct biological group but rather from the much simpler conceptions of white superiority, hypodescent, and racism. It is not, after all, as if Humphries were a nonracist who approved equally of whites and Afro-Americans, but disapproved of interracial dating and marriage. Rather, his disapproval was directed at the Afro-American element in such relations. As such, it constituted anti-Afro-American racism, and such discrimination is tracked most effectively by the standard federal categories.

To provide another example, in March 1996 in Thomasville, Georgia, Whitney Elaine Johnson was born without a skull and lived only nineteen hours. She was buried in the cemetery of the all-white Barnetts Creek Baptist Church. However, when church elders discovered that although the child's mother was white, her father was Afro-American, they informed family members that the child's body would be disinterred and reburied elsewhere. The family's refusal to comply, coupled no doubt with the national outrage sparked by news reports of the incident, led church leaders to drop their demand.

Yet again, this was not a case of bigotry directed against multiracial identity but simply the same variety of anti-Afro-American racism that has for so long informed events and institutions in the United States. The church's deacon, Logan Lewis, was quoted as saying, "That's a 100 percent white cemetery, and that's the way it's going to stay,"[30] while the pastor of the church, Leon Van Landingham, explained the decision to disinter the child as "trying to do what God wanted us to do . . . and that's what got us into trouble."[31] Ordinary racism against Afro-

Americans is the fuel for the bigotry demonstrated by the leaders of Barnetts Creek Baptist Church. The only issue here, as in the Wedowee case, is white superiority and racism directed at non-whites. It is no more complex than that.

In the United States, racism follows the race construct and is directed against people as members of large, diverse, and biologically meaningless groups. In general, bigots are interested in no more than that portion of a person's ancestry they have chosen to hate. Steven Carbo explains that "the relevant issue is how people are treating others. The gentleman who is multiracial may be perceived as being Black," with the result that this person "may be discriminated against on the basis of that perception of him as being African American. That's the relevant point that we need to keep sight of."[32] To take Carbo's Afro-American example in a slightly different direction, according to Graham's logic, all racial discrimination against Afro-Americans should be considered multiracial discrimination since it is common knowledge that Afro-Americans have mixed ancestry. On Graham's account, then, most antiblack racism in the United States is anti-multiracial discrimination. In seeking to distinguish multiracials as a distinct category of people, however, multiracial advocates do not welcome this logical extension of their own arguments.

The second reason Graham's call for a multiracial category for discrimination tracking purposes is flawed is that since phenotype is the most likely basis for racist judgments, efforts to move persons from the statistical categories (Native American, Asian, black, white, Hispanic) that motivate the racist's behavior to a category (multiracial) that effectively masks the perceived distinctions that are the basis for the racist's actions would cripple antidiscrimination efforts. Even a cursory examination of Graham's assertion that a multiracial category is needed to monitor discrimination against multiracial persons demonstrates that her proposal would establish a category that in all likelihood is not a specific target of discrimination, while simultaneously disabling a system that has worked very effectively to monitor civil rights compliance in the United States since the 1960s.

In summary, the 1993 Project RACE proposal sought to add a multiracial category that was not to be broken down further without high-level authorization, and also sought the immediate and complete elimination of observer identification for purposes of compliance monitoring. Especially important are two statements Graham made to the congressional subcommittee during her testimony. At one point she testified in a written response to a question posed by Representative Sawyer: "More importantly, I object to any format that does not include the term 'multiracial,'"[33] while stating during her testimony: "I also think that it's important to point out that we're not trying to make a separate or a new category of people."[34] Given Graham's insistence on a stand-alone multiracial identifier that would require federal approval in order to be further disaggregated, her statement that Project RACE is "not trying to make a separate or a new category of people" is simply not credible, since the sole purpose of the proposed category was precisely to create a new racial classification.

Along with Project RACE, AMEA also testified before Congress on June 30, 1993. The primary difference between the two organizations' proposals was that although both called for a multiracial category—as opposed to some other alternative, such as an open-ended or mark-all-that-apply option using the standard categories—AMEA did not insist on forbidding the collection of sub-category data on respondents as did Project RACE. The AMEA proposal was presented by the organization's president at the time, Carlos Fernández, and was altogether more sophisticated than that of Project RACE in that the AMEA plan at least attempted to recognize several of the very real practical concerns associated with altering OMB 15. Fernández attempted to address the concern that minority benefit programs might be affected by such a change, as well as the concern that the continuity of government records might be disrupted if persons who previously identified one way subsequently shifted to a multira-cial category. According to Fernández: "Our proposal takes both of these ques-tions into account by requiring that the races/ethnicities of parents be signified for each individual identifying as multiracial or multiethnic."[35] The specific language of the multiracial category check-box as proposed by AMEA was as follows:

Multiracial
(persons of more than one of the listed groups only)
For respondents in this category, specify races of parents.[36]

Here, however, the inevitable contradiction inherent in multiracial ideology becomes apparent, for having asserted before the same subcommittee that most Afro-Americans are multiracial (see Chapter 3), Fernández, with this proposal, required multiracially identifying Afro-Americans to identify their Afro-Ameri-can parents—who, by Fernández's own definition, are just as multiracial as the respondents—monoracially. Avoiding this inaccuracy would require, according to the proposal's logic, another subcategory level for grandparents, and possibly yet another for great-grandparents, and so on. Thus, on the one hand the presi-dent of AMEA asserted before Congress that Afro-Americans are de facto mul-tiracial, while on the other he presented a proposal that assumed that Afro-Amer-icans are unproblematically unmixed and should be identified as black in the OMB 15 format.

Several of the major themes discussed in Chapter 3 are illustrated by the re-spective AMEA and Project RACE proposals. It is clear that advocating a federal multiracial category requires acceptance of race as a biological reality, since mul-tiraciality is consistently defined as referring to persons with parents from two different racial groups. As demonstrated in Chapter 3, this is a biological, and not a social, rationale for identification. Additionally, these advocacy groups apply a selective form of hypodescent that categorizes Afro-Americans as black while classifying any children they may have with persons of other races as multiracial, even though Afro-Americans are themselves the most genetically heterogeneous group in the United States.

Within two years, however, AMEA and Project RACE had altered portions of their respective 1993 proposals and submitted a joint recommendation to OMB. In this new proposal, the multiracial category option would read on various forms as follows:

> *Multiracial:* Please specify the combination of your origins from the list
>   below that best describes your multiracial identification:
> _____American Indian or Alaskan Native
> _____Asian or Pacific Islander
> _____Black
> _____Hispanic
> _____White[37]

In order to develop this joint proposal, Project RACE acceded to the listing of subcategories and AMEA removed the specific requirement to identify one's *parents* monoracially, but the insistence on eliminating observer identification was carried over from the 1993 Project RACE proposal. These compromises were not minor and marked an important turning point in the brief history of the multiracial movement. In particular, the instruction to "specify the combination of your origins" was a far cry from the contradictory and somewhat ominous nature of AMEA's earlier requirement to "specify races of parents." Further, the joint proposal allowed the two organizations to better make the claim that together they represented the interests of a purported multiracial community.[38] In a joint letter to Katherine Wallman, statistical policy chief of OMB's Office of Information and Regulatory Affairs, Susan Graham and AMEA president Ramona Douglass stated that their model was "acceptable to Project RACE, AMEA, and most members of the multiracial community."[39] However, the data instrument utilized to determine that "most members of the multiracial community" supported this specific proposal, or even knew of its existence, is not revealed in the letter.

Afro-American Responses to
a Federal Multiracial Category

It is interesting that while many self-identifying multiracial persons who favor a multiracial category are Afro-American, the strongest opposition to such an initiative also comes from Afro-American individuals and organizations.[40] It will be useful, therefore, to examine the disagreement that comes from this quarter. Afro-American opposition to a multiracial category is essentially composed of three lines of argument: (1) that it is a method of denial used by those who are ashamed of their own or their children's blackness, (2) that it is a conspiracy by the far right to split and dilute Afro-American political strength, and (3) that it would spell disaster for antidiscrimination efforts that are given substance by the federal race categories.

Afro-American opposition to a multiracial category is centered not on people who identify multiracially per se, but specifically on Afro-Americans who do so. The concern is the potential effect of a multiracial category on people who are perceived as black but who might choose to identify as multiracial. The fact that some people who consider themselves Asian/white or Native American/Hispanic choose to identify as multiracial has no effect, except in the very broadest sense, on Americans who identify as black. Instead, Afro-Americans are concerned that many Americans who identify as black may instead choose to identify as multiracial, that this change in identification may lead to decreased political strength and increased social misery for Afro-Americans, and that there may be serious disruptions to federal antidiscrimination efforts.

Retreating from Blackness

On the popular level at least, much Afro-American criticism of a multiracial category is less than compelling, as a brief review of several Afro-American-oriented magazines illustrates. The cover of the January 1996 issue of *Emerge* announces that "'Multiracial' Grouping Undermines Black Clout," while the August 1995 *Ebony* asks: "Is There a Plot to Create a 'Colored' Buffer Race in America?" Fitting in with this uncritically sensationalist idiom are the comments of Halford Fairchild, a psychology professor at Pitzer College who believes that regardless of their ancestral mixture, people of African descent should maintain an *African* identity. Fairchild further contends that "the desire for alternative racial classification is due to individuals wanting to retreat from their Blackness."[41] This sort of perspective is based on an acceptance of hypodescent, and on its underlying, though likely unrecognized, foundation of white purity and black impurity. Thus, multiracial advocates and their Afro-American opponents who deploy Fairchild's line of argument engage in a pitched battle on the fallacious field of biological racial identity. Because both sides are fully complicit with the American racial construct, neither is capable of venturing outside the racial hegemony that so oppresses them.

Despite the fact that there is no essential or biological blackness from which to retreat, some multiracial advocates may in fact see the proposed category as an escape route from just such an identity. *Interrace* magazine editor Candace Mills, who is critical of essentialist constructions of race and would therefore not agree with Fairchild's sentiments, suggests nonetheless that much of the impetus for multiracial identity politics can be attributed to an aversion to black racial identification. She points in particular to many parents of multiracial children, saying that it is they "who have the identity problem, not the children themselves. . . . Many of these multiracial activists, both black and white, want to minimize their child's African heritage. I think they see a multiracial category as a way to elevate their children, to say, 'You're not black. You're better than that.' Now, I ask you, what's so bad about being called black?"[42] Columnist Lisa Jones concurs, characterizing multiracial identity politics as a movement based on self-esteem rather than political conviction and asserting that advocates of the new designation are seeking to have it "move them away from the stigma of Blackness."[43]

In another scenario, some white parents in interracial marriages may advocate multiracialism, not because they are averse to blackness, but because they are dissatisfied with being left out of their child's "racial portfolio." According to Barbara McIntyre, a white woman married to an Afro-American man, with whom she has had a child: "There may be some parents who like the multiracial idea because they want their children to be better than black, but there are also plenty like me who just want to be acknowledged. I'm part of this kid, too, no matter who he looks like."[44] Yet surely the problem here lies in the racial construct itself and not in making adjustments to what is no more than a taxonomic fallacy. In possessing European ancestry, McIntyre's son is no different from the average Afro-American child since, excepting perhaps recent immigrant families from Africa, virtually all Afro-Americans have at least some European ancestry. The mixture of course varies from individual to individual, but this is not relevant in any case. Since the multiracial argument is founded on biology—on so-called race mixing—intermixture is intermixture, whether it occurred in 1699, 1799, 1899, or 1999. The question that must be asked and that is continually avoided by multiracial advocates is: Why should people such as McIntyre's son be considered any differently from those Afro-Americans whose ancestral mixture is one, two, five, or more generations removed? This is the perpetual mystery of multiracial ideology—how multiracial advocates determine which genetically mixed Afro-Americans are multiracial and which genetically mixed Afro-Americans are merely black.

However, according to at least one of the national multiracial advocacy organizations, there is no mystery. In a failed 1996 bid to add a separate multiracial category to the California State Government Code, Project RACE revealed a multiracial category proposal that flies in the face of multiracial arguments for hereditary accuracy and medical exigency. The proposal AB 3371, "An Act to Add Section 11092.7 to the Government Code, Relating to State Agencies," was introduced by state assembly member Robert Campbell on February 23, 1996.[45] The bill was sponsored by Project RACE and supported by Georgia representative Newt Gingrich.[46] The proposed bill required "any form, application, questionnaire, or any other written or electronic document that is produced by any state agency that requests information on the racial or ethnic identification, to include the classification 'multiracial' among the selections provided."[47]

In its 1993 presentation to the congressional subcommittee, Project RACE proposed allowing subcategories under a multiracial box only if deemed necessary by federal agencies on a case-by-case basis. The organization's 1996 California proposal went even farther by not allowing subcategories at all. Under this proposal, "if the federal agency rejects the 'multiracial' classification, the reporting state agency will redesignate individuals under this category by allocating those persons to racial or ethnic classifications approved by the federal agency in the same ratio that those classifications occur within the general population of the group from which the information was solicited."[48] It is important to see that in pursuing this proposal, Project RACE apparently was so obsessed with having a stand-alone multiracial box that it was ready to consent to having multiracial statistics proportionally redistributed and therefore lost—qua multiracial statistics—rather than allow respondents to check multiple subcategory responses. Given that this was a state, and not a federal, proposal and that OMB 15 did not recognize a multiracial category, Susan Graham was well aware that even if her proposal were approved, all multiracial responses in the state of California would be proportionally redistributed for federal reporting purposes and therefore rendered moot. This fact must be borne in mind when considering arguments made by Project RACE regarding accuracy and the supposed importance of medically relevant multiracial data.

Furthermore, the Project RACE bill specified that all documents with racial check-boxes were to "contain a definition of the term 'multiracial' which this bill defines as 'having biological parents, grandparents, or great-grandparents of more than one race.'"[49] All the inherent contradiction of multiracial ideology is exposed with this bill proposal, which went on to state that "(1) multiracial persons are presently faced with selecting a category that denies the rest of their racial heritage; (2) the lack of proper racial and/or ethnic classification presents self-esteem problems, especially for children; [and] (3) without accurate racial designations, multiracial children are at risk for improper medical screening [for diseases] that affect certain racial groups."[50]

Surely, however, there is no concern whatsoever for accuracy of heritage when the multiracial category line is drawn arbitrarily at the level of great-grandparents. According to the logic of the Project RACE California proposal, an Afro-American with one white great-grandparent would qualify for the multiracial category, whereas an Afro-American with five white great-great-grandparents might not. One can see immediately that the claim made above regarding the pressing medical imperative for a multiracial designator is made a mockery of by the very bill in which it is expressed.[51] If the medical screening argument is a real concern, if it is something more than just a political hot-button issue and magnet for sympathy without real substance, then an Afro-American having five white great-great-grandparents should be at least as significant a medical issue, if not more so, than another Afro-American having a single white great-grandparent.

Yet for Project RACE to allow individuals to go farther back in ancestry to qualify for the multiracial category would only make more obvious the fact that Afro-Americans are all already multiracial. To allow the multiracial category to extend even two or three generations farther back would be tantamount to an admittance that there is no justifiable distinction to be drawn between so-called first-generation black/white multiracials and the average Afro-American. That being an unacceptable alternative, however, Project RACE chose arbitrarily, with no scientific or medical justification, to draw the line at great-grandparents. Among other things, one is struck here by the similarity of Project RACE's California proposal to the discussions of whiteness as an exclusionary identity in Chapter 1.

The arbitrariness of the exclusionary cutoff line is ironic in light of the California bill's defining multiracial as "having biological parents, grandparents, or great-grandparents of more than one race," reaffirming once again that multiracial ideology is based on the mythology of race as a biological reality. Ironic as well is the fact that as regards definitions, Graham's failed bill essentially reflects the thinking of the 1705 Virginia Colonial Assembly, which declared that the "child, grand child, or great grand child, of a negro shall be deemed, accounted, held and taken to be a mulatto."[52] It is telling indeed that the trajectory of Project RACE's California proposal takes one not forward, but rather three centuries into the past. In this light, the purported progressiveness of Project RACE is thrown seriously into question.

There is another aspect of the attempt to restrict entrance to the multiracial category that has not yet been fully addressed: the question of succeeding generations of so-called multiracial persons. The issues of whether only first-generation multiracials are qualified for a multiracial category, and whether the children, grandchildren, and further descendants of multiracials would be considered multiracial as well, have been raised in the national debate, but these issues have generally been discussed rhetorically rather than substantively. In essence, these are the same questions being looked at from two different temporal perspectives. The issue I have addressed above, the inconsistency of attempting to limit multiracial identity exclusively to first- or recent-generation multiracial individuals, is the perspective that looks back at the past. The same criticism in reverse, as it were, can be made of the multiracial project in considering the status of individuals two, three, or more generations into the future.

At what point and based on what criteria would the descendants of a multiracial individual no longer be considered multiracial? If a so-called black/white multiracial person has a child with a black person, is that child multiracial or black? What if that child in turn marries a black person and bears grandchildren? This is the same problem, but in the opposite generational direction, as the question of when ancestral mixture no longer counts toward multiracial status. The irony of the Project RACE California proposal, when taken to its logical conclusion, is that by the proposal's own definition multiracial status is only maintainable for several generations at best before individuals no longer qualify for the category, since the same rearward-looking exclusivity that was built purposefully into the proposal must apply from a forward-looking perspective as well. The only way to avoid this conclusion would be to enforce some kind of group endogamy on multiracially identifying persons. Ultimately, the failed Project RACE California proposal is likely to fuel increased criticism of multiracial identity as a "retreat from blackness" strategy, especially in light of the exclusivity stemming from the arbitrary parameters of the proposed category.

The "retreat from blackness" argument not only appears in the sensationalist journalism of popular magazines but has made its way to more respectable forums as well. Arthur Fletcher presented a version of this argument before Representative Sawyer's congressional subcommittee when he predicted

> a whole host of light-skinned Black Americans running for the door the minute they have another choice. And it won't necessarily be because their immediate parents are Black, White, or whatever, but all of a sudden they have a way of saying, "I am something other than Black." Now, what kind of problem that will produce I don't know, but I am ready to bet that if that [multiracial] category were added you would see a significant diminution in the number of Black Americans who under the present set of circumstances are identified as Black.[53]

Despite the correctness of his views on the multiracial category's potentially deleterious effect on compliance monitoring efforts, Fletcher is clearly engaging in hyperbole here. It is alarming that the chair of the Commission on Civil Rights would make such an exaggerated and inflammatory assertion. If his prediction of a mass desertion of light-skinned Afro-Americans from the black category proved accurate, one would then have to question the justification for not letting them go, since in Fletcher's account these people are practically being held against their will. Further, Fletcher's specific assertion that a "host of light-skinned Black Americans" would run for the door the minute the multiracial category was instituted is an extremely troubling statement that perhaps says more about Fletcher than it does about light-skinned Afro-Americans. Certainly, there are undertones of "retreating from blackness" in the implications of some multiracial arguments—their continual use of selective hypodescent in categorizing Afro-Americans is one example—but Fletcher's blunt suggestion of mass desertion by light-skinned Afro-Americans is unsubstantiated and reprehensible, especially considering his position. As it turns out, however, not only is Fletcher's prediction not borne out by the results of the Current Population Survey (CPS), National Content Survey (NCS), and Race and Ethnic Targeted Test (RAETT), but it is in fact wildly inaccurate.[54]

Not far removed from Fletcher's prediction of a mass desertion of the black category by light-skinned Afro-Americans—perhaps merely the other side of the same coin—is the nearly colonial attitude of Charles Stewart, an official of the California state government, who asserts that "Today there are few affirmatives in being designated black . . . but we've paid the price for that designation, and we have a right and a *need* to claim to those numbers."[55] Identity politics at such a low level of sophistication can be oppressive to an ironic degree. Stewart's idea that all Americans of sub-Saharan African descent can be appropriated for his politics, regardless of their particular ancestries or personal desires, is stunning in its audacity, to say the least.

It is important to make the distinction between challenging a multiracial category from an antiracial perspective and opposing it based on hypodescent and racial politics. Stewart's reasons for opposing the category stem from a politics based on racial mythology and hypodescent, and from a desire to increase the population figures and subsequent political power of Afro-Americans.[56] His opposition must be distinguished from that founded on an antiracial philosophy, which holds that an identity politics of biological race is wrongheaded no matter what the category in question might be. Nonetheless, Stewart's asserted right to claim so-called multiracial persons of African descent for a black political agenda finds echoes in many Afro-American arguments against a multiracial category. As long as such arguments take place within the context of the American racial paradigm, there would seem to be no room for a satisfactory resolution. The racial hegemony of this arrangement is so successful and so complete that the tool of hypodescent is defended with the utmost passion by those it oppresses the most.[57]

Conspiracy Theories

The second general Afro-American complaint against a multiracial category is the charge that it is a component of right-wing machinations to undermine Afro-American political power; in fact, that it is a plot to create an apartheid-like "colored" buffer race in America. Lisa Townsel explains this concern in the November 1996 issue of *Ebony:* "If mixed-race people who regularly choose Black on the census form now choose the new designation, it is feared that Black economic, social and political power will be seriously diluted and that the establishment of a new category could create a privileged 'colored society' similar to what existed in the old South Africa."[58] Writing in *Emerge*, Karen Bates reports that "many African Americans who are sympathetic to multiracial Americans' wish for enhanced self-definition worry that in its weakening grasp on the levers of power, white American society is embracing the multiracial movement as a convenient divide-and-conquer mechanism—another way of buying time before their time is finally up."[59] Covering the multiracial category initiative for *Ebony,* Lynn Norment notes the charge that "right-wing conservatives and other civil rights opponents are pushing the move in a deliberate effort to divide and dilute Black political power."[60] "Moreover," she adds, "there is apprehension that the push for a multiracial category could lead to a 'colored' class, or Black-White buffer zone, of individuals similar to that which was the legacy of apartheid now abolished in South Africa."[61]

In *Emerge*, Michael Frisby relates that "privately, some Black leaders contend the multiracial families pushing this movement are pawns for racists, whose real goal is to eliminate racial categories altogether, pushing the nation toward this delusion of a color-blind society."[62] This kind of sensationalism is not restricted to glossy magazines; it has found a home in local politics as well. Michigan State Representative Ed Vaughan, a proponent of the conspiracy school regarding the multiracial proposal, explains that "it seems a rather innocent thing to say, 'I have parents of different backgrounds, so I'll call myself multiracial.' . . . But underneath is something much more sinister."[63] According to Vaughan, "This is a very serious and critical issue that we need to deal with because the real plan is to make a colored race in America by the year 2000. . . . If that happens, it will further divide the African American community by separating us according to skin color."[64]

Needless to say, the existence of such a conspiracy is implausible. Although far-right bigots may indeed welcome the deleterious effect a multiracial category would have on civil rights compliance monitoring, there is no evidence or reason to suspect that the multiracial category initiative is part of some larger, organized, anti-Afro-American conspiracy. As for the specific claim that the initiative is connected to an organized far-right plot to create a colored buffer race in America, no generous reading is even possible—it is an utterly nonsensical assertion. One can understand the frustration of multiracial advocates in having to defend themselves against this type of inanity. Although a multiracial category is fraught with significant philosophical contradictions and seemingly insurmountable practical problems, it certainly is not a vehicle for anything as ridiculous as the buffer race fantasy.[65]

Civil Rights Compliance Concerns

The third Afro-American argument against a federal multiracial category that I shall consider in some detail is the concern that civil rights compliance monitoring efforts would be negatively affected by the institution of such a designation. Of the three criticisms examined in this chapter, the compliance monitoring concern is the only serious one. As detailed above, the conspiracy–buffer race argument is sensationalist nonsense, while the "retreat from blackness" argument suffers from a dependence on the same hegemonic fallacy of biological race that invalidates multiracial ideology. Concerns about antidiscrimination compliance monitoring, however, are legitimate and extend well beyond Afro-American individuals and organizations. Such concerns apply to all minorities in the United States and are the central reason for the opposition of federal agencies to a multiracial category.

Arthur Fletcher provides the Commission on Civil Rights view of a multiracial category: "The Commission finds the race and ethnicity categories in Directive No. 15 to be satisfactory as minimum standards for data collection and reporting. . . . However, the Commission believes that the addition of a new race category is likely to undermine efforts to enumerate and characterize racial groups, without necessarily yielding useful new information."[66]

Norma Cantú, assistant secretary for civil rights of the U.S. Department of Education, explains some of the problems suggested by Fletcher's comments:

> Adding another racial/ethnic category would take students from the current categories. This would reduce the number of students in these other categories. One problem in analyzing civil rights data is the small number of cases in each category cell. Adding another category would make analyses more difficult by reducing cell sizes. In addition, having one category of multiracial could lead to less information than is currently available about students. We would have no information about the composition of the multiracial category. Different combinations of minorities or minority/nonminority may face differing problems of discrimination, but all would be included in the one proposed category.[67]

Concern for the effects of a multiracial category on compliance monitoring extends to nonfederal organizations as well, as the NAACP, the National Urban League, the National Council of La Raza, and the Lawyers' Committee for Civil Rights Under Law all registered opposition to a multiracial category.[68] Sonia Pérez, senior policy analyst for the National Council of La Raza, outlined her organization's concerns to Representative Sawyer's congressional subcommittee, suggesting that the subcommittee

> proceed with caution regarding new categories of "mixed," "biracial," or "multiracial." The Bureau and the Committee should carefully review and test such categories to determine their accuracy. Moreover, careful consideration must be given to the implications such categories would have on civil rights issues involving equitable representation and affirmative action, for which Census data is often used to determine coverage according to affected group. Double-counting of an individual (for two-protected groups) may or may not present a problem.[69]

A similar worry was expressed by Rachel Joseph, interim director of the National Congress of American Indians:

> By ancestry, major portions of the American people are "multi-racial." This includes many Indian people, as well as Hispanics and a potentially growing number of Asian and Pacific Islander people. If an unknown portion of any of these populations were to shift their responses to the current race question from the present categories to a "multiracial" category, this would very seriously damage the use of Census Bureau data in assessing the socio-economic status of all groups. In the case of the Indian population, any such shift would make it much more difficult to measure the socio-economic status of the Indian and Alaska Native population and therefore the extent to which the unique federal responsibilities to our people are being met. . . . We have also made major strides in the way the data is tabulated and presented, with information now available for all types of reservation, trust land and Alaska Native areas.

We are, understandably, reluctant to jeopardize this progress. We need to know the effects of any changes before we break the continuity of all the data series we now have on population characteristics and distribution by race.[70]

There is reason to believe, as a result of the May 1995 Current Population Survey (CPS), conducted by the Bureau of Labor Statistics, that Native American representation would indeed suffer as a result of instituting a multiracial category. The CPS is a "monthly survey of the population using a scientifically selected sample of close to 60,000 households . . . representative of the civilian non-institutional population of the United States."[71] A series of initial face-to-face and telephone interviews are conducted over a period of four consecutive months, followed by no interviews for eight months, and then more interviews for another four consecutive months. The first project of the Research Working Group of OMB's Interagency Committee for the Review of Racial and Ethnic Standards was to administer a supplement to the CPS, designed to evaluate new panels of race and ethnicity questions. The May 1995 CPS supplement was concerned with three items: "(1) the effect of having a multiracial category among the list of races; (2) the effect of adding 'Hispanic' to the list of racial categories; and (3) the preferences for alternative names for racial and ethnic categories."[72] The CPS supplement design consisted of four panels as follows:

Panel 1: Separate race and Hispanic-origin questions; no multiracial category.
Panel 2: Separate race and Hispanic-origin questions, with a multiracial category.
Panel 3: A combined race and Hispanic-origin question; no multiracial category.
Panel 4: A combined race and Hispanic-origin question with a multiracial category.[73]

The multiracial category in panels 2 and 4 resulted in a little more than 1.5 percent of respondents identifying as multiracial, which brings up the interesting question of whether this category should be considered important enough to add to the federal racial scheme if it garnered such a low number of responses.[74] Also, the proportion of those identifying as Asian/Pacific Islander was affected only slightly by either the Hispanic or the multiracial options, and the proportion of those identifying as black was not significantly affected at all.[75] Contrary to the popular prediction offered by Fletcher and others that there would be mass numbers of Afro-Americans moving from the black to the multiracial category, all of the categories remained stable with the exception of the Native American/Alaskan Native group, which experienced a decline in those panels offering a multiracial option.

These results are confirmed when comparing the supplement measurements with the initial CPS interviews: "Regardless of the panel, almost 95 percent of those identifying as 'Black' in the CPS question also identify as 'Black' in the supplement. The level of consistency for whites is about 96 percent in panels 1 and 2 but drops to below 91 percent in panels 3 and 4, where some whites select 'Hispanic' instead. The agreement for Asian or Pacific Islander respondents ranges between 86 and 93 percent, but no detectable pattern emerges across panels."[76]

The Native American/Alaskan Native category, however, suffered a remarkable decline with the addition of the multiracial designation. Specifically, "in contrast to the other racial categories, the agreement rate between the CPS and the supplement for the American Indian, Eskimo, or Aleut category never reaches more than 75 percent in any panel. It is only 60 percent when multiracial is included as a category in panels 2 and 4."[77]

This drop is a major concern for Native American groups, as "the apparent decline in the number of people calling themselves American Indians has caused alarm among some of the nation's 500 tribes as well as intertribal organizations. Joann K. Case, executive director of the National Congress of American Indians and a member of the Mandan and Hidatsa tribes of North Dakota, says that a drop in the Government's official count of Native Americans 'would have a devastating impact on our communities.'"[78]

The National Content Survey (NCS) was conducted by the Census Bureau between March and June 1996 and was designed to test the sequencing of race and Hispanic-origin questions that might be used in the 2000 census. Unlike the CPS, the NCS found that the "addition of a multiracial category *had no statistically significant effect on the percentage of persons who reported as White, as Black, as American Indian, or as Asian or Pacific Islander* in either the race-first or the Hispanic origin-first sequence."[79] However, "the NCS sample was not designed to detect possible effects of different treatments on relatively small population groups, such as American Indians and Alaska Natives."[80]

What is significant about the NCS, though, is its consistency with the CPS in one of its major findings: "About one percent of persons reported as multiracial in the versions of the race question that included a multiracial or biracial response category."[81] This is remarkably close to the 1.5 percent of respondents who identified as multiracial on the CPS, demonstrating the inappropriateness of adding a multiracial category to the system of federal racial classification. In addition to the fact that a multiracial category does not meet the criteria for which these categories were originally established (to identify those groups that have suffered oppression at the hands of the U.S. government, as well as the one group that did not suffer such oppression), two government surveys both found that not even 2 percent of the U.S. population would identify in such a way. The addition of a multiracial category, selected in test surveys by such a minuscule portion of the U.S. population, is unfitting and trivializes past government oppression ranging from chattel slavery to genocide directed against already designated minority groups.

The Race and Ethnic Targeted Test (RAETT), conducted from June to September 1996 also by the Census Bureau, was designed with small groups in mind. Using census tracts to gather a sample of 112,100 households (of which approximately 53 percent responded), the RAETT targeted black, Native American, Alaskan Native, Asian and Pacific Islander, Hispanic origin, and white ethnic populations.[82] As a targeted test, however, the RAETT's results are not generalizable to the national population or to the specific racial and ethnic populations under consideration, but only to the "areas of relatively high concentrations of the targeted populations used to select each sample."[83] Nonetheless, the results of the RAETT are concordant in important ways with those of both the CPS and the NCS:

> The RAETT results were consistent in two important ways with findings from previous research on adding a multiracial category to the race question. First, the RAETT found that neither the multiracial category nor the options to mark more than one box had any statistically significant effects on the percentages of persons who reported as White or as Black in their respective targeted samples. . . . Second, the RAETT found that the panels with the multiracial reporting options had significant effects on reporting by two groups for whom either the CPS or the NCS also provided some evidence of possible effects: American Indians and Alaska Natives, and Asians and Pacific Islanders. . . . Taken together, the results from the CPS Supplement, the NCS and the RAETT suggest that providing multiracial reporting options would not affect the percentages reporting as White or as Black, but may well affect reporting in populations with higher intermarriage rates, most notably American Indians and Alaska Natives, and Asians and Pacific Islanders.[84]

The results of these three government surveys argue strongly against the addition of a multiracial category to the federal racial classification system for at least two reasons. First, there is good reason to believe that data on Native Americans, Alaskan Natives, Asians, and Pacific Islanders would be degraded by adding the new category. It would be unconscionable to risk the accuracy of data on historically oppressed groups for the sake of another group's self-esteem. Second, it appears that only a small percentage of Afro-Americans, who make up the majority of so-called multiracial persons, would choose the new category. It would not be judicious to add a new category for such a small population.

The federal race categories are not designed to capture every possible gathering of people who consider themselves a distinct group. They are designed expressly to facilitate the monitoring of discrimination against a select number of historically specific groups. Furthermore, should the number of Afro-Americans who might choose a multiracial category increase over time, then the reliability of data on Afro-Americans would be subject to the same disruption as predicted for the other populations.

In the fall of 1994, a coalition of civil rights groups opposed to a multiracial category circulated their concerns in a statement whose signatories included the NAACP, the Lawyers' Committee for Civil Rights Under Law, the National Urban League, and the Joint Center for Political and Economic Studies. This statement outlined several areas of disagreement with a federal multiracial category, some of which coincide with the problems discussed above; in fact, the statement appeared to be an attempt to cluster a large number of plausible and implausible arguments against a multiracial category into a single document. Among the less convincing arguments, for instance, was the coalition's warning that the institution of a multiracial category might lead to a caste system, and the further suggestion that an apartheid-like "colored" category might be established in America as a result.[85] Such scenarios, though, are no more plausible in the mouths of leaders of distinguished organizations than they are when found in the pages of glossy magazines.

The coalition statement did make important points when considering civil rights compliance monitoring, however, and it is in this regard that the statement is most effective. Citing the positive work of compliance monitoring in reducing discrimination and diluting the pervasive effects of racism, the coalition statement warned that "any effort that threatens to complicate, retard, or thwart further progress toward a true equal opportunity society must be resisted. We believe that the multiracial proposal poses such risks as it would make the collection of useful data on racial classifications difficult, if not impossible."[86]

Given the concordance between the federal categories and public understandings of race, the dilemma of how to move away from racial categorization without undermining civil rights compliance monitoring again becomes apparent. In the context of this dilemma, a multiracial category is likely to further cement both the existing categories and racial classification in general. From an intellectual perspective, a multiracial category is as illusory as the standard racial categories and would work to make the dismantling of the American racial paradigm an even more difficult task than it already is. From a practical perspective, a multiracial category would have the immediate effect of disrupting civil rights compliance monitoring for the sake of self-esteem issues for a very small percentage of the U.S. population.

Precisely how widespread the negative effects of a multiracial category would be on civil rights compliance monitoring cannot be known unless the category is actually instituted. Clearly, in addition to conducting tests on how respondents would react to data collection instruments containing a multiracial option, the federal government should devise and conduct tests of the category's likely effects on civil rights compliance monitoring. The available evidence, however, as well as the statements of those agencies and interested parties that currently have a stake in such monitoring, suggest overwhelmingly that the category's effect on the battle against racist discrimination would be a negative one. Additionally, it would appear that Native American statistical representation would be damaged severely by the proposed category. The most that multiracial advocates have done to counter these worries is to state that no negative effects would occur, without providing any reason for this conclusion or any real response to the many specific concerns already raised by individuals, agencies, and organizations interested in maintaining the integrity of antidiscrimination monitoring.

Interrogating the Self-Esteem Argument

Much effort has been expended by multiracial advocates in making the case that a purported right to self-identify is denied to multiracial persons by the lack of a federal multiracial category. As Ramona Douglass puts it, "I have a right to have a category."[87] In being limited to the available choices on forms that have racial check-boxes (which are usually the standard federal categories, as most agencies and nonfederal users tend not to avail themselves of the option of making finer distinctions), multiracial advocates claim that people who identify as multiracial are forced to deny part of their heritage. Carlos Fernández provides a typical rendition of this complaint:

> First, when the government compels the multiracial, multiethnic family to signify a factually false identity for their child, it invades their fundamental right of privacy. Every multiracial/ethnic family is entitled to safeguard its integrity against unwarranted intrusions by the government. No child should be forced to favor one parent over the other by any governmental agency. Second, it violates a fundamental right of privacy of the multiracial/ethnic individual to require that they deny their factual identity and heritage, including the right to their own distinctive identity as a multiracial/ethnic person. Such a requirement offends personal dignity and interferes in a negative way with the development of self-esteem of multiracial/ethnic students.[88]

Beyond the obvious fact that anyone who questions the taxonomic validity of the federal categories could make a similar claim of being classified imprecisely, there are several particular assertions in Fernández's statement that bear closer scrutiny. First, no one is forced to signify anything. Racial check-boxes are always voluntary, and no person is ever compelled to mark a choice. Thus, the notion that some "fundamental right of privacy" is being violated by a particular configuration of categories is simply false. According to Fernández, his 1993 multiracial category proposal "avoids unnecessary and unwarranted government influence and interference in the very sensitive and private matter of personal identity."[89] This statement is no more than the appropriation of rhetoric in order to distort an issue, because the federal categories are not a "private matter of personal identity." They are devices very specifically intended for the purpose of tracking discrimination.

By framing discussion of the categories as a matter of private identity, Fernández attempts to subvert the issue, as when, for instance, he states that the lack of a federal multiracial category violates the "fundamental right" of self-identified multiracial persons to "their own distinctive identity." However, the idea that a presumed "right to self-identify" is being denied to some Americans because there is no federal multiracial category is a claim that requires analysis. Nowhere is a case made for this alleged right, which is simply asserted as if such assertion were by itself enough to confer legitimacy. Yet what does a "right to self-identify" mean? Of what would such a right consist? If it means having the freedom to proclaim one's selected identity, then it is superfluous since all Americans already have this right. I currently have the right to define myself any way I wish. If I am not comfortable with the options on a form featuring the federal categories, I can refuse to answer that portion of the form, or I can write in my own response and leave it up to the data collection agency to sort my answer out (recognizing, of course, that such an action would undermine civil rights compliance monitoring). Multiracial category advocates seem particularly unable to appreciate that the very thing they oppose (broad categories containing people of diverse heritages, not all of whom are described adequately by the category names) has led them to pursue a multiracial category that would be no more than precisely the same thing (a broad category containing people of many diverse heritages, not all of whom would be described adequately by the category name).

The federal government does not define people. It does not validate identity, nor is it in the business of ensuring individual self-esteem. Sally Katzen, explaining the purpose of OMB's review of federal racial categorization, makes the same point: "OMB's role is not to define how an individual should identify himself or herself when providing data on race and ethnicity. Rather, we are trying to determine what categories for aggregating data on race and ethnicity facilitate the measuring and reporting of information on the social and economic conditions of our Nation's population groups for use in formulating public policy."[90]

If some "right to self-identify" actually were guaranteed by the Constitution, then each of the 250 million people in the United States would have a right to a single, unique, identification category, since no two people are exactly alike. Rather, language about a "right to self-identify" is an attempt to shift discussion of federal racial classification from what it is to what it is not—to shift what is essentially a matter of facilitating the statistical tracking of racial discrimination to a special pleading for personal appropriation of one of the basic mechanisms of civil rights compliance monitoring. When multiracial advocate Linda Mahdesian says of the multiracial category initiative, "We are fighting for our existence," she demonstrates the hegemonic effect of the American racial paradigm as well as the shallowness of people's identity and their willingness to seek validation of that identity from, of all sources, the federal government.[91] Responding to Mahdesian's comment, Pacific Union College psychology professor Aubyn Fulton offers: "Of course, I am no more 'multiracial' than I am 'other'; and if I could never really truly identify myself before, I doubt a box on the census will suddenly let me identify myself in the future."[92] Self-identity, if the term is to mean anything, can only be conferred by the individual, and not by check-boxes on a federal form.

The charge that the absence of a federal multiracial category compels children to choose or favor one parent over the other is another familiar, and essentially unanalyzed, claim. Despite the fact that young children generally do not fill out their own school registration paperwork, proponents of multiracial ideology claim repeatedly that children suffer serious emotional damage via this avenue. For instance, according to multiracial advocate Marvin Arnold, "Whether in school or in other parts of the community, multiracial children are constantly being reminded that they have no official racial identity."[93] In terms of younger school children especially, since they do not fill out their own admissions paperwork, one wonders how they are being damaged emotionally by the federal categories. One wonders too whether these complaints are not in fact about the parents, since the entire classification process in a school entrance context is completely transparent to children, unless their parents specifically bring it up before them.

There are of course stock horror stories of children being embarrassed by some insensitive administrator who comes to the classroom announcing an intention to determine the child's race once and for all; yet the rareness of such incidents is highlighted by the fact that one hears the same handful of cases invoked time and time again.[94] According to Susan Graham, "When a child has to pick the race of one of their parents, they are in essence being forced to deny the other parent."[95] Similarly, University of Illinois graduate student Phil Vernon says: "I'm biracial. I cannot look to Norway without rejecting my father and I cannot look to Africa without rejecting my mother."[96] Vernon's lament is a false dilemma, however, for it is in no sense evident why acknowledging one parental heritage, even momentarily, should necessitate a rejection of the other. Such a position can only be based on strict essentialism and crude biological racial mythology, serving as an example, again, of the tendency for multiracial ideology to be complicit with rather than oppositional to the artificial and arbitrary racial lines drawn in the United States.

A strong argument against the "denial of parent" thesis as a justification for a multiracial category comes from multiracial activist Deb Smyre, who, while supporting multiracial identity in general, is nonetheless critical of the "denial of parent" argument. In her view, "identifying as one race does not mean you have disowned one of your parents. If that were true, then multiracials are essentially disowning BOTH of their parents, at the same time. Too easy."[97] She is, of course, correct, for since the point of the "denial of parent" argument is that a child allegedly suffers distress by checking a box that is different than that of *one* parent, it stands to reason that the same or more distress should occur if the child checks a box that is different than those of *either* parent. Yet it is precisely the latter option that multiracial advocates are striving to implement. This inconsistency provides an opportunity to acknowledge yet again the extent to which multiracial ideology is complicit with and dependent upon biological racial constructions of identity. It is indeed too simple to hang so much of personal identity on the peg of race, when people are constantly proving that racial identifiers do not and cannot perform the task of describing them adequately.

Racial Destabilization and Political Recognition

Is it possible to destabilize racial categorization while simultaneously seeking political recognition of multiracialism based on that very same system of racial categorization? One would not think so; however, this is precisely the strategy of many multiracial advocates. Leaving aside for the moment the falseness of the destabilization claim, it will be useful to consider it together with the argument for the distinct political recognition of multiracial people.

One is hard pressed to understand how explicit political acknowledgment based on racial classification is supposed to lead to the breakdown of the race concept. If multiracial activists were to gain political recognition and political power as a racial group distinct from all other racial groups, what would inspire multiracial leaders to then initiate the racial destabilization process? It is important to see that their goal of acquiring political recognition based on their multiracial status is completely dependent on there being a racial structure to accommodate them. To destabilize the racial structure at that point would defeat the purpose of their having gained political recognition in the first place.

Far from doing away with race as an organizing principle, multiracial advocates seek to become part of the organization. According to Carlos Fernández, establishing and continuing to occupy racial political space is the very goal of the multiracial movement: "Carving out a political space? Are we getting a little hysterical? OF COURSE we want to carve out a political space, the bigger the better! It's our right."[98] The question Fernández does not answer, of course, is how the maintenance and expansion of political space by multiracial persons would lead to the breakdown of the race concept. Clearly, the new multiracial occupants of those race-based seats of power would not be interested in facilitating the destabilization of the very racial borders that make possible their newfound status.

As is made evident throughout this book, the assertions of multiracial advocates are not often challenged on the basis of their accuracy. Opponents will argue that the assertions are irrelevant or are outweighed by other factors, but rarely are the basic assertions themselves subjected to rigorous critical analysis. For example, Fernández, past president and current legal counsel of AMEA and a highly placed leader of the multiracial movement, has claimed that multiracial recognition will lead to the destabilization of the American racial paradigm (see Chapter 3) while at the same time stating that the goal of multiracial advocates is to carve out as much race-based political space for themselves as possible. Despite the utter contradiction of these two positions, they have heretofore not been challenged. By combining these kinds of statements with the "right to self-identify" and "denial of parent" theses, one begins to see an emerging pattern of false claims and invalid arguments chimerically supporting much of multiracial ideology.

The Multiracial Medical Fallacy

Of all the arguments presented on behalf of a federal multiracial category, the one that at first glance appears most compelling is the concern over medical screening. The claim here is that the lack of a federal multiracial category threatens the health and even the lives of Americans who identify as multiracial. Responding to a *New York Times* article on the multiracial category initiative, Ramona Douglass offered the following in a letter to the editor: "Your article overlooks a key medical concern of multiracial people. We are invisible statistically to the medical research community and will remain so as long as our well-being is secondary to politics."[99] Precisely how key is this medical thesis, however? Is there any validity to this highly emotional line of argument, or does it sound worthier than it actually is?

The problem with the medical thesis, as with the "right to self-identify" and "denial of parent" arguments, is that it has not been analyzed or intellectually challenged; it has simply been accepted without debate. The following argument by Susan Graham for a federal multiracial category on the basis of racially differentiated birth weights is a case in point of reasoning that is medically invalid:

> The result of one study has shown the relative odds of low birthweight based on race of the married mothers and fathers, specifically of white and black non-Hispanic marriages in the United States from 1984 to 1988. The odds were the best for children of a white mother/white father; worse for those with a white mother/black father; even worse for those with a black mother/white father; and worst of all for children of black mothers/black fathers. This is critical health information, yet it does not take other racial combinations or socioeconomic factors into consideration. Should multiracial children be placed at high risk medically because OMB Directive No. 15 excludes them?[100]

Douglass takes a similar line of reasoning in asserting that "every OB/GYN professional in the country knows that black babies have a higher mortality and lower birth weight averages than white babies. But who is tracking the birth weights and mortality rates of multiracial/multiethnic children? . . . Without the ability to count or monitor multiracial infants, research on our community won't be forthcoming and our children will remain at risk. This inequity and oversight cannot continue."[101]

The reality is that low birth weights are due to poverty, lack of prenatal care, and the generally lower disposable assets of Afro-American couples who may nonetheless have relatively high combined incomes. The pairings cited by Graham can be correlated with the likely disposable assets and social statuses of the respective couples, and suggest economic rather than genetic causes for low birth weights. Although correctly pointing out that the study she refers to does not take social factors into account, Graham nonetheless ignores the importance of those same social factors herself when she calls for a multiracial category on the basis of the supposed biological relevance of race in considering low birth weights. Similarly, the disparities cited by Douglass are attributable to the same causes.

Moreover, even if Douglass's thesis were correct, it is unclear how the multiracial "community" she is concerned about would be served in a medical sense by a designation that placed people of Asian/white, black/white, and Native American/Asian heritage, for example, all in the same statistical category. Since Douglass is arguing that racial biology is medically relevant, assembling a statistical category containing such various and disparate mixtures of heritage would be counterproductive, as any information gleaned from such a category would be worthless statistically. In any case, the point is moot since race is not medically relevant in the way that Graham and Douglass want it to be.[102]

Paul Wise, discussing infant mortality and the confusion between factors that affect mean birth weight and those that affect the probability of high-risk birth weight (under 1,500 grams), takes the position that "not only has this problem generated considerable disorder in identifying the major causes of disparate infant mortality rates in the United States but it has also contributed to the confusion surrounding possible biologically determined causes of disparate infant mortality, including inherited influences."[103]

The simplistic notion that disparate birth weight rates in the United States are attributable primarily to biological race, rather than to the host of social factors surrounding racism and racial categorization, must be rejected. Though focusing on the lack of correlation between racial biology and infant mortality, Wise's criticism extends to the elementary linking of race and birth weight as well:

> Despite speculation, little current evidence supports the contention that racial disparities in infant mortality are based on genetic, or otherwise biologically determined, pathways. . . . Nevertheless, the notion that racial disparities in infant mortality are generated by immutable biologic forces continues to reverberate in scientific and political circles. The profound tragedy here is that this specious debate has continued to distract policymakers and freeze local agencies in their efforts to address disparities in infant survival.[104]

While Graham was making unfounded claims about race, birth weight, and the need for a federal multiracial category, two medical professionals in Illinois were conducting a study demolishing such arguments. Richard David and James Collins assessed the birth weights of children born to black women of U.S. birth, black women of West African birth, and white women of U.S. birth. The idea for their study was straightforward. Reasoning that Afro-Americans are descended mostly from West African heritage and to a lesser extent from European heritage, one would expect, if race were actually a factor in low birth weights, that the Afro-American incidence of low birth weight would fall between that of African-born black women and U.S.-born white women. In other words, using Graham's logic of medically relevant race, one would expect African-born black women to have the smallest babies, Afro-American women the next smallest (but closer in size to the African-born black women), and U.S.-born white women the largest. This is not what David and Collins found, however.

Not only were the babies of African-born black women the middle group with respect to birth weight, but they were closer to babies of U.S.-born white women than they were to those of U.S.-born black women. David and Collins elaborate:

> Our findings challenge the genetic concept of race as it relates to birth weight. The African-born women in our study were new immigrants from the same region from which the ancestors of most U.S. blacks came, but without the estimated 20 to 30 percent admixture of European genetic material that has occurred since the mid–17th century. If genetics played a prominent part in determining black-white differences in birth weight, the infants of the African-born black women should have had lower birth weights than those of the U.S.-born black women. We found the opposite.[105]

The probable explanation for this result, according to David and Collins, is that their African-born sample was representative of a relatively highly educated African immigrant population in Illinois, and that many of these women were likely "born into affluent families."[106] Therefore, socioeconomic factors tied to education, class, and access to prenatal care were the critical determinants of birth weights—not fallacious appeals to biological race.

To answer Graham's argument, there is no health risk associated with the lack of a federal multiracial category since there is no biological link between race and low birth weight. Introducing multiracialism here only obscures the real dynamics of a very serious problem by reinforcing the fallacy that race is a meaningful biological concept. Simplistic and "sweeping biologic explanations" are dangerous and irresponsible, as they tend to relieve policymakers of their accountability for addressing the actual social causes of many poor health outcomes that have nothing to do with biology.[107]

There is vital work to be done in the field of medical screening. Project RACE has sponsored bone marrow screening clinics in the hope of providing matches for people who identify multiracially. Bone marrow donor drives are a worthwhile cause, but not for the reason Project RACE suggests. They are valuable in creating a large donor pool so that as many needy persons as possible can be matched with suitable bone marrow donors. This has nothing to do with racial or multiracial categories on forms, however. Multiracial advocates often invoke the tragic death of former professional baseball player Rod Carew's daughter from leukemia in the spring of 1996 as a justification for specific multiracial medical screening, but the same point applies here. Michelle Carew died not because there is no specific multiracial bone marrow database, but because there simply are not enough donors registered with the National Marrow Donor Program. If the donor pool had been large and diverse enough, a person could have been found who might have met Carew's specific donor needs; the donor's racial self-identification would have been immaterial. More people of all backgrounds and ancestries must register so that tragedies such as the death of Michelle Carew do not recur due to the lack of suitable donors.

As with other medical issues, what is needed is for persons to give their health care providers as detailed a personal and family medical history as possible (and for health care providers to consider this information appropriately) so that intervention decisions can be made based on the best and most complete medical information available. The fact that a particular person identifies as white, black, Native American, or Asian is less important medically than the specifics of that person's medical profile, which may include traits not normally associated with the presumed race in question or ancestors who identified as members of a different race. The answer is not to add a meaningless and potentially confusing multiracial category, but rather to remove biological racial mythology from the practice of medicine altogether. Frequently, multiracial advocates will point out that black/white multiracial persons usually are considered black by health care providers, with no attention given to their other heritage(s), and that this tendency is justification enough for instituting a federal multiracial category. The problem here, however, is that health care practitioners should not make *any* assumptions about patients based on perceived race. The emphasis should be on individuals and their family histories, not on mythic groups.

A perfect example of such misplaced emphasis comes by way of a newspaper article that Representative Newt Gingrich, in support of Representative Thomas Petri's multiracial category bill (H.R. 830), entered into the *Congressional Record* on July 11, 1997. The article relates that Ramona Douglass, "part Italian American, part American Indian and part African American, was once almost given the wrong anesthesia before a major surgery because doctors had incorrectly assumed that she suffered from sickle-cell anemia, a disease common among African Americans. As a result, Douglass was forced to call off the surgery."[108]

In her own account of the incident, Douglass explains that the white admissions clerk listed her as white, the South Asian resident listed her as black, and the lab technician decided that she "needed to be listed as sickle cell positive, but the test was never done."[109] Had she not been a "vocal and conscious patient," says Douglass, she might have "been given the wrong anesthesia."[110] What this harrowing example demonstrates, however, is not any medical need for a multiracial category, but rather that Douglass was at the mercy of incompetent physicians and staff. No better case could be made for the fact that basing medical intervention decisions on the fallacy of race, rather than on tests and medical histories, is tantamount to medical malpractice.

The same type of misinformation based on the fallacy of racial grouping is evident in the example of cardiovascular disease. Graham once again engages in gross oversimplification in an attempt to justify a federal multiracial category: "Black people are at greater risk of high blood pressure than the general population. Blacks get the disease one third more often than whites, they get it earlier in life, and they suffer it far more severely. Are multiracial people at high risk for some diseases? How can we know without accurate data?"[111]

Again, multiracial ideology takes precedence over actual causes of health risks such as environmental and social factors. It is not the case that race and cardiovascular disease are as neatly correlated as suggested by Graham. In an editorial in the *New England Journal of Medicine*, Richard Gillum explains that the general "understanding of the ethnic distribution of cardiovascular disease and the appropriate public health response has been undermined by a neglect of the dynamic aspects of the problem and the heterogeneity of rates of cardiovascular disease among blacks."[112] His comment is substantiated by an article focusing on cardiovascular mortality, birthplace, and race in the same issue of the *Journal*. Studying the different cardiovascular mortality rates of New York City blacks born in the South, the Northeast, and the Caribbean, and the rate for Northeast-born whites, Jing Fang, Shantha Madhavan, and Michael Alderman found that these rates varied among blacks depending on birthplace:

> Mortality rates in New York City differ substantially according to race and sex. The disadvantage of blacks as compared to whites is well known. What has not previously been noted, however, is the striking heterogeneity of mortality rates within the black population that is revealed through simple stratification by birthplace. In fact, the apparent interracial differences actually obscure larger variations within the black population.[113]

Blacks born in the Southern United States had the highest rates of cardiovascular disease, whereas those born in the Caribbean had the lowest rates. "Our data show that even the youngest Caribbean-born blacks of both sexes had rates of death from coronary heart disease well below—and Southern-born blacks well above—those of whites born in the northeast."[114] Proving once again that there is more difference within so-called racial groups than there is among them, and thereby undermining the very justification for the groupings in question, the authors conclude "that the variation in mortality from cardiovascular disease within the black population according to birthplace far exceeds the interracial differences between blacks and whites."[115]

Richard Cooper, chair of the Department of Preventive Medicine and Epidemiology of Loyola University Medical School, concurs when he writes, "it is possible that a person classified as black could be more dissimilar from another black than from a member of the white population."[116] Challenging the view that simplistic notions of biological race have medically relevant significance, Cooper explains that "black Americans are most closely related to West Africans genetically, yet the latter do not share high rates of the major disease syndromes common in the United States, including coronary heart disease, hypertension, diabetes, and lung cancer."[117] Although published two years earlier, Cooper's words perfectly complement the findings of Fang, Madhavan, and Alderman.

Although mortality from hypertension among Caribbean-born blacks was consistently greater than that of northeastern whites, it was nonetheless always lower than the rates among Southern-born blacks. However, in the case of Caribbean-born black men younger than sixty-five years, the rate of hypertensive mortality was much closer to that of correspondingly aged white men than it was to that of either Northern- or Southern-born black men. Thus, Graham's assumption that hypertension is determined primarily by race instead of by other factors such as environment and diet, and that therefore the lack of a federal multiracial category poses a health risk for people who identify as multiracial, is clearly not supported by empirical evidence. As in the case of low birth weight, biological race is not a determining factor in this particular health outcome. Rather, social and environmental conditions that may be affected by racial categorization, racism, and culture play a more significant role in determining the health outcomes of particular socially defined groups of people.

The claim that persons identifying as multiracial suffer health risks due to the lack of a federal multiracial category is without foundation. On March 1 and 2, 1993, the Centers for Disease Control and Prevention and the Agency for Toxic Substances and Disease Registry conducted their Workshop on the Use of Race and Ethnicity in Public Health Surveillance. One of the general principles agreed upon by workshop participants was that "the concept of race as assessed in public health surveillance is a social measure. Biological or genetic reference, or both, should be made with extreme caution."[118] Clearly, the call for instituting a multiracial category for purposes of disease screening is medically insupportable. According to epidemiologists and workshop participants Robert Hahn and Donna Stroup, medical screening by biological race is not desired since "what is *measured* as 'race' in public health surveillance is not a biological characteristic, but rather a self-perception for which phenotypic characteristics may be one among many criteria. . . . Even were distinctive biological markers of race determined, it would be difficult, if not impossible, to assess such markers in common surveillance processes and in the census."[119]

Race comes into play in public health in the sense that American society's stratification by race leads to inequities in social environment and in access to health care. Race is a social, and not a biological, factor, as explained by conference participants David Williams, Risa Lavizzo-Mourey, and Rueben Warren: "We focus on differences in skin color, not because the genes linked to skin color have been shown to be critical determinants of disease patterns, but because in our society skin color (race), is a centrally determining characteristic of social identity and obligations, as well as a key determinant of access to desirable resources."[120]

The authors further describe the fallacious nature of biological race as a factor in regard to public health, demonstrating that ideological arguments for the necessity of a federal multiracial category in order to facilitate medical screening are meritless because "the genetic model of racial differences in health is based on three assumptions that are all of dubious scientific validity. They are that race is a valid biological category, that the genes that determine race are linked to those that determine health, and that the health of a population is largely determined by the biological constitution of the population."[121]

The claim of multiracial advocates that persons who identify as multiracial suffer health risks due to the lack of a federal multiracial category is based on precisely the above misconceptions. Since medical screening by biological racial category is not a reliable predictor of disease, the establishment of a federal multiracial category for the same purpose will produce no data that is medically useful. The Afro-American case again demonstrates the implausibility of the multiracial position. Since Afro-Americans are such a heterogeneous population, with varying degrees of intermixture from recent times to several centuries ago, one cannot present a coherent argument for treating Afro-Americans as a biologically different population from black/white multiracials for purposes of medical screening. In this sense, the multiracial category is redundant, and certainly geared more toward self-esteem than medical relevance.

Assessments

Public debates are rarely pure, dialectical discussions. They are sometimes won and lost on the basis of how their parameters are set. In the case of the multiracial category debate, it is necessary to analyze carefully the validity of each claim presented, no matter the ideology of the presenter. Several of the reasons presented by Afro-American individuals and organizations for rejecting a multiracial category are not credible. In particular, assertions that there will be a mass desertion of lighter-skinned Afro-Americans from the black category, and that the multiracial category initiative is part of an organized plot to establish a "colored" caste in America, are preposterous and ultimately unhelpful. The most convincing practical reason for opposing a multiracial category is the destructive effect it would have on civil rights compliance monitoring.

Incorrectness is apparent on both sides of the debate. Claiming the need for a federal multiracial category on the basis of public health screening is simply a poor argument. The assumptions concerning the viability of biological race in screening patients are incorrect, thereby invalidating the collateral assertion that a multiracial category is required for proper medical screening. In addition to the logical errors and inconsistencies that are coextensive with multiracial ideology, though, there are attempts to distort the debate and to shift the issues under consideration away from what they are, thereby reframing the discussion in terms that are not valid. One sees this when multiracial advocates attempt to turn federal racial classification from a civil rights compliance monitoring tool into a vehicle for the enhancement of self-esteem and the validation of personal identity. It is apparent also when proponents of multiracial ideology invoke an alleged "right to self-identify" without providing any philosophical argument as to why such a right, even were it to exist, would be satisfied by the addition of a single new category to the federal standards.

Generally, the inconsistencies and logical errors of the multiracial position have not been part of the debate. Rather, the opponents of a federal multiracial category have accepted without question the distorted parameters set by multiracial advocates. In this chapter, I have outlined practical objections to instituting a multiracial category, the most prominent being the harmful impact on civil rights compliance monitoring that would ensue. In doing so I have subjected federal multiracial category arguments to a level of analysis they heretofore have not been required to endure. The stakes here, which include the crucial need to maintain momentum in the battle against overt and covert racial discrimination in the United States, demand nothing less.

Notes

1. House Subcommittee on Census, Statistics, and Postal Personnel, Committee on Post Office and Civil Service, *Hearings on the Review of Federal Measurements of Race and Ethnicity,* testimony by Steven Carbo on June 30, 1993, 103d Cong., 1st sess., April 14, June 30, July 29, and November 3, 1993, 194.

2. Executive Office of the President, Office of Management and Budget, "Standards for the Classification of Federal Data on Race and Ethnicity," by Sally Katzen, *Federal Register* 59, no. 110 (June 9, 1994): 29832.

3. Reading the text of the congressional hearings held on the OMB 15 review in 1993 by Representative Thomas Sawyer, and in 1997 by Representative Stephen Horn, one comes upon agency after federal agency expressing satisfaction with the existing federal race categories as minimum standards.

4. House Subcommittee on Census, Statistics, and Postal Personnel, Committee on Post Office and Civil Service, *Hearings on the Review of Federal Measurements of Race and Ethnicity,* 103d Cong., 1st sess., April 14, June 30, July 29, and November 3, 1993.

5. House Subcommittee on Census, Statistics, and Postal Personnel, Committee on Post Office and Civil Service, *Hearings on the Review of Federal Measurements of Race and Ethnicity,* testimony by Sally Katzen on July 29, 1993, 103d Cong., 1st sess., April 14, June 30, July 29, and November 3, 1993, 220.

6. National Research Council, Committee on National Statistics, *Spotlight on Heterogeneity: The Federal Standards for Racial and Ethnic Classification, Summary of a Workshop,* ed. Barry Edmonston, Joshua Goldstein, and Juanita T. Lott (Washington, D.C.: National Academy Press, 1996), v.

7. Executive Office of the President, Office of Management and Budget, "Standards for the Classification of Federal Data on Race and Ethnicity," by Sally Katzen, *Federal Register* 60, no. 166 (August 28, 1995): 44674.

8. Executive Office of the President, "Standards for Classification," June 9, 1994, 29832–29833.

9. Executive Office of the President, "Standards for Classification," August 28, 1995, 44675.

10. Ibid., 44674. The National Content Test referred to above was called the National Content Survey (NCS) when it was actually conducted.

11. House Subcommittee on Government Management, Information, and Technology, Committee on Government Reform and Oversight, *Hearings on Federal Measures of Race and Ethnicity and the Implications for the 2000 Census*, 105th Cong., 1st sess., April 23, May 22, and July 25, 1997.

12. House Subcommittee on Government Management, Information, and Technology, Committee on Government Reform and Oversight, *Hearings on Federal Measures of Race and Ethnicity and the Implications for the 2000 Census*, testimony by Sally Katzen on April 23, 1997, 105th Cong., 1st sess., April 23, May 22, and July 25, 1997, 56–57.

13. House, *A Bill to Amend the Paperwork Reduction Act*, 105th Cong., 1st sess., H.R. 830, *Congressional Record*, 143, no. 21, daily ed. (February 25, 1997): H628.

14. House, *A Bill to Amend the Paperwork Reduction Act*, 104th Cong., 2nd sess., H.R. 3920, *Congressional Record*, 142, no. 114, daily ed. (July 30, 1996): H8982.

15. House Subcommittee on Government Management, Information, and Technology, Committee on Government Reform and Oversight, *Hearings on Federal Measures of Race and Ethnicity and the Implications for the 2000 Census*, testimony by Thomas Petri on April 23 and July 25, 1997, 105th Cong., 1st sess., April 23, May 22, and July 25, 1997, 225–226, 524.

16. House Subcommittee on Census, Statistics, and Postal Personnel, Committee on Post Office and Civil Service, *Hearings on the Review of Federal Measurements of Race and Ethnicity*, testimony by Susan Graham on June 30, 1993, 103d Cong., 1st sess., April 14, June 30, July 29, and November 3, 1993, 115.

17. Susan Graham, "The Real World," in *The Multiracial Experience: Racial Borders As the New Frontier*, ed. Maria P. P. Root (Thousand Oaks, Calif.: Sage Publications, 1996), 44–45.

18. It is critical to recognize that these categories are to some degree determined by the actions of bigots who continue to oppress others based on phenotype, culture, or language. Thus, although race is a fallacy, many people are discriminated against because they are perceived to be black, Asian, or Native American.

19. House Subcommittee on Census, Statistics, and Postal Personnel, Committee on Post Office and Civil Service, *Hearings on the Review of Federal Measurements of Race and Ethnicity*, testimony by Paul Williams on November 3, 1993, 103d Cong., 1st sess., April 14, June 30, July 29, and November 3, 1993, 271.

20. House Subcommittee on Census, Statistics, and Postal Personnel, Committee on Post Office and Civil Service, *Hearings on the Review of Federal Measurements of Race and Ethnicity*, testimony by Arthur A. Fletcher on November 3, 1993, 103d Cong., 1st sess., April 14, June 30, July 29, and November 3, 1993, 258.

21. House Subcommittee, testimony by Susan Graham, 115.

22. House Subcommittee, testimony by Steven Carbo, 182.

23. House Subcommittee, testimony by Susan Graham, 115.

24. Ibid.

25. House Subcommittee, testimony by Arthur A. Fletcher, 257.

26. House Subcommittee on Census, Statistics, and Postal Personnel, Committee on Post Office and Civil Service, *Hearings on the Review of Federal Measurements of Race and Ethnicity,* testimony by Tony E. Gallegos on November 3, 1993, 103d Cong., 1st sess., April 14, June 30, July 29, and November 3, 1993, 285.

27. Graham, "The Real World," 43. Note also Graham's implication that multiracial people as well as "interracial families" (by which I take her to mean the ostensibly mono-racial people who would constitute the partners in an interracial marriage) would be tracked by a multiracial category. It is not clear how Graham would justify placing a mul-tiracial person, as well as a white woman and her Afro-American husband, for instance, all in the same multiracial category, yet this is precisely the implication of her wish to gather "data for this segment of the population," which she has categorized as "multiracial people and interracial families."

28. Alan Patureau, "Principal Called Mixed-Race Pupil a 'Mistake,'" *Atlanta Journal-Constitution,* March 10, 1994, A3.

29. Ibid.

30. Quoted in Dennis McCafferty, "No Resting in Peace for Infant," *Atlanta Journal-Constitution,* March 28, 1996, D1.

31. Ibid.

32. House Subcommittee, testimony by Steven Carbo, 193.

33. House Subcommittee, testimony by Susan Graham, 119.

34. Ibid., 170.

35. House Subcommittee on Census, Statistics, and Postal Personnel, Committee on Post Office and Civil Service, *Hearings on the Review of Federal Measurements of Race and Ethnicity,* testimony by Carlos Fernández on June 30, 1993, 103d Cong., 1st sess., April 14, June 30, July 29, and November 3, 1993, 134.

36. Ibid., 137.

37. Ramona Douglass (AMEA) and Susan Graham (Project RACE) to Katherine Wall-man (Office of Information and Regulatory Affairs, OMB), September 29, 1995.

38. The existence of such a community as a political entity is debatable. The fact that multiracial advocacy organizations exist does not in itself entail that some sort of mul-tiracial community also exists. It is important to maintain a distinction between special interest groups that have a certain number of constituents and what might more properly be termed true social communities. Much has been assumed by the language of multira-cial advocacy that has not undergone serious intellectual challenge. Part of my aim in this chapter is to examine the appropriation of terminology that sets the parameters of debate on this issue.

39. Douglass and Graham, to Katherine Wallman.

40. Another large group of multiracial advocates are the self-identifying white parents of so-called multiracial children (i.e., white partners in interracial relationships), a phe-nomenon that is itself the seat of some controversy.

41. Quoted in Lynn Norment, "Am I Black, White, or In Between?" *Ebony,* August 1995, 110.

42. Quoted in Linda Mathews, "More Than Identity Rides on a New Racial Category," *New York Times,* July 6, 1996, A7.

43. Quoted in Norment, "Am I Black," 110–112.

44. Quoted in Mathews, "More Than Identity," A7.

45. California State Legislature, "An Act to Add Section 11092.7 to the Government Code, Relating to State Agencies," California Legislature Public Access Computer, AB 3371 Assembly Bill: Introduced, December 26, 1998 [ftp://leginfo.public.ca.gov/].

46. California State Legislature, "An Act to Add Section 11092.7 to the Government Code, Relating to State Agencies," California Legislature Public Access Computer, AB 3371 Assembly Bill: Bill Analysis, December 26, 1998 [ftp://leginfo.public.ca.gov/].

47. Ibid.

48. Ibid.

49. Ibid.

50. Ibid.

51. I shall take up the often cited, but rarely analyzed, medical concerns later in this chapter.

52. William Waller Hening, ed., The Statutes At Large; Being a Collection of All the Laws of Virginia, from the First Session of the Legislature in the Year 1619, vol. 3 (Richmond, Va.: Samuel Pleasants, 1812), 252. This section, covering legislation from October 1705, gives the text of "an act declaring who shall not bear office in this country."

53. House Subcommittee, testimony by Arthur A. Fletcher, 273.

54. I shall address the results of the CPS, NCS, and RAETT later in this chapter.

55. Quoted in Karen G. Bates, "Color Complexity," *Emerge*, June 1993, 38.

56. Ibid.

57. I refer here to both groups. In general, Afro-Americans use hypodescent to assert that the black/white multiracial person is black, whereas multiracial advocates utilize the mechanism selectively in order to posit black people who can produce multiracial children.

58. Lisa Jones Townsel, "Neither Black Nor White: Would a New Census Category Be a Dangerous Diversion or a Step Forward?" *Ebony*, November 1996, 45.

59. Bates, "Color Complexity," 39.

60. Norment, "Am I Black," 108.

61. Ibid., 110.

62. Michael K. Frisby, "Black, White, or Other," *Emerge*, December 1995–January 1996, 49–50.

63. Quoted in Kenneth Cole, "'Multiracial' Box on Job, School Forms Riles Critics," *Detroit News*, June 28, 1995, 3D.

64. Quoted in Marc C. Tilles, "Multiracial Category Becomes Law," *Michigan Chronicle*, September 20-26, 1995, 1A.

65. I am making a distinction here between it being the explicit goal of either multiracial advocates or the far right to institute a buffer race, and the possibility that such an outcome might be desired by some. There are certainly many people in the United States, especially far-right politicians, who would welcome the idea. Such extremist support, however, is not the same as a large-scale organized plot.

66. House Subcommittee, testimony by Arthur A. Fletcher, 256–257.

67. House Subcommittee on Census, Statistics, and Postal Personnel, Committee on Post Office and Civil Service, *Hearings on the Review of Federal Measurements of Race and Ethnicity*, testimony by Norma V. Cantú on November 3, 1993, 103d Cong., 1st sess., April 14, June 30, July 29, and November 3, 1993, 264–265.

68. Mathews, "More Than Identity," A7.

69. House Subcommittee on Census, Statistics, and Postal Personnel, Committee on Post Office and Civil Service, *Hearings on the Review of Federal Measurements of Race and Ethnicity,* testimony by Sonia M. Pérez on June 30, 1993, 103d Cong., 1st sess., April 14, June 30, July 29, and November 3, 1993, 177.

70. House Subcommittee on Census, Statistics, and Postal Personnel, Committee on Post Office and Civil Service, *Hearings on the Review of Federal Measurements of Race and Ethnicity,* testimony by Rachel A. Joseph on July 29, 1993, 103d Cong., 1st sess., April 14, June 30, July 29, and November 3, 1993, 239.

71. Department of Labor, Bureau of Labor Statistics, *A Test of Methods for Collecting Racial and Ethnic Information: May 1995,* USDL 95-428 (Washington, D.C., October 26, 1995), 1.

72. Ibid.

73. Ibid., 2.

74. Ibid.

75. Ibid., 2–3.

76. Ibid., 3.

77. Ibid., 3–4.

78. Mathews, "More Than Identity," A7.

79. Department of Commerce, Bureau of the Census, *Findings on Questions on Race and Hispanic Origin Tested in the 1996 National Content Survey,* Population Division Working Paper no. 16 (Washington, D.C., December 1996), 15.

80. Ibid., 1.

81. Ibid.

82. Department of Commerce, Bureau of the Census, *Results of the 1996 Race and Ethnic Targeted Test,* Population Division Working Paper no. 18 (Washington, D.C., May 1997), 1-6.

83. Ibid., 1-23.

84. Ibid., 1-24–1-25.

85. Lawyers' Committee for Civil Rights Under Law, National Association for the Advancement of Colored People, National Urban League, and Joint Center for Political and Economic Studies, *Coalition Statement on Proposed Modification of OMB Directive no. 15,* Fall 1994, 4.

86. Ibid., 8–9.

87. Quoted in Elizabeth A. Bowman, "'Multiracial' Category Sparks Controversy," *Detroit News,* April 13, 1995, 2C.

88. House Subcommittee, testimony by Carlos Fernández, 130.

89. Ibid., 129.

90. House Subcommittee, testimony by Sally Katzen, April 23, 1997, 10.

91. Quoted in Paul Shepard, "Year 2000 May Bring Census with New Mixed-Race Category," *Atlanta Journal-Constitution,* April 3, 1997, A8.

92. Aubyn Fulton, online posting, Interracial Individuals Discussion List, April 3, 1997 [ii-list@hcs.harvard.edu].

93. House Subcommittee on Census, Statistics, and Postal Personnel, Committee on Post Office and Civil Service, *Hearings on the Review of Federal Measurements of Race and Ethnicity,* testimony by Marvin C. Arnold on June 30, 1993, 103d Cong., 1st sess., April 14, June 30, July 29, and November 3, 1993, 161.

94. None of this is to suggest that such incidents ought not to be taken seriously, and administrators and teachers disciplined appropriately when they occur, but rather to point out that these cases are extremely rare. They should not be considered the norm, which is how multiracial advocates often paint them.

95. Quoted in Rogers Worthington, "'Multiracial' Census Category Is Sought," *Chicago Tribune*, July 13, 1994, sec. 1, 15.

96. Quoted in Janita Poe, "Multiracial People Want a Single Name That Fits," *Chicago Tribune*, May 3, 1993, sec. 1, 13.

97. Deb Smyre, online posting, Interracial Individuals Discussion List, February 24, 1997 [ii-list@hcs.harvard.edu].

98. Carlos Fernández, online posting, Interracial Individuals Discussion List, February 5, 1996 [ii@gnu.ai.mit.edu].

99. Ramona Douglass, "Multiracial People Must No Longer Be Invisible," *New York Times*, July 12, 1996, A14.

100. Graham, "The Real World," 41.

101. House Subcommittee on Government Management, Information, and Technology, Committee on Government Reform and Oversight, *Hearings on Federal Measures of Race and Ethnicity and the Implications for the 2000 Census*, testimony by Ramona Douglass on May 22, 1997, 105th Cong., 1st sess., April 23, May 22, and July 25, 1997, 386.

102. By July 1997, Douglass had moved away from the contradictory position that a stand-alone multiracial category, composed of multiple combinations of mixture, would provide medical screening benefits. She has maintained her stance that race is a reliable predictor of health outcomes, however (see Chapter 5).

103. Paul H. Wise, "Confronting Racial Disparities in Infant Mortality: Reconciling Science and Politics," *Racial Differences in Preterm Delivery: Developing a New Research Paradigm* (supplement), *American Journal of Preventive Medicine* 9, no. 6 (November-December 1993): 11.

104. Ibid., 14.

105. Richard J. David and James W. Collins, "Differing Birth Weight Among Infants of U.S.-Born Blacks, African-Born Blacks, and U.S.-Born Whites," *New England Journal of Medicine* 337, no. 17 (October 23, 1997): 1213.

106. Ibid.

107. Wise, "Confronting Racial Disparities," 14.

108. *Congressional Record*, 105th Cong., 1st sess., 143, no. 98, daily ed. (July 11, 1997): E1408. Article submitted by Representative Newt Gingrich of Georgia in extension of remarks.

109. House Subcommittee, testimony by Ramona Douglass, 383.

110. Ibid.

111. Graham, "The Real World," 41.

112. Richard F. Gillum, "The Epidemiology of Cardiovascular Disease in Black Americans," *New England Journal of Medicine* 335, no. 21 (November 21, 1996): 1597.

113. Jing Fang, Shantha Madhavan, and Michael H. Alderman, "The Association Between Birthplace and Mortality from Cardiovascular Causes Among Black and White Residents of New York City," *New England Journal of Medicine* 335, no. 21 (November 21, 1996): 1549–1550.

114. Ibid., 1550.

115. Ibid., 1545.

116. Richard S. Cooper, "A Case Study in the Use of Race and Ethnicity in Public Health Surveillance," *Public Health Reports* 109, no. 1 (January-February 1994): 49.

117. Ibid.

118. Reuben C. Warren, Robert A. Hahn, Lonnie Bristow, and Elena S. H. Yu, "The Use of Race and Ethnicity in Public Health Surveillance," *Public Health Reports* 109, no. 1 (January-February 1994): 5.

119. Robert A. Hahn and Donna F. Stroup, "Race and Ethnicity in Public Health Surveillance: Criteria for the Scientific Use of Social Categories," *Public Health Reports* 109, no. 1 (January-February 1994): 13.

120. David R. Williams, Risa Lavizzo-Mourey, and Rueben C. Warren, "The Concept of Race and Health Status in America," *Public Health Reports* 109, no. 1 (January-February 1994): 28.

121. Ibid., 27.

5

Final Proposal, Final Recommendation, Final Decision

Will look forward to giving you and ii [the Interracial Individuals Discussion List] updates in the weeks ahead and I encourage them all to make their feelings known—to be supportive of the interagency recommendations so we don't get lost in the "politics" of others who do not wish us well and only wish to manipulate our community for their own personal or political goals.

—Ramona Douglass, president, Association of MultiEthnic Americans[1]

Proposal

The challenge for America lies in determining how to move away from the fallacy of race while remaining aggressive in the battle against racism. As an aspect of civil rights compliance monitoring, federal racial classification ironically works against the former goal while serving the latter especially well. Any alteration to federal racial classification therefore demands the closest scrutiny. The claim of multiracial advocates that a federal multiracial category would destabilize race and at best do no harm to antidiscrimination monitoring efforts is not credible. The reality is that a federal multiracial category would not serve these purposes, but would instead inhibit them both by cementing the idea of race further in place while simultaneously reducing the effectiveness of civil rights compliance monitoring.

One of the more interesting developments to emerge from the 1997 congressional hearings on revising OMB Directive No. 15 was the abandonment in May of that year of an explicit multiracial category by Project RACE in favor of a "mark all that apply" (MATA) alternative, and the subsequent support of that alternative by the Association of MultiEthnic Americans (AMEA).[2] This development represented no less than a fundamental strategic shift in approach by the primary multiracial advocacy organizations in the United States. Whether this modification was voluntary in the sense of being the result of considered changes of heart, or whether it was involuntary in the sense of being the result of successive retrenchments in the face of opposition to the earlier proposals, is debatable.[3] What we can note, though, is the fact that the option proposed by these groups to OMB in 1997 was completely unacceptable to these same organizations only one year earlier.

Additionally, it is worth mentioning that the massive review of federal racial classification between 1993 and 1997, including seven congressional subcommittee hearings, was undertaken in part due to insistent lobbying by AMEA and Project RACE for a separate multiracial category, and cost millions of dollars. The Race and Ethnic Targeted Test (RAETT) alone had an estimated annual cost of $2.2 million.[4] The abandonment of a separate multiracial classification by AMEA and Project RACE in favor of a MATA approach, after millions of dollars had been spent precisely because these two organizations had argued for a separate category, is significant. This is not to say that the cost of the entire review can be placed at the feet of these two organizations, however.

In Chapter 4, I detailed the implications of adding a separate multiracial category to the system of federal racial classification. In order to evaluate the MATA option, it will be useful to review the several specific multiracial category options that had been proposed previously. Multiracial advocates proposed three different options, including MATA, to OMB between 1993 and 1997. In Chapter 4 I detailed two of them—a separate multiracial category with no subcategories, and a multiracial category with subcategories. The former is the multiracial check-box option proposed by Project RACE alone in 1993, and it remains the only proposal that presents the multiracial selection as an exclusive, stand-alone choice with no subcategories.[5] The latter is the format submitted by AMEA in 1993, and jointly by AMEA and Project RACE in 1995. I shall refer to the latter option as B+MATA (box plus "mark all that apply"), in order to distinguish it from the exclusive multiracial check-box proposal of 1993 and the MATA option proposed in 1997.

MATA is the only option that does not include an actual multiracial check-box; instead, it invites respondents to simply mark all the boxes that might apply to their ancestry, and thus it does not overtly establish a multiracial designation as an explicitly distinct biological racial group.[6] I say it does not do this *overtly*, since of course selecting this option does imply a distinctness from those respondents who would mark only a single, monoracial choice. This is perhaps the closest that an institutionalized assertion of multiracial identity can come to being a subversive force, as one might argue that under the MATA option the monoracial paradigm can be challenged without establishing an explicit multiracial category, thereby undermining the notion of fixed races. I shall take up this point in Chapter 6 when discussing the sense in which the multiracial idea, considered in the abstract, can possess a measure of subversive power.

From the multiracial advocacy perspective, a separate multiracial check-box would be the most favored choice, because it would grant fully equivalent status to the multiracial category. With an exclusive check-box, multiracial advocates would achieve full complicity with the American monoracial paradigm by fitting themselves into this paradigm rather than challenging it. In effect, the multiracial classification itself would be transformed into a de facto monoracial classification, losing any subversive power it might have possessed to disrupt the paradigm and thereby becoming as biologically reifying as the racial categories whose ranks it would join.

The B+MATA option, on the other hand, would introduce a sense of qualification to a multiracial classification by requiring a sublisting of the standard categories that applied to the respondent. In this scenario, the multiracial classification would be different from the other classifications, not sharing the same status due to being qualified by, and thus somewhat subordinate to, the standard racial categories. Although both B+MATA and the separate check-box depend fully on the standard categories for their existence, this dependence would be more visible, on the form itself, in the case of B+MATA.

A brief review of the multiracial proposals will help establish the context of the 1997 alternative. In 1993, AMEA and Project RACE each favored a different option in their respective congressional testimonies, with AMEA proposing B+MATA and Project RACE proposing a stand-alone multiracial check-box. By 1995, the two organizations had agreed to a joint proposal in which they endorsed a version of B+MATA somewhat modified from the 1993 AMEA proposal. In her congressional testimony of May 22, 1997, Susan Graham, executive director of Project RACE, again changed proposals and endorsed a MATA option. The 1997 Project RACE MATA proposal was presented as follows:

Check one. If you consider yourself to be biracial or multiracial, check as
    many as apply:
_____American Indian or Alaskan Native
_____Asian or Pacific Islander
_____Black or African-American
_____Hispanic
_____White[7]

Not long afterward, AMEA endorsed Project RACE's proposal. During the Third Multiracial Leadership Summit, held in Oakland, California, on June 7, 1997, AMEA and six other multiracial advocacy organizations adopted the following resolutions:

- We the undersigned organizations represent the intersection of traditional racial communities comprised of individuals and families who identify with more than one racial background.

- We advocate a "check one or more" format for the collection of racial data which will not adversely affect existing civil rights protections. We do not advocate a stand-alone multiracial category at the federal level.
- A "check one or more" format will enable all Americans to respond truthfully on the census and other forms that collect racial data.
- A "check one or more" format will ensure the identification of all Americans who may be at risk for life-threatening diseases for which genetic information is critical.[8]

By June 21, 1997, thirteen multiracial organizations, as well as the NAACP chapter of Mid-Peninsula, California, had endorsed the Project RACE MATA proposal.[9] The endorsement of a MATA option by Project RACE and AMEA was a significant development so late in the OMB 15 decisionmaking process as, prior to 1997, MATA was far from being the preference of either organization. This is understandable, as the exclusive check-box option would go farther in establishing a multiracial classification that was the biological equivalent of the monoracial categories. Although Graham stated in July 1996 that "Project RACE has always advocated for a check all that apply," this is not borne out by the proposals the organization had submitted prior to that assertion.[10] In her 1993 congressional testimony, Graham submitted an exclusive multiracial category proposal that required a high-level federal variance for approving the addition of subcategories, and only for particular data collection agencies. She submitted an even more exclusive proposal, with no subcategories allowed under any circumstances, in her unsuccessful California multiracial category bid of 1996.[11] Moreover, in her congressional testimony of 1997, she stated that "the myth is that on a federal level we only want the term multiracial and nothing more. The reality is that when we testified in 1993 we suggested a format for federal purposes that instructed a multiracial person to *ALSO* choose their racial combinations from a list of categories listed underneath the multiracial category."[12]

This certainly is not what one finds, however, in the congressional subcommittee testimony of 1993, in which Graham argued explicitly for an exclusive multiracial designation that allowed a variance for the listing of subcategories only "if the agency can demonstrate a reasonable necessity for civil rights compliance reporting, general program administrative reporting or statistical reporting."[13] This was clearly an argument for an exclusive multiracial check-box, with subcategories allowable only if granted by variance on an agency-by-agency basis. In no sense can this 1993 testimony be understood as a suggestion to implement a generalized B+MATA format. In describing Project RACE's 1993 proposal four years later, Graham was seemingly describing the AMEA proposal of that year instead.

In addition, during the Committee on National Statistics (CNSTAT) workshop of 1994, Graham detailed quite plainly Project RACE's preference for an exclusive multiracial category with no subcategories: "The Project RACE proposal for a revised directive differs from that of some other organizations. We propose the addition of the classification multiracial to the five basic racial and ethnic categories without further breakdown. In other words, multiracial children would only check multiracial and not be forced to list the race and ethnicity of their mothers and fathers."[14] As is quite evident in her own words, Graham had always advocated a separate multiracial check-box with no option (or a very limited option) to indicate subcategories. Graham's 1997 congressional testimony, suggesting that she had proposed a B+MATA option in 1993, is simply not reconcilable with the historical record.

AMEA did not propose a stand-alone multiracial check-box in 1993, opting instead for the B+MATA version I outlined in Chapter 4. By 1995, AMEA and Project RACE had submitted a joint B+MATA proposal to OMB, which AMEA president Ramona Douglass endorsed as follows: "I've spoken of AMEA's goals, Project RACE's goals, and so have Susan Graham and Carlos Fernández. I said that there were those of us who do not wish to be fractionalized or equivocate on our choice of an identifier—'Multiracial' with the option of checking all that apply."[15]

During this time, both AMEA and Project RACE felt that a MATA option without a multiracial check-box was not an acceptable alternative. In the words of Susan Graham: "Multiple check-offs without a multiracial heading is unacceptable."[16] Furthermore, she stated that "the rationale behind the Project RACE model is simple: Marking all that apply without putting those choices under the 'multiracial' umbrella leaves the multiracial population undercounted, miscounted, or rendered invisible. . . . 'Mark all that apply' or 'Check as many as applicable' alone would still render a multiracial person invisible, and merely serve to collapse numbers back into the five existing categories."[17]

These criticisms of MATA are not persuasive, however. It seems obvious that if a person marked more than one response, that person could easily be counted as multiracial by data collectors.[18] Clearly, today's database and data processing programs are capable of handling such a simple operation. The MATA option would allow all those who marked more than one category to be aggregated without requiring a separate multiracial check-box. It is perhaps merely the fact that MATA would not feature an explicit multiracial check-box that explains Project RACE's opposition to it. Given Project RACE's 1993 federal proposal, which consisted of an exclusive multiracial check-box with subcategories allowed only on a case-by-case basis, as well as the 1996 California proposal, which had no provision for subcategories, this explanation seems most likely.

Significantly, Project RACE's 1996 criticisms of MATA were not mentioned in the organization's 1997 endorsement of that very same option. On the contrary, the endorsement spoke highly of the accuracy and functionality of the "mark all that apply" option: "Numbers would be allocated accordingly. It only adds 14 small words. It is clear. It is precise. It is accurate and it would yield results that could easily be coded and tabulated."[19]

This major shift in preference from B+MATA to the formerly "unacceptable" MATA format is notable. Not only did Project RACE term the MATA option "unacceptable" one year and "accurate" the next, but Project RACE as well as AMEA had stated in an earlier letter to OMB of September 29, 1995, that their B+MATA proposal was acceptable to their organizations and to "most members of the multiracial community."[20] There was no authentication for this claim of broad acceptance of B+MATA in 1995, or for that matter any verification in 1997 that "most members of the multiracial community" now favored MATA.

Finally, given the fact that Graham had signed a joint letter in September 1995 endorsing a B+MATA proposal as being acceptable to Project RACE and to "most members of the multiracial community," there is then no justification for her California proposal only five months later in which she argued for a separate multiracial check-box with no subcategories. One is hard pressed to determine which of these conflicting proposals truly represented the interests of the multiracial community that Project RACE claimed to serve. For a major national multiracial advocacy organization to claim in one venue that B+MATA was acceptable to itself and to "most members of the multiracial community," while promoting a stand-alone check-box option in another venue, is enough to bring into question the true goals and motivations of that organization.

The specific instruction that accompanied the 1997 Project RACE MATA proposal ("If you consider yourself to be biracial or multiracial, check as many as apply") bears examination as well. Graham's explanation for the instruction is puzzling at best: "Why the terminology 'if you consider yourself to be'? Consider means to give serious thought to, to come to view, or classify. The Merriam-Webster Thesaurus lists the *contrasted* words 'to consider' as: disregard, ignore, neglect, overlook, slight—words that define exactly what it means *not* to allow multiracial individuals the right to consider themselves multiracial."[21]

Of course, the unspoken assumption for all the designations is that their respective respondents consider themselves to be related to the categories they signify. By marking a check-box, respondents indicate their association with that particular category. Therefore, Graham's reasoning does not justify going out of the way to provide a specific instruction for those who consider themselves biracial or multiracial, as opposed to inviting respondents to simply mark all that apply. If accuracy is as important an issue as multiracial advocates claim, then an individual—any individual—of mixed ancestry, whether that person identifies as multiracial or not, should mark all the boxes that apply. Rather, the purpose of the proposed special instruction is likely to be found elsewhere.

There is a difference between acknowledging a diverse ancestry and identifying as multiracial. For instance, many Afro-Americans openly acknowledge European and Native American ancestry, but prefer to as identify as black rather than multiracial. Additionally, many whites—whether accurately or not—claim Native American ancestry, but use it more as an ornament than a personal identity. They too, in spite of a diverse ancestry, do not identify as multiracial. What I want to focus on in examining the instruction for the 1997 MATA proposal is whether it was aimed at accuracy or self-esteem, the tension between which I have already pointed out as a fundamental contradiction of multiracial ideology.

The Project RACE MATA proposal, with its special instruction, would in effect replicate the B+MATA option, since it would tend to elicit multiracial-identifying responses while discouraging persons who acknowledge multiple ancestries— but who do not necessarily identify as multiracial ("If you consider yourself to be biracial or multiracial, check as many as apply")—from checking all that apply.[22] The author of this proposal—through the special instruction—attempted to construct an exclusive, multiracially identifying constituency as opposed to the inclusive, multiple-ancestried one that would result from the same option without the limiting instruction.

This latter, inclusive result is what Lise Funderburg had in mind when she wrote: "I don't think of myself as multiracial; I think of myself as black and white. A multiracial identity should not be exclusive, but inclusive. People of mixed heritage (which includes up to 75 percent of African-Americans) should be able to check any boxes that apply. Let all Americans speak truthfully about who they are."[23] Funderburg's call for an inclusive MATA option is noticeably different than the Project RACE MATA proposal, which, rather than inviting all people of mixed ancestry to mark all categories that apply, would have invited only those who actively considered themselves "biracial or multiracial." The goal of the Project RACE instruction was self-esteem, not accuracy.

One of the foundations of the multiracial category initiative is the expectation of increased accuracy in racial labeling that a federal multiracial category would provide. I have already detailed why the call for accuracy is contradictory to the call for self-esteem, and my examination of the instruction accompanying this MATA option illustrates this very point. Multiracial advocates argue for accuracy in regard to the medical screening issue, which is a fiction, as pointed out in Chapter 4. For the purpose of illustration, I will again invoke the medical accuracy argument, if only to make a point within the context of multiracial ideology. A sincere concern for accuracy in terms of medical screening would require that one should mark all ancestries that apply to one's family history regardless of whether one expresses a multiracial identity or not. However, the instruction "If you consider yourself to be biracial or multiracial, check as many as apply" degrades medical accuracy, since there is no medical relevance to how one identifies personally. The important issue would be accuracy for the sake of medical screening, regardless of whether one considers oneself to be multiracial or not.

Therefore, in order to be consistent with the argument for accuracy, the instruction should not have contained language pertaining to how the respondent identifies, but should simply have invited respondents to mark all categories that apply. As it stands, however, the version of MATA proposed by Project RACE in 1997 comes as close as possible to being B+MATA without having an explicit multiracial check-box. This is so because the instruction would have served to discourage those persons of mixed ancestry who did not identify personally as multiracial from marking all choices that applied. The proposal's sponsor, therefore, would seem to be more interested in aggregating those individuals who identify personally as multiracial than in collecting what has been claimed is critical medical data for an undocumented population. A central point of this book has been my assertion that the contradiction between accuracy and self-esteem is integral to multiracial ideology; whenever one is invoked, the other serves as a counterexample. The two readings of the MATA proposal illustrate this contradiction.

But what of a MATA option without the objectionable instruction contained in the Project RACE proposal? Would a truly inclusive MATA option, one that simply invited all respondents to mark all categories that apply, be a workable alternative? Would it satisfy people's desire to not be constrained to a single choice when filling out forms with racial check-boxes? There is a seductiveness to MATA that we must acknowledge, as it appears to be a neutral and benign method of allowing people to identify all their heritages; yet this is where a critique of this option must begin. The primary purpose of maintaining federal racial statistics is civil rights compliance monitoring, not self-identification or self-esteem. Any benefits in these latter areas that may accrue from implementing MATA are secondary to the proposal's effects on the functioning of compliance monitoring.

Even without the exclusive instruction, however, a MATA option, while perhaps nonobjectionable on the census, presents problems with respect to the primary purpose of federal racial statistics. From the perspective of compliance monitoring, the objection to MATA is somewhat different than the objection to an exclusive multiracial check-box. In the latter case, racism is masked when persons are discriminated against as members of a particular category but are statistically counted as multiracial. In the case of MATA, the problem lies in what sort of algorithm data collectors and analyzers would use to recode multiple responses for compliance monitoring purposes. B+MATA, as a combination approach, evinces both problems, depending on how it is applied to compliance monitoring. If the data of persons listed as multiracial is not reaggregated but left in the multiracial category, racism would be masked just as with the exclusive multiracial check-box. If the data is recoded into the standard categories, the same algorithm problems as with MATA would result. Both MATA and B+MATA allow the counting of persons as multiracial by data instruments such as the census without masking the constituent ancestries, but compliance monitoring concerns would not be met unless the multiple responses were recoded into single categories. The problem is how to accomplish this when one Asian/white might be discriminated against as Asian while another Asian/white might be perceived as white. Nothing in the responses on the form would indicate the respondent's phenotype or the way that person is perceived by others. Therefore, any algorithm for recoding multiple responses would necessarily be arbitrary, and would likely be objectionable.[24]

These objections need not signal the disqualification of MATA as a potential format for federal race statistics, however. At least it appears to do no harm in terms of further validating race. In the inclusive form it merely invites respondents to mark any racial categories that might apply to them, as opposed to OMB 15, which allows only a single choice. It should be clear, though, that because of its exclusive instruction, the MATA option proposed by Project RACE is equivalent to the addition of a multiracial check-box, and on that basis would operate on the same presumptions as the B+MATA option. If statistical recoding problems could be solved, however, an inclusive MATA format might hold promise in that it would at least not cement race further or interfere with civil rights compliance monitoring efforts. Additionally, a MATA configuration does not seem to affect observer identification, as there would be good reason in an observer identification scenario to restrict choices to a single, standard category since any multiple responses would likely have to be recoded for reporting purposes anyway.

Clearly, though, it would be a mistake to implement even an inclusive version of MATA without first conducting federal studies of potential recoding problems. The studies conducted by the Bureau of Labor Statistics and the Census Bureau as part of the OMB 15 review were all geared toward examining how people choose to identify themselves; they did not investigate any potential effects on compliance monitoring. For example, would it be the responsibility of individual businesses to recode the multiple responses of their employees, or would such responses be recoded at a farther remove by federal workers or computer programs? Either scenario presents important tabulation problems in obtaining useful data for civil rights compliance monitoring purposes. Although some would doubtless bemoan a call for further studies, the importance of civil rights compliance monitoring must take priority, since this is the primary reason for maintaining federal racial statistics. At the very least, "marking all that apply" must be proven harmless to antiracism efforts before being seriously considered as a modification to the federal format. If such studies prove promising, MATA might well represent an intermediate step on the path to full liberation from the false consciousness of race.

The preceding course of events, had it been followed, would have been ideally rational. However, as we shall see, the rapidly unfolding events of 1997 overtook any such sensible deliberations regarding the MATA option.

Recommendation

On July 9, 1997, OMB published the recommendations of the interagency committee it had commissioned to review possible changes to the standards for classifying federal data on race and ethnicity. The committee's major announcement was that it had rejected the option of adding a multiracial category to the federal scheme. In the words of Representative Thomas Sawyer, chair of the 1993 congressional subcommittee examining the OMB 15 categories: "The

OMB task force was composed of 30 federal agencies which regularly use racial and ethnic data. The panel recommended *unanimously* to OMB that a 'multiracial' category *not* be used when collecting racial and ethnic data."[25] The specific recommendations of the interagency committee as to a multiracial category were as follows:

Recommendations Concerning Reporting More Than One Race

- When self-identification is used, a method for reporting more than one race should be adopted.
- The method for respondents to report more than one race should take the form of multiple responses to a single question and not a "multiracial" category.
- When a list of races is provided to respondents, the list should not contain a "multiracial" category.
- Two acceptable forms for the instruction accompanying the multiple response question are "Mark one or more * * *" and "Select one or more * * *."
- If the criteria for data quality and confidentiality are met, provision should be made to report, at a minimum, the number of individuals identifying with more than one race. Data producers are encouraged to provide greater detail about the distribution of multiple responses.
- The new standards will be used in the decennial census, and other data producers should conform as soon as possible, but not later than January 1, 2003.[26]

The interagency committee recommended a MATA option—not B+MATA or a stand-alone multiracial check-box. Of no small concern was the fact that this recommendation was made with no firm procedures in mind for the tabulation of multiple responses, my major apprehension as discussed above. According to the interagency committee report: "Instructions for interviewers, the wording of questions, and specifications for tabulations are not addressed in the recommendations."[27] The recommendations stated further:

More research still is needed. . . . Tabulation methods are particularly important in the case of reporting more than one race, and Federal and state agencies are encouraged to work together, under the auspices of OMB, to develop methods that would produce consistent results for program purposes and for comparisons with historical data. These guidelines would be particularly useful for those charged with civil rights enforcement. In addition, much thought should be given to the appropriate way to tabulate multiple responses for official purposes.[28]

Criticism of the interagency committee and OMB for recommending this change to federal racial classification without having considered the mechanics of tabulation was not long in coming. Representative Sawyer took up the issue just over two weeks later during the July 25, 1997, subcommittee hearings: "While I believe the recommendations properly address the concerns of those on both sides of the 'multi-racial' issue, I would encourage OMB to address the equally critical issue of establishing guidelines for how Federal agencies should tabulate, publish, and use the data once it is collected."[29]

Sawyer went on to consider concrete examples such as those discussed above, asking, "If the census data on race and ethnicity for a given census tract includes a percentage of residents who checked off 'White' and 'Black' or 'Asian American,' the question is, should the Justice Department consider that portion of the population to be 'minority' or 'non-minority' for purposes of determining whether there is a pattern of discrimination in that neighborhood?"[30]

Likewise, Representative Carrie Meek displayed a deep concern over the issue of tabulating multiple responses:

I applaud the Office of Management and Budget for its hard work. It gets an "A" for effort. But we cannot yet give it *any* grade for accomplishment. That is because the proposed regulation does not answer in detail a critical question—how will the data be tabulated and presented if individuals are instructed that they can check several racial categories on the census form? . . . I applaud OMB's decision to not create a multiracial category. But I am very troubled by OMB's alternative of letting people check as many racial categories as they desire. I understand that this alternative allows the children of racially-mixed marriages to avoid choosing between their parents when answering the census questions. But we must remember that the primary purpose of the racial questions on the census is to permit enforcement of both the equal protection provision of the 14th amendment of the Constitution and the anti-discrimination laws that past Congresses have enacted.[31]

Tabulation of multiple responses will have a direct impact on compliance monitoring, as Sally Katzen, administrator of OMB's Office of Information and Regulatory Affairs, makes clear:

Equal employment opportunity and other anti-discrimination programs have traditionally provided the numbers of people in the population by selected characteristics, including racial categories, for business, academic, and government organizations to use in evaluating conformance with program objectives. Because of the potentially large number of categories that may result from application of the new standards, many with very small numbers, it is not clear how this need for data will be best satisfied in the future.[32]

Beyond the tabulation issue, more uncertainty was injected into the developing situation by an abrupt turnaround on the part of Project RACE. Throughout their relatively brief histories, AMEA and Project RACE have rarely occupied the same strategic or tactical space. Although they submitted a joint proposal to OMB in 1995, and although AMEA endorsed Project RACE's 1997 proposal, those instances were more temporary marriages of convenience than anything else. It should be clear from the statements made by the spokespersons of these two organizations that they possess differing ideological bents. Although AMEA's proposals and public statements were somewhat less consistent logically under the leadership of Carlos Fernández than under his successor, Ramona Douglass, under either of these first two presidents the organization has been far more cogent than Project RACE.

The latter's inconsistency has been to some degree unavoidable since the organization has always pushed for a separate multiracial check-box based on arguments for both accuracy and self-esteem—a combination replete with logical contradiction. One of my primary concerns in this book has been to point out that arguing for a federal multiracial category for the sake of self-esteem forces one to take positions that make a mockery of arguments for racial accuracy, and vice versa. If the position of Project RACE is to be taken seriously, the argument for self-esteem would require for multiracial people a stand-alone check-box with no subcategories; yet such a check-box would obscure the allegedly medically relevant racial data on which the argument for accuracy supposedly relies. This contradiction is integral to multiracial ideology, but because opponents have generally failed to challenge the bases of that ideology, concentrating instead on perceived threats to racial solidarity, the philosophical validity of multiracial ideology has heretofore not been scrutinized adequately.

In any case, although the basic ideology of multiracialism is flawed, one can still draw important distinctions between the major advocacy organizations. These differences were made clear by their respective reactions following the July 9, 1997, announcement of the interagency committee's recommendations.

On the one hand, AMEA's Douglass began immediately organizing people and groups in support of the interagency committee recommendations. By July 11, 1997, two days after the MATA recommendation was announced, she requested that multiracial interests be represented on the OMB Tabulations Working Group; coordinated with Katherine Wallman, statistical policy chief of OMB's Office of Information and Regulatory Affairs; received a written endorsement of the MATA proposal from the Japanese-American Citizens League; secured a commitment from the NAACP to draft a joint letter of support by multiracial advocacy groups and traditional civil rights organizations; and announced that she wanted to meet with multiracial Native Americans in order to become better acquainted with treaty issues.[33] In short, Douglass dedicated herself to ensuring that the interagency committee's recommendation of the MATA option proposed by Project RACE and endorsed by AMEA (less the special instruction) would be accepted by OMB.

On the other hand, Project RACE's response to the MATA recommendation was somewhat different. On July 13, 1997, four days after the interagency recommendations were made public, Executive Director Graham posted a message to her readers on the Project RACE World Wide Web site:

> Now that the Office of Management and Budget (OMB) has made its recommendation on the multiracial classification, I would like to take this opportunity to talk about it and where we go next.
>
> The OMB recommendation is NOT to have a multiracial classification. But, they are recommending a "check all that apply" format on the U.S. Census and federal forms. It is the first time in the history of this country that the "check one" mandate will disappear. It is definite PROGRESS! We got HALF of what we asked for. . . . The Board of Directors of Project RACE has unanimously voted to NOT stop with "half a loaf." It IS important to be recognized as multiracial children and adults, not just as "check all that apply" persons.[34]

Despite Graham's suggestion that the MATA recommendation indicated progress, Project RACE's actual position would soon be made very clear. On July 25, 1997, Graham testified again before the congressional subcommittee regarding the MATA recommendation, which, less the special instruction, was in essence what she herself had proposed before the same subcommittee only two months earlier. This time, however, she denounced the MATA option and argued instead for a B+MATA format.[35] Throughout the history of the multiracial category debate, Project RACE has made several inconsistent and contradictory statements, but the foregoing is especially confusing.

It is not clear in what sense Graham's organization received only half of what it asked for. With the exception of the special instruction ("If you consider yourself to be biracial or multiracial, check as many as apply"), the recommendation of the interagency committee was exactly what Graham had asked for in her May 22, 1997, congressional testimony. In May 1997, Graham described the MATA option as clear, precise, and accurate; in July 1997, however, it was only "half a loaf." By voting unanimously to "NOT stop with 'half a loaf,'" Project RACE's board of directors acted to reject the very proposal they had made to OMB only two months earlier. Adding to the confusion is Graham's complaint in her July 25, 1997, testimony that the "compromise for 'check one or more' without a multiracial identifier was not a compromise with the multiracial community. It was a compromise with the opponents of a multiracial category."[36] Yet it was Graham herself who had unilaterally put forth a proposal consisting of "'check one or more' without a multiracial identifier" in her previous testimony.

Assuming that Project RACE was sincere in its 1997 MATA proposal, the organization's consequent rejection of the interagency committee's MATA recommendation must therefore have been based solely on the omission of the special instruction, which as I pointed out earlier would have worked to discourage any but those who identified personally as multiracial from marking more than one check-box. It appears likely that it was only that particular special instruction that made the MATA proposal palatable to Project RACE.

The riddle of why Project RACE would reject a multiple response option similar to the very one it proposed, and that was endorsed by AMEA and many other multiracial advocacy organizations, is not difficult to solve. The answer lies in the results at the state level that Project RACE had already achieved. Because of Project RACE's involvement, seven states were using a multiracial category in 1997.[37] These multiracial designations were meaningless above the state level, however, as the states were required to report statistical information in accord with the standard racial categories of OMB 15. In addition to any purported medically relevant data being lost at the federal level, civil rights compliance monitoring in these seven states would have been disrupted to the extent that the multiracial category served to mask covert and institutional discrimination.

However, Project RACE had succeeded in instituting a multiracial check-box in those seven states, and therein lies the organization's problem with the interagency committee's MATA recommendation. If OMB decided to adopt the interagency committee's recommendation, all agencies, institutions, and businesses having federal reporting requirements would be obligated to utilize the new format. Despite the fact that seven states had added a multiracial designator, in the context of a federal MATA format that designator would become instantly redundant and would likely not be readopted by those states. In other words, the work that Project RACE had undertaken to bring a multiracial category to those seven states would in a single stroke be undone. Project RACE's hostility to the MATA option, especially in the face of its endorsement by so many other multiracial advocacy organizations, is easy to understand (though not to justify) in this context.

Relevant as well to Project RACE's May–July 1997 turnabout on the MATA proposal is a private meeting that Susan Graham had in June with Republican representative and Speaker of the House Newt Gingrich, who had helped her sponsor the failed 1996 California proposal: "[Gingrich] confirmed that he is in favor of the multiracial classification and will immediately work toward its implementation."[38] Gingrich's entry into the federal multiracial category debate was an ominous sign. On June 18, 1997, he announced ten practical steps for "building a better America," among which included "adding a multiracial category to the census" and "doing away with affirmative action."[39]

In Chapter 3 I suggested a parallel between the early-twentieth-century political manipulation of mulattoes by Edward Reuter and the modern appropriation of the multiracial category debate by political factions otherwise unconcerned with minority interests. Gingrich's entry into the federal multiracial category debate is a case in point. The people attracted to Gingrich's brand of neoconservatism would have been all too pleased to support anything that would limit the effectiveness of civil rights compliance monitoring. Thus, Gingrich's support of a federal multiracial category is not surprising. Although certainly not the stuff of conspiracy theories, the interest of Gingrich in a federal multiracial category was nonetheless akin to exploiting a target of opportunity. Project RACE's embrace of Gingrich is another example of the degree to which at least some multiracial activists are willing to sacrifice civil rights enforcement for the sake of self-esteem. Gingrich's record on civil rights issues leaves no doubt as to precisely why he would support a multiracial category. Asserting otherwise goes far beyond even naïveté or wishful thinking.

All of this is consistent with the aim of establishing a federal multiracial category for the sole purpose of enhancing the self-esteem of those who identify as multiracial. Accuracy of heritage has never been a primary interest of Project RACE, just as supposed concerns for medically relevant multiracial data are shown to be unfounded every time the organization proposes a stand-alone multiracial category or attempts to limit the listing of racial subcategories. The goal instead has been a separate multiracial category for self-esteem purposes. This represents the greatest difference between Project RACE and other multiracial organizations.

On July 14, 1997, Ramona Douglass stated:

I am already very aware of the problems with "alignment" with the Republican "Right Wing." It has sent too many mixed messages: on the one hand embracing our multicultural/multiethnic community efforts and simultaneously working to dismantle existing Civil Rights protections (i.e., Affirmative Action). . . . This was one of the reasons AMEA and Project RACE formally disassociated from one another prior to the OMB interagency recommendations because—contrary to the pledges made at the 3rd Multiracial Leadership Summit (June 7, 1997), Project RACE went to the Summit, got all the information on what our community was thinking regarding endorsement of the "check one or more" format, was one of the original eight organizations to endorse it, then announced just before its Executive Director's (Susan Graham's) independent and undisclosed discussion with the Speaker of the House that Project RACE was against the Summit Statement, demanded that their name be taken off the Summit Statement, and fully endorsed HR 830 which has only a "stand-alone" multiracial/multiethnic category. . . . AMEA was left with no choice—due to a blatant breach of trust on Project RACE's part but to announce we were no longer associated with Project RACE and its leadership since we could not count on where Project RACE would be standing regarding our multiracial community interests from one week to the next.[40]

Acknowledging the inherent contradiction I have drawn attention to throughout this book between advocating a stand-alone multiracial category on the basis of self-esteem and arguing for the accuracy of racial heritage, Douglass continued:

> We also came out with a formal letter to Congressman Petri acknowledging his support of our community with HR 830 but made it clear that in its present "stand-alone" multiracial/multiethnic format AMEA would have to oppose the Bill since it would not distinguish our multiracial/multiethnic community for purposes of public health—racial/ethnic breakdown is essential for life-threatening diseases that require more specific detail than any stand-alone category would give. The stand-alone category would only perpetuate the racist rule of "hypodescent" which we were not interested in preserving or carrying into the 21st century—and lastly we were not interested in introducing a "stand-alone" multiracial/multiethnic model on the federal level since it might in fact adversely impact existing civil rights protections.[41]

Finally, by asserting that a "'stand-alone' multiracial/multiethnic category was not distinguishable . . . in any practical sense from just another 'Other,'" Douglass affirmed the inescapable ambiguity inherent in a catchall multiracial category.[42] Her recognition that a stand-alone multiracial check-box would do nothing to facilitate accuracy or medical screening makes even more clear the fact that Project RACE's interest in such a check-box has been driven purely by the issue of self-esteem and by the desire to create a new racial category.

In commenting on Project RACE's rejection of the MATA recommendation and AMEA's willingness to embrace that option, Aubyn Fulton wrote:

> I have been assuming all along that Susan's primary goal was some mechanism that would allow iis [interracial individuals] to "identify themselves" and "be counted." Since MATA does this, and since it looks like that is what we are going to get, one would think she would be happy, since whatever incremental self-esteem benefit she thinks would accrue from the exclusive category must be small when compared to what she has apparently won. It must be that she really does want to establish a new race category.[43]

Continuing his commentary, Fulton pinpointed the primary difference between AMEA and Project RACE: "It appears then that there are at least two currents in the 'multiracial movement,' running in opposite directions: one that hopes, in one way or another that 'multiraciality' becomes at least a nail in the coffin of the idea of RACE; the other hoping to actually reinforce the idea of RACE by institutionalizing yet another racial classification. I suppose we should have taken the name of Susan's organization more literally."[44]

Decision

On October 30, 1997, OMB published its announcement that it would accept the interagency committee's recommendations for revising federal race classifications, with two modifications. These were: "(1) the Asian or Pacific Islander category will be separated into two categories—'Asian' and 'Native Hawaiian or Other Pacific Islander,' and (2) the term 'Hispanic' will be changed to 'Hispanic or Latino.'"[45] Most significantly, OMB had accepted the recommendations of the interagency committee that a multiracial category be rejected and that a "mark all that apply" approach be adopted instead.[46]

OMB also resolved the thorny problem of the lack of a proper reference to OMB 15 (see Chapter 2) by removing the point of confusion altogether. By dropping the designation "Directive No. 15," which was based on a series of Department of Commerce directives stemming from the transfer of certain statistical functions from OMB to the Department of Commerce in the late 1970s, this problem was thereby eliminated. Additionally, the title of the policy was changed from *Race and Ethnic Standards for Federal Statistics and Administrative Reporting* to *Standards for Maintaining, Collecting, and Presenting Federal Data on Race and Ethnicity*.[47]

Despite the sense of compromise that permeated the announcement, it would be wrong to view this change as satisfactory to many of the individuals, institutions, and agencies that had a stake in its outcome. Indeed, practically all who were genuinely concerned in one way or another with the revision to OMB 15 had problems with the decision.

Persons opposed to a multiracial category on the ground that it would work to further solidify the fallacy of race as opposed to dismantling it still face the difficult task of arguing against race while taking care not to undermine civil rights compliance monitoring, as OMB's decision moved them no closer to responsibly doing away with race and racial categorization. For the racial skeptic, then, the challenge remains as daunting as ever.

Those who opposed a multiracial category based on concerns over civil rights compliance monitoring found themselves left with legitimate worries regarding tabulation issues that were not resolved or even considered prior to the acceptance of MATA by OMB. If the tabulation problem is not resolved effectively, MATA may prove to be as damaging to antiracist efforts as a federal multiracial category would have been. For these critics, the "mark all that apply" decision represents a step into the darkness, a step that should not have been taken since they were generally satisfied with OMB 15 the way it was.

There are also those for whom OMB's decision did not go far enough. Those who found that they could accept the MATA alternative but who would have preferred a multiracial header above a listing of racial subcategories (B+MATA) may very well choose to reconstitute their resources and lobby for such a change prior to the 2010 census. AMEA in particular falls into this category, as its leaders—

despite their acceptance of the MATA compromise—have made plain their preference for a B+MATA option.[48] AMEA may view MATA for 2000 as an intermediate step toward the goal of B+MATA for 2010. It remains to be seen how satisfactory OMB's decision will prove to be for this branch of the multiracial movement.

Finally, the more extreme position exemplified by Project RACE and other peripheral groups promises that there will be at least some agitation for a separate multiracial check-box as attention turns to the 2010 census. These groups' single-minded determination to install a stand-alone multiracial category, despite the contradiction inherent in their twin calls for accuracy and self-esteem, serves to delineate the border between mainstream and fringe currents within the multiracial movement. The potential impact of these fringe elements is difficult to predict. Clearly, Project RACE has, by its inconsistencies and turnarounds, acted to remove itself from the inner circle of serious multiracial organizations, just as OMB's acceptance of MATA has rendered moot the multiracial category that Project RACE helped bring into existence in seven states. Nonetheless, those individuals who believe in the myth of biological race and who view the self-esteem derived from a separate multiracial category as a higher priority than federal antidiscrimination efforts will remain drawn to Project RACE's ideology.

Another fringe entity, although not an organization, is the online publication *Interracial Voice,* posted by Charles Byrd. Here, unreflective anger and frustration at the American monoracial paradigm find varying degrees of expression. Not surprisingly, the same contradiction that exemplifies Project RACE's ideology is evident; in a single sentence in Byrd's September-October 1996 editorial, race is assailed as an "artificial construct" and a "social reality," and elsewhere in the same editorial the purported "special medical considerations" of multiracial people based on the reality of biological race are appealed to.[49] As is typical of this ideological position, any claim—no matter how false, irrelevant, or contradictory—is deployed for the sake of promoting a stand-alone multiracial category.

Interracial Voice represents both the best and the worst possibilities of the electronic communications medium. On the positive side, one can utilize the site to locate links to documents and other related sites containing legitimate information that might otherwise be difficult to find. On the negative side, however, much undocumented and unreviewed misinformation is spread through the site's editorials and articles. Examples of this more unfortunate aspect are Byrd's references to the "AMEA/Hapa Forum/NAACP *federación socialista*"[50] and his assertion that AMEA and the Hapa Issues Forum were "the two organizations responsible for cutting a behind-closed-doors deal with the NAACP, 'paving the way' for acceptance of this *check all that apply* scheme."[51] As we know, a MATA option was in fact proposed unilaterally by Project RACE on May 22, 1997. *Interracial Voice* is a forum where individuals of a certain ideological bent can go to read things they already agree with, without having to face the threat of challenge or logical refutation.

Unfortunately, there is a real danger that this kind of misinformation can do great harm. In his January-February 1998 editorial, Byrd advises his readers to do any of the following with their year 2000 census forms: "Check White!" "Check Anything But Black!" "Check Every Box On The Form!" "Don't Return A Census Form At All!" "Check Hispanic!" and "Check American Indian!"[52] While it is possible to read various harmful impulses into any of these suggestions, particularly the one to "Check Anything But Black!" one is struck by the insensitivity and self-ishness required to consciously do harm to Native Americans by purposely advocating the destabilization of their numbers and the undermining of the protections and benefits based on those numbers.

Project RACE and *Interracial Voice* will likely persevere in their call for a separate multiracial category. In all probability, this call will continue to be driven by self-esteem issues, seasoned as before with contradictory and insincere arguments about accuracy and medical screening. But OMB's MATA decision is not satisfactory as an end result for any of the interested parties I have discussed. Future proposals by some factions to institute a stand-alone multiracial category, a B+MATA option, or even a return to the pre-MATA OMB 15 format will be met by dogged resistance and counterproposals by other factions. In this sense, OMB's 1997 decision represents perhaps only the beginning of newer and potentially more divisive debates over race and federal racial categorization.

Notes

1. Ramona Douglass, e-mail to author, July 14, 1997.

2. House Subcommittee on Government Management, Information, and Technology, Committee on Government Reform and Oversight, *Hearings on Federal Measures of Race and Ethnicity and the Implications for the 2000 Census,* testimony by Susan Graham on May 22, 1997, 105th Cong., 1st sess., April 23, May 22, and July 25, 1997, 290; and Ramona Douglass, e-mail to author, June 3, 1997.

3. This major change of direction by these two organizations came less than two months before the recommendations of OMB's interagency committee were finalized and made public. These were hardly secret deliberations, and it is likely that the direction in which the interagency committee was leaning became known to both AMEA and Project RACE, with the organizations reacting based on that knowledge.

4. Department of Commerce, Bureau of the Census, "1996 Race and Ethnic Targeted Test (RAETT) and Its Content Reinterview, Also Identified As the 1996 Census Survey," by Gerald Taché, *Federal Register* 60, no. 231 (December 1, 1995): 62011.

5. This proposal would have allowed subcategories only if granted by high-level federal authority on an agency-by-agency basis. There was a clear intention in this proposal to discourage the use of subcategories.

6. Also important is the *way* one invites respondents to answer, an issue that I shall take up when discussing in detail the MATA option proposed by Project RACE.

7. House Subcommittee, testimony by Susan Graham, May 22, 1997, 290.

8. Bridget Bielinski, e-mail to author, July 11, 1997.

9. Ibid.

10. Susan Graham, online posting, Interracial Individuals Discussion List, July 17, 1996 [ii-list@hcs.harvard.edu].

11. I examined both of these proposals in some detail in Chapter 4.

12. House Subcommittee, testimony by Susan Graham, May 22, 1997, 289.

13. House Subcommittee on Census, Statistics, and Postal Personnel, Committee on Post Office and Civil Service, *Hearings on the Review of Federal Measurements of Race and Ethnicity,* testimony by Susan Graham on June 30, 1993, 103d Cong., 1st sess., April 14, June 30, July 29, and November 3, 1993, 114.

14. Susan Graham, "The Real World," in *The Multiracial Experience: Racial Borders As the New Frontier,* ed. Maria P. P. Root (Thousand Oaks, Calif.: Sage Publications, 1996), 44.

15. Ramona Douglass, online posting, Interracial Individuals Discussion List, February 12, 1996 [ii@gnu.ai.mit.edu].

16. Susan Graham, online posting, Interracial Individuals Discussion List, January 27, 1996 [ii@gnu.ai.mit.edu].

17. Susan Graham, online posting, Interracial Individuals Discussion List, January 29, 1996 [ii@gnu.ai.mit.edu].

18. A person marking more than one check-box would be counted as multiracial in terms of population, but this would not solve the masking problems regarding civil rights compliance monitoring that occur when people are discriminated against as *X,* but are listed as *Y.* Also, implementing MATA would necessitate devising algorithms for the re-coding of multiple responses for compliance monitoring purposes.

19. House Subcommittee, testimony by Susan Graham, May 22, 1997, 291.

20. Ramona Douglass (AMEA) and Susan Graham (Project RACE) to Katherine Wallman (Office of Information and Regulatory Affairs, OMB), September 29, 1995.

21. House Subcommittee, testimony by Susan Graham, May 22, 1997, 291.

22. Note the similarity of this special instruction to the B+MATA option proposed by AMEA and Project RACE in 1995: "Multiracial: Please specify the combination of your origins from the list below that best describes your multiracial identification."

23. Lise Funderburg, "Boxed In," *New York Times,* July 10, 1996, A15.

24. In the "mark one only" scenario, this problem is addressed by the respondent's se-lecting a single category, hopefully the same category that others perceive.

25. House Subcommittee on Government Management, Information, and Technology, Committee on Government Reform and Oversight, *Hearings on Federal Measures of Race and Ethnicity and the Implications for the 2000 Census,* testimony by Thomas Sawyer on July 25, 1997, 105th Cong., 1st sess., April 23, May 22, and July 25, 1997, 520.

26. Executive Office of the President, Office of Management and Budget, "Recommen-dations from the Interagency Committee for the Review of the Racial and Ethnic Stan-dards to the Office of Management and Budget Concerning Changes to the Standards for the Classification of Federal Data on Race and Ethnicity," by Sally Katzen, *Federal Register* 62, no. 131 (July 9, 1997): 36937.

27. Ibid.

28. Ibid., 36943.

29. House Subcommittee, testimony by Thomas Sawyer, 519.

30. Ibid., 521.

31. House Subcommittee on Government Management, Information, and Technology, Committee on Government Reform and Oversight, *Hearings on Federal Measures of Race*

and Ethnicity and the Implications for the 2000 Census, testimony by Carrie Meek on July 25, 1997, 105th Cong., 1st sess., April 23, May 22, and July 25, 1997, 537.

32. Executive Office of the President, Office of Management and Budget, "Revisions to the Standards for the Classification of Federal Data on Race and Ethnicity," by Sally Katzen, *Federal Register* 62, no. 210 (October 30, 1997): 58788.

33. Ramona Douglass, e-mail to author, July 11, 1997.

34. Susan Graham, Project RACE World Wide Web site, July 14, 1997 <http://www.projectrace.mindspring.com/hot_news.html>.

35. House Subcommittee on Government Management, Information, and Technology, Committee on Government Reform and Oversight, *Hearings on Federal Measures of Race and Ethnicity and the Implications for the 2000 Census,* testimony by Susan Graham on July 25, 1997, 105th Cong., 1st sess., April 23, May 22, and July 25, 1997, 547, 551–556.

36. Ibid., 553.

37. Ibid., 554. By July 1997, five states (Georgia, Illinois, Indiana, Michigan, and Ohio) had enacted legislation establishing a multiracial category, and two states (Florida and North Carolina) had adopted the category by administrative mandate. Susan Graham, Project RACE World Wide Web site, December 26, 1998 <http://www.projectrace.home.mindspring.com/state.html>.

38. Graham, Project RACE World Wide Web site, July 14, 1997.

39. Rick Christie, "Gingrich Lists His Action Plan for Racial Gulf," *Atlanta Journal-Constitution,* June 19, 1997, A3.

40. Douglass, e-mail to author, July 14, 1997. Douglass asked me to post this e-mail message to the Interracial Individuals Discussion List (on which she was no longer an active participant) for public dissemination.

41. Ibid.

42. Ibid.

43. Aubyn Fulton, online posting, Interracial Individuals Discussion List, July 11, 1997 [ii-list@hcs.harvard.edu].

44. Ibid.

45. Executive Office of the President, "Revisions to the Standards," 58782.

46. Ibid., 58782, 58784.

47. Ibid., 58788; and Suzann Evinger, telephone conversation with author, January 4, 1999.

48. Douglass, e-mail to author, July 14, 1997; and House Subcommittee on Government Management, Information, and Technology, Committee on Government Reform and Oversight, *Hearings on Federal Measures of Race and Ethnicity and the Implications for the 2000 Census,* testimony by Carlos Fernández on July 25, 1997, 105th Cong., 1st sess., April 23, May 22, and July 25, 1997, 573.

49. Charles Byrd, "Compensation's Secret," *Interracial Voice,* December 26, 1998 <http://www.webcom.com/~intvoice/editor7.html>.

50. Charles Byrd, "Census 2000 Protest: *Check American Indian!" Interracial Voice,* January 7, 1998 <http://www.webcom.com/~intvoice/editor.html>.

51. Charles Byrd, "Government Officially Nixes Multiracial Category," *Interracial Voice,* December 26, 1998 <http://www.webcom.com/~intvoice/editor.html>.

52. Byrd, "Census 2000 Protest."

6

Thinking About Transcending Race

I wish you would tell us what a "multiracial" identity is. When I talk about a "pluralistic" identity, I don't mean that I walk around thinking of myself as a "pluralistic." I mean that I hold many different identifications simultaneously. Some of those are "racially" situated, some ethnically, some occupationally, etc. But what does it mean when "multiracial" is transformed from an adjective to a noun, from having an identity which is multiracial, to identifying as multiracial?

—Aubyn Fulton, professor of psychology, who describes himself as black and Jewish[1]

Identity is not a single, unitary construct. When we speak of this or that person's identity, we oversimplify a very complex phenomenon. There is no single or overarching identity; rather, there are identities. A person may simultaneously consider several such identities to be of primary importance to his or her self-concept. Certainly, the identities of woman, man, parent, employer, student, debtor, recovering alcoholic, home owner, and so on are important ways in which people see themselves. It is a gross oversimplification, though, to see people in terms of only a single identity. Surely a woman's full identity is not revealed without describing more of her than just her sex. Her sex is obviously an important aspect of her total identity, yet so are her occupation, interests, age, educational level, nationality, and a host of other predicates.

Of course, there are times and places where an emphasis on one or another of these identities is appropriate or necessary, but my interest here is in focusing on what I have argued is a false identity—racial identity. Of the three main social organizing forces in the United States (gender, class, and race), race is the most suspect. The myth of race exists in the minds of its believers, but it is not part of the physical world. Clearly, organizing socially by race is neither natural nor necessary. It is a learned activity based on acceptance of a biological fallacy. I am certainly not denying that people do in fact organize themselves by race, and that people commit acts—sometimes horrible ones—based on a belief in race. I am arguing instead that such racial organization, and the racism that accompanies it, are founded on a fantasy that has no more reality than an infinite number or a flat Earth. Kwame Anthony Appiah makes an important point when he offers that "there is a danger in making racial identities too central to our conceptions of ourselves; while there is a place for racial identities in a world shaped by racism . . . if we are to move beyond racism we shall have, in the end, to move beyond current racial identities."[2]

That people organize by race at all is unfortunate, and the extent to which such organization has become one of the central pillars of American life is a profoundly tragic phenomenon. Here, I would invoke the image of Galileo and suggest that it is the responsibility of intellectuals to reject the incorrect received opinion, demonstrate why it is wrong, and continue asserting the truth that must eventually find universal acceptance. This is no small task in the case of the American race construct, yet we may take heart in the example of the medieval European geocentric paradigm—long defunct—which was ascribed to even more fundamentally by people in its time than is the notion of biological race today. Believing that we can move beyond race, and thinking about how to do it, are the first steps toward ultimate liberation from the fallacy. And I want very specifically to distinguish the idea of moving beyond race from the often criticized notion of color blindness. Moving beyond race does not require ignoring racism or pretending that phenotypic differences do not exist. Rather, it involves recognizing that any system of classifying modern humans by skin color, ancestry, or biology is completely foundationless.

Standing on the threshold of a new millennium, Americans, had they thought about it, might have considered whether to at last shed the nineteenth-century constructions of race that so characterize their society, as opposed to carrying these fallacies along into the twenty-first century. Unfortunately, America has not shown any desire to opt for the more progressive course. It is perhaps unrealistic to expect a sudden break with race, a concept embedded so deeply in the American consciousness and in American institutions. Yet even though American society has invested too much in race to summarily deny it, it is possible nonetheless to *think* about moving away from race. This kind of thinking does not come naturally, however. Although some may debate the existence of race, or the meaningfulness of calling race a social reality, such arguments are rooted invariably in the past and the present. People may imagine an America without race, but there is no concerted effort to think about how such a vision might become reality, no consideration of how to get from here to there.

One important thing we can learn from the multiracial category debate is that in the closing years of the twentieth century, the federal government has suffered from a myopic engagement with racial categorization. The congressional hearings in 1993 and 1997 on whether to change the federal race categories demonstrated a singular focus on the past and the present, with no view toward the future. The critical question is not what federal racial categorization should look like next year or on the next census, but rather what it should look like twenty, thirty, or fifty years into the future. That segment of society most knowledgeable about the supposed makeup of race—biologists, geneticists, and physical anthropologists—has correctly declared it a myth. It remains for the rest of the population to become aware of and accept this reality. Unfortunately, such awareness and acceptance is made more difficult by federal racial categorization, which tends to reinforce the myth of race by validating the categories via seemingly innumerable check-boxes on both federal and nonfederal forms.

The proliferation of racial check-boxes has its beginnings in the mid-1960s, when the Civil Rights Act of 1964 and the Voting Rights Act of 1965 inspired the use of racial statistics for civil rights compliance monitoring. Since that time the government has uncovered and eliminated much covert and institutional racial discrimination via such monitoring, although much still remains. It is this very success that makes federal racial categorization a double-edged sword, exposing patterns of racial discrimination on the one hand while validating biological racial categorization on the other. Ironically, the limitations and inconsistencies of the American racial paradigm are rightly pointed out by adherents of a federal multiracial category, while those same adherents—as they work to become complicit with that paradigm—simultaneously disregard the damage to compliance monitoring that such a category would precipitate.

The debate surrounding the multiracial category initiative has centered on two issues, the potential damage to civil rights compliance monitoring on one side and multiracial arguments for self-esteem on the other, but this debate has not been balanced. These two issues are both connected to the multiracial question, of course, but they are actually separate conversations that neither the government, the media, nor the general public has done an effective job of distinguishing between. By setting the parameters of the debate such that the "right to self-identify" and the "denial of parent" theses became the central issues, multiracial advocates succeeded in masking the most important function of federal racial classification—compliance monitoring—and thereby shifted this critical debate onto the frivolous ground of self-esteem and the federal validation of personal identity. This strategic victory allowed multiracial ideology to rise, at least temporarily, above the voices inside and outside the government that are concerned about civil rights enforcement. In particular, the Statistical Policy Office of OMB's Office of Information and Regulatory Affairs is an excellent source of information on the purpose of the federal categories and the potential effects of altering them. Additionally, during the congressional hearings, many federal agencies expressed deep concerns about the continued usefulness of federal racial data should a multiracial category be established. But these voices strained to find the wider audience that multiracial advocacy apparently had found, and it appeared that the core issue of compliance monitoring had become a secondary, or even tertiary, concern.

My opposition to a federal multiracial category is explicitly based on the damage such a category would do to civil rights compliance monitoring and on the way it would validate the race concept, and not on some notion of the loss of Afro-American numbers or political power. The compliance monitoring concern and the loss of numbers concern are not the same thing. The effectiveness of compliance monitoring as currently configured is dependent on people's statistical data matching the fallacious racial categories that racists in America have for centuries believed in and utilized. On the other hand, arguments expressing concern about the dilution of Afro-American numbers and the consequent loss of Afro-American political power are specious in my view, and do not address the real issue.

Advocates of multiracial ideology were aided in their endeavor in no small measure by the stunning success of professional golfer Tiger Woods, who is of Thai, Chinese, European, Native American, and Afro-American descent. Indeed, Woods has seen himself appropriated from all sides—by Afro-Americans, who hail him as the first black Masters Tournament champion, as well as by multiracial advocates, who have declared him the symbol of their struggle for a federal multiracial category. This appropriation is evident in the words of Association of MultiEthnic Americans (AMEA) president Ramona Douglass: "Whether he wants to or not, he is sort of becoming the poster person for multiracial identity."[3] In the same vein, Project RACE executive director Susan Graham offered that "Tiger Woods could not have come at a better time. The public can now see a face of what it means to be multiracial."[4] Finally, if there is any doubt concerning the appropriation of Woods, one need look no farther than Representative Thomas Petri, who named his multiracial category bill (H.R. 830) the "Tiger Woods Bill."[5]

In terms of popular understandings of the multiracial category debate, it would be a mistake to underestimate Woods's influence. This is not to say that Woods ever agreed to be a spokesperson for multiracial advocacy, but by focusing on his racial identity, and by doing so with a distinct lack of critical tools, the popular media redirected the national spotlight onto simplistic conceptions of race as well as multiraciality. For instance, the cover of the May 5, 1997, issue of *Time* magazine reads "Tiger and Race," while the article itself opens with a two-page photograph of Woods seated in a golf cart with his parents.[6] An article in that same week's *Newsweek* contains a photograph of Woods and leads with the following: "Tiger Woods is the exception that rules. For his multiracial generation, hip isn't just black and white."[7]

These journalistic attempts to cover the multiracial category debate inevitably lack depth and are geared more toward presentation through color graphs and photographs than through anything approaching deep or rigorous analysis.[8] Nevertheless, many Americans have educated themselves about the multiracial category debate through this kind of shallow, popular journalism. Thus, Woods's impact at the popular level, while having no effect on scholarly interpretations of the multiracial issue or on the factors that OMB took into account when rendering its decision on revising the federal race categories, remains a phenomenon that works to present the multiracial category debate as solely an issue of self-esteem and federal validation of personal identity.

This shift of focus away from the actual purpose of the federal categories has revealed the tenuous nature of multiracial ideology as well as its inherent inconsistency. In general, the leaders of multiracial advocacy groups as well as individuals who write and speak in favor of multiracial ideology will, in the course of an extended conversation, admit that Afro-Americans do not actually constitute a monoracial biological group.[9] In the words of former AMEA president Carlos Fernández: "Yes, race as a biological concept is illogical. . . . Arguing for a 'multiracial' category should not be read as an endorsement of race as a biological concept."[10] Fernández is precisely wrong here, however; for a multiracial category can neither be argued for nor even conceived of without acknowledging some notion of biological race. Indeed, and in no uncertain terms, arguing for a multiracial category can *only* be read as an endorsement of race as a biological concept. To assert otherwise, as Fernández does, is no more than logical nonsense.

Ramona Douglass as well seems very clearly to disavow the notion of biological race when she asserts:

Race itself is simply a conversation people either align with or they don't. It is real only in our speaking of it—not in science. . . . The 'one drop rule' is an irrational notion born out of economic greed exploitation and repression over 200 years old. It is time to let it die once and for all in our hearts and in our minds. To continue to speak [of] it as if it is real or has any merit only serves to limit the possibilities that human diversity has for today and for all our tomorrows.[11]

Yet multiracial ideology clearly requires the explicit acknowledgement of biological race in order to arrive at the alleged existence of multiracial individuals. This, again, is the internal contradiction of multiracial identity politics that cannot be denied. Even Douglass, after her eloquent argument against biological race, invokes race—and presumably hypodescent—when she says that "the blood running through the veins of black children cannot be distinguished from the blood running through the veins of other children no matter what color they are or what culture they eventually embrace."[12] The unanswered question, of course, is to what does she appeal in making the black children in her example black, if not biological race?

Moreover, as I have pointed out previously, even if one accepts for the sake of argument the idea of racial groups, it is a logical and biological impossibility to posit Afro-Americans as pure blacks, whatever "pure blacks" might be. The long history of Native American and European admixture in the ancestry of Afro-Americans, as well as their tremendous phenotypic diversity, militates against any conception of them as making up a monoracial group. Given the apparent acceptance of this reality by multiracial adherents, how does the ideology then account for its distinction between Afro-Americans and black/white multiracial individuals? It does so in one of two ways. First, it might follow the logic of Project RACE's California proposal by arbitrarily drawing an exclusionary line at great-grandparents. Second, it might assert that racial identity is subjective, such that multiracial Afro-Americans who identify as black are black and multiracial Afro-Americans who identify as multiracial are multiracial. These justifications illustrate the extent to which multiracial ideology—contrary to the statements its spokespeople make on behalf of the importance of accuracy, especially medically relevant accuracy—is in fact not concerned with accuracy but is instead driven by issues of self-esteem. When proper identification depends not on physical facts but on personal preference, the argument for accuracy is exposed as the red herring it is.

A brief return to the *Time* and *Newsweek* articles mentioned above will demonstrate the extent to which accuracy on the issue of race in general, and multirace in particular, is an illusion. Each piece contains a color graph illustrating the supposed rise of interracial marriages in the United States. Each article also graphs the percentage of black/white interracial marriages in America. A profound question must be asked about these graphs, a question the respective editors apparently failed to grasp. What exactly is an interracial marriage? What assumptions do people take for granted when categorizing this or that marriage as interracial? What the editors of *Time* and *Newsweek* did in their graphs was to deploy the racist apparatus of hypodescent by perpetuating the idea that the extremely diverse people of African descent in the United States, the vast majority of whom possess European and Native American ancestry as well, all constitute a single biological race. There is, after all, no way to have a black/white interracial marriage unless one of the partners is black.

Simplistic journalism is not the only party guilty of acquiescence to hypodescent on the question of interracial marriages. The Census Bureau's 1997 report on the Race and Ethnic Targeted Test (RAETT) claims:

> An increase in interracial marriages [has] led to a higher proportion of the population being of mixed race or ethnicity. Census data show that there were about 1.5 million interracial couples in 1990. In all but 8 percent of these interracial couples, one spouse (or unmarried partner) was White. In 14 percent of interracial couples, the other spouse was Black. . . . Census data also show that the number of children in interracial families increased from less than 500,000 in 1970 to about two million in 1990.[13]

It cannot be stated emphatically enough that the foregoing analysis is biological nonsense. It is not possible to arrive at the above numbers, or to conceptualize the relevant relationships in the 14 percent of interracial marriages in which one partner was Afro-American, without appealing to hypodescent. Consider one of the children mentioned in the last sentence of the above passage, a child having one white and one black parent, in accord with the race concept utilized by the author. Now let us consider as well an ancestor of the black parent—a white ancestor.[14] In order for the Census Bureau statement to be valid, one would have to demonstrate that the child with one black and one white parent is multiracial in a way that the black parent, who also has black and white ancestry, is not. My argument throughout this book has been that such a demonstration is a logical and physical impossibility. The unchallenged acceptance of statements such as that of the Census Bureau, and of the *Time* and *Newsweek* graphs, regarding the rise of multiracials as a suddenly appearing, new population flies in the face of what we know to be the history of genetic mixture in the ancestries of African-descended people in the United States.

This idea of a suddenly rising multiracial population merely reinscribes the race fallacy while simultaneously upholding the racist notion of hypodescent. What does it mean, what sense does it make, when a person who possesses both European and African ancestries is categorized as black, as if the European component did not exist? What does it mean when such a person is said—because she procreated with a white partner—to have given birth to a multiracial child, when that child is no more the product of genetic mixture than she herself is? This kind of interpretation only means that a selective hypodescent has been deployed in the case of the parent, but not in the case of the child.

The assertion that multiracial births increased from fewer than 500,000 to about 2 million over several decades is a meaningless fantasy that ignores both past and present population mixture and internal miscegenation, as we know that at least 30 million Afro-Americans of mixed ancestry have been born in the United States in the past 100 years. Not only are Afro-Americans not "pure" blacks (whatever that might mean) but they are the most biologically heterogeneous population in the United States. If multiracialism were valid (which it most assuredly is not), then the 30 million Afro-Americans in the United States would already be multiracial, not black, and the idea of a suddenly rising multiracial population would therefore be moot.

People who accept the notion of a new and rising multiracial population merely reinforce hypodescent and the corrupt idea of white racial purity on which it is based. Americans will not advance from their backward belief in biological race if they validate the idea of multiracial people as being the products of differently raced parents, especially when the blackness of black parents is based on the racist fallacy of hypodescent. When a very dark-skinned person with tightly kinked hair and brown eyes and a very light-skinned person with naturally straight hair and blue eyes can each be uncritically considered the black partner in an interracial marriage, the concepts of race, interracial marriage, and multiracial people are all exposed as absurd fantasies, divorced from biological reality.

The vast majority of Afro-Americans have individuals like the so-called black/white multiracial child of today in their ancestries, so the distinction between them and that child is illusory. By deploying a selective hypodescent, multiracial advocates, *Time* and *Newsweek* editors, the Census Bureau, and many others perpetuate the myth of race and the continuing construction of monoracially black people by an after-the-fact excision of European, Native American, and other admixtures from Afro-American ancestries. Whatever number of black/white multiracial children anyone claims were born in a given year, these infants are no different from many millions of Afro-American children born in the United States since the early seventeenth century.[15] Both alleged black/white interracial mating and internal miscegenation result in precisely the same thing—a child with both African and European ancestry. I am by no means claiming that today's so-called black/white multiracial people are in fact black and that they should therefore "just get over it." Rather, I am asserting very specifically that race is a fallacy and that there is no logical or biological validity in distinguishing between Afro-Americans and black/white multiracials on the basis of genetic mixture.

It should be clear therefore, that rather than destabilizing racial categorization, a federal multiracial category would reinforce the fallacious categories already in use by requiring their continuing validity for its own existence. The path toward ultimately eliminating the race concept in American society is not through the establishment of a federal multiracial category, as Aubyn Fulton explains:

> I think the existence of iis [interracial individuals] is corrosive to and undermining of the current racial status quo (in this context I think that "corrosive" and "undermining" are *good* things, since I think that the current racial status quo is a bad thing and should be corroded and undermined). I think this undermining effect of iis is mitigated when "multiracial" is portrayed as just another "racial" category, of which only one can be checked, since such categories are mutually exclusive of each other.[16]

A federal multiracial category would create yet another non-white race in America, thereby doing nothing to alter the present axis of America's oppressive racial hierarchy. There is no doubt that the American racial paradigm could incorporate such a new non-white category, since even though it would be a multiracial category it would nonetheless have no effect on the status of the white category that drives the hierarchy. Thus, Fulton is correct to point out that whatever destabilizing effect the notion of multiraciality might have, such an effect would be lost were *multiracial* to become institutionalized as one of the standard federal categories. In other words, the maintenance of any insurgent character on the part of multiraciality depends on its challenging the paradigm from without.

The multiracial idea can be an effective reductio ad absurdum argument against the notion of race, since it demonstrates the absurdity of fixed and exclusive racial categories. In this sense I am referring specifically to multiraciality as a kind of abstract, insurgent idea—a hypothetical counterexample that serves to invalidate the idea of race. If one holds that races are distinct and pure entities, for instance, one must account for the categorizations of people having mixed racial heritages. Invariably, such can only be accounted for through the use of an inconsistent and racist tool such as hypodescent. Conversely, if one accepts that races are not pure and distinct, one must then account for the maintenance of racial boundaries, since persons of mixed ancestry might well be all seen as members of different races, each having but a single member. Thus, the multiracial idea is most effective and most subversive as a hypothetical counterexample to racial categorization. However, multiraciality can only exist in this kind of abstract state. Once it invalidates the idea of distinct and exclusive racial groups, it must of necessity invalidate itself as well, since it depends on these same fixed categories for its own existence.

Ironically, the attempt to instantiate the multiracial idea renders it fully impotent. This is so because, once established on federal forms, multiraciality would have an entirely different existence. Far from being an abstract idea that would invalidate the racial construct, thus necessitating its own dissolution, it would become a standard, accepted, biological racial choice relying explicitly on the other choices for its own existence. Unlike its abstract configuration, a federal multiracial category would not challenge the other categories, since its goal would be merely to exist among them. Moreover, due to the power and legitimacy that derive from federal requirements and official forms, respondents would not see a multiracial choice as challenging the idea of race but rather as simply one among several biological choices. Clearly, by collaborating with the paradigm and becoming established as one of the formal racial categories, multiraciality would lose its disruptive, subversive power in this regard.

Beyond the question of whether the tabulation issues of the "mark all that apply" (MATA) decision will eventually be resolved, the challenge remains to transcend the myth of racial categorization altogether. Certainly, the path toward eventually moving away from race is not through institutionalizing a federal multiracial category (whether through a stand-alone multiracial check-box, a separate multiracial check-box with subcategories, or in diluted form through the Project RACE MATA proposal with its exclusive special instruction), but rather via a concerted effort to think—in both philosophical and practical terms—about what it would require to establish a society where race is regarded as a myth, yet where there are still effective means to uncover and respond to the prejudices and hatreds of those who insist on living in the nineteenth century. Such an effort should begin with a panel or commission consisting of intellectuals, OMB officials, representatives of federal agencies concerned with civil rights enforcement, and other interested parties, who would be tasked to undertake long-term brainstorming about racial categorization in the United States. Looking only one, five, or ten years into the future is not looking far enough ahead.

Such thinkers must make a serious examination of, and suggest some difficult choices with respect to, civil rights compliance monitoring. It is essential that we not simply dismantle compliance monitoring while moving away from race. Yet it is just as certain that continuing such monitoring in the same form will prohibit the breakdown of race. Although there may seem to be no other method of ensuring compliance with civil rights laws, it is also true that alternatives have not been intensively considered since monitoring was initiated in the mid-1960s. It is obvious that summarily jettisoning federal racial categorization is not a reasonable option. Some kind of transition period will be necessary in order to accommodate changes to compliance monitoring; perhaps several stages of changes would have to be implemented. These issues should be considered by a combination of intellectuals, federal officials, and civil rights organizations in a future-oriented atmosphere, guided by the explicit goal of disconnecting race from American institutions while maintaining an attitude of intolerance toward racism of any kind.

Multiracial ideology, like the monoracial ideology it depends on, is a false consciousness. The frustration its adherents feel would be better directed at criticizing the American racial paradigm itself rather than at attempting to modify the paradigm's configuration. A modified paradigm, one containing a multiracial category, would be as fallacious as one without a multiracial category. As long as the idea of race has legitimacy, and as long as the racial hierarchy remains undisturbed, nothing will really change.

Notes

1. Aubyn Fulton, online posting, Interracial Individuals Discussion List, April 20, 1997 [ii-list@hcs.harvard.edu].

2. Kwame Anthony Appiah and Amy Gutman, *Color Conscious: The Political Morality of Race* (Princeton: Princeton University Press, 1996), 32.

3. Quoted in Janita Poe, "Woods Spotlights Multiracial Identity," *Chicago Tribune*, April 21, 1997, sec. 2, 2.

4. Quoted in Jeffry Scott, "Race, Labels, and Identity," *Atlanta Journal-Constitution*, May 6, 1997, D1.

5. Thomas Petri, press release, April 23, 1997 <http://www.house.gov/petri/press/census.htm>. Petri's H.R. 830 never received floor action in the House and was not passed by the 105th Congress. The identical fate had previously befallen the same bill, which Petri had introduced as H.R. 3920 in the 104th Congress.

6. Jack E. White, "'I'm Just Who I Am,'" *Time*, May 5, 1997, 32–33.

7. John Leland and Gregory Beals, "In Living Colors," *Newsweek*, May 5, 1997, 58–59.

8. The *Time* and *Newsweek* articles each contain two color graphs as well as numerous photographs.

9. I, as well as others, have debated these very issues with Ramona Douglass, Susan Graham, and Carlos Fernández on the Interracial Individuals Discussion List, and I feel confident that no current leader of a legitimate multiracial organization would assert directly that biological race exists. This is quite separate from the fact that the multiracial ideology these leaders espouse absolutely requires their acceptance of biological race at some level, again illustrating that multiracial advocacy is an inherently contradictory enterprise.

10. Carlos Fernández, online posting, Interracial Individuals Discussion List, January 22, 1996 [ii@gnu.ai.mit.edu].

11. House Subcommittee on Government Management, Information, and Technology, Committee on Government Reform and Oversight, *Hearings on Federal Measures of Race and Ethnicity and the Implications for the 2000 Census,* testimony by Ramona Douglass on May 22, 1997, 105th Cong., 1st Sess., April 23, May 22, and July 25, 1997, 385.

12. Ibid., 386.

13. Department of Commerce, Bureau of the Census, *Results of the 1996 Race and Ethnic Targeted Test,* Population Division Working Paper no. 18 (Washington, D.C., May 1997), 1-3.

14. It must be remembered here that a person has 256 six-times great-grandparents, 512 seven-times great-grandparents, 1,024 eight-times great-grandparents, and so on. The phenomenon of internal miscegenation widens the possibilities of ancestral diversity considerably more than people might realize.

15. Certainly, the farther one goes back into the American past, the more possible it becomes to differentiate between Africans and Afro-Americans. My point here is that at the present moment, no such differentiation is possible (with the exception of recent African immigrants). Although a relatively high proportion of Afro-American children born in the British North American colonies may have had two unmixed African parents, this proportion became smaller and smaller through the centuries. The likelihood of an Afro-American tracing her genealogy back through the seventeenth century, or even the eighteenth or nineteenth centuries, and finding only unmixed Africans is so small as to be infinitesimal.

16. Aubyn Fulton, online posting, Interracial Individuals Discussion List, May 30, 1997 [ii-list@hcs.harvard.edu].

Bibliography

Alcoff, Linda. "Mestizo Identity." In *American Mixed Race: The Culture of Microdiversity*, ed. Naomi Zack, 257–278. Lanham, Md.: Rowman and Littlefield, 1995.

Angeles, Peter A., ed. *Dictionary of Philosophy*. New York: Barnes and Noble, 1981. S.v. "reification/reism."

Appiah, Kwame Anthony. *In My Father's House: Africa in the Philosophy of Culture*. Oxford: Oxford University Press, 1992.

Appiah, Kwame Anthony, and Amy Gutman. *Color Conscious: The Political Morality of Race*. Princeton: Princeton University Press, 1996.

Azoulay, Katya G. *Black, Jewish, and Interracial: It's Not the Color of Your Skin, but the Race of Your Kin, and Other Myths of Identity*. Durham, N.C.: Duke University Press, 1997.

Bates, Karen G. "Color Complexity." *Emerge*, June 1993, 38–39.

Bond, Horace Mann. "Two Racial Islands in Alabama." *American Journal of Sociology* 36 (1930-1931): 552–567.

Bowles, Dorcas D. "Bi-Racial Identity: Children Born to African-American and White Couples." *Clinical Social Work Journal* 21, no. 4 (Winter 1993): 417–428.

Bowman, Elizabeth A. "'Multiracial' Category Sparks Controversy." *Detroit News*, April 13, 1995, 2C.

Brandes, O. Jean. "Racial/Ethnic Categories for Educational Statistics." *Statistical Reporter* 76, no. 3 (September 1975): 51–52.

Brown, Nancy G., and Ramona Douglass. "Making the Invisible Visible: The Growth of Community Network Organizations." In *The Multiracial Experience: Racial Borders As the New Frontier*, ed. Maria P. P. Root, 323–340. Thousand Oaks, Calif.: Sage Publications, 1996.

Budget and Accounting Procedures Act of 1950. U.S. Statutes at Large 64 (1950-1951).

Cartwright, Samuel A. "Diseases and Peculiarities of the Negro Race." In *The Cause of the South: Selections from De Bow's Review, 1846–1867*, ed. Paul F. Paskoff and Daniel J. Wilson, 26–43. Baton Rouge: Louisiana State University Press, 1982.

Christie, Rick. "Gingrich Lists His Action Plan for Racial Gulf." *Atlanta Journal-Constitution*, June 19, 1997, A3.

Civil Rights. U.S. Code. Vol. 21, secs. 1981–2000 (1994).

Civil Rights Act of 1957. U.S. Statutes at Large 71 (1957).

Civil Rights Act of 1964. U.S. Statutes at Large 78 (1964).

Civil Rights Commission. U.S. Code. Vol. 21, sec. 1975 (1994).

Cole, Kenneth. "'Multiracial' Box on Job, School Forms Riles Critics." *Detroit News*, June 28, 1995, 3D, 6D.

Collection and Publication of Statistics. U.S. Code. Vol. 5, secs. 41–103 (1994).

Community Reinvestment. U.S. Code. Vol. 23, secs. 2901–2907 (1994).

Congressional Record. 105th Cong., 1st sess., 143, no. 98, daily ed. (July 11, 1997): E1408. Article submitted by Representative Newt Gingrich of Georgia in extension of remarks.

Cooper, Richard S. "A Case Study in the Use of Race and Ethnicity in Public Health Surveillance." *Public Health Reports* 109, no. 1 (January-February 1994): 46–52.

Coordination of Federal Information Policy. U.S. Code. Vol. 24, secs. 3501–3520 (1994).

Cranston-Gonzalez National Affordable Housing Act. U.S. Statutes at Large 104 (1990).

David, Richard J., and James W. Collins. "Differing Birth Weight Among Infants of U.S.-Born Blacks, African-Born Blacks, and U.S.-Born Whites." *New England Journal of Medicine* 337, no. 17 (October 23, 1997): 1209–1214.

Davis, F. James. *Who Is Black? One Nation's Definition.* University Park: Pennsylvania State University Press, 1991.

Degler, Carl. *Neither Black Nor White: Slavery and Race Relations in Brazil and the United States.* Madison: University of Wisconsin Press, 1971.

Diamond, Jared. "Race Without Color." *Discover,* November 1994, 82–89.

Douglass, Ramona. "Multiracial People Must No Longer Be Invisible." *New York Times,* July 12, 1996, A14.

Douglass, Ramona (AMEA), and Susan Graham (Project RACE). To Katherine Wallman (Office of Information and Regulatory Affairs, OMB). September 29, 1995.

Elective Franchise. U.S. Code. Vol. 21, secs. 1971–1974 (1994).

Evinger, Suzann. "How Shall We Measure Our Nation's Diversity?" *Chance* 8, no. 1 (Winter 1995): 7–14.

_____. "How to Record Race." *American Demographics,* May 1996, 36–41.

_____. "Results of CPS Research on the Measurement of Race and Ethnicity." *Chance* 9, no. 2 (Spring 1996): 53–56.

Fair Housing. U.S. Code. Vol. 21, secs. 3601–3631 (1994).

Fang, Jing, Shantha Madhavan, and Michael H. Alderman. "The Association Between Birthplace and Mortality from Cardiovascular Causes Among Black and White Residents of New York City." *New England Journal of Medicine* 335, no. 21 (November 21, 1996): 1545–1551.

Farley, Reynolds. "A Single Census Question to Measure Race, Spanish-Origin, and Ancestry." *Poverty and Race* 4, no. 1 (January-February 1995): 14–15.

Ferber, Abby L. "Exploring the Social Construction of Race." In *American Mixed Race: The Culture of Microdiversity,* ed. Naomi Zack, 155–167. Lanham, Md.: Rowman and Littlefield, 1995.

Fernández, Carlos A. "La Raza and the Melting Pot: A Comparative Look at Multiethnicity." In *Racially Mixed People in America,* ed. Maria P. P. Root, 126–143. Newbury Park, Calif.: Sage Publications, 1992.

_____. "Government Classification of Multiracial/Multiethnic People." In *The Multiracial Experience: Racial Borders As the New Frontier,* ed. Maria P. P. Root, 15–36. Thousand Oaks, Calif.: Sage Publications, 1996.

Financial Institutions Reform, Recovery, and Enforcement Act of 1989. U.S. Statutes at Large 103 (1989).

Flores-Hughes, Grace. "Why the Term 'Hispanic'?" *Hispanic,* September 1996, 64.

Flowers, Gary. "New Racial Classifications: A Setback for Civil Rights Enforcement?" *Committee Report* 6, no. 1 (Winter 1994-1995): 1–6.

Forbes, Jack D. *Africans and Native Americans: The Language of Race and the Evolution of Red-Black Peoples.* Urbana and Chicago: University of Illinois Press, 1993.

Foucault, Michel. *The Order of Things: An Archaeology of the Human Sciences.* New York: Vintage Books, 1973.

Frisby, Michael K. "Black, White, or Other." *Emerge,* December 1995–January 1996, 48–54.

Funderburg, Lise. *Black, White, Other: Biracial Americans Talk About Race and Identity.* New York: William Morrow, 1994.

_____. "Boxed In." *New York Times,* July 10, 1996, A15.

Genovese, Eugene D. *Roll, Jordan, Roll: The World the Slaves Made.* New York: Vintage Books, 1974.

Geronimus, Arline T., John Bound, Timothy A. Waidmann, Marianne M. Hillemeier, and Patricia B. Burns. "Excess Mortality Among Blacks and Whites in the United States." *New England Journal of Medicine* 335, no. 21 (November 21, 1996): 1552–1558.

Gillum, Richard F. "The Epidemiology of Cardiovascular Disease in Black Americans." *New England Journal of Medicine* 335, no. 21 (November 21, 1996): 1597–1599.

Glazer, Nathan. "On the Census, Race, and Ethnic Categories." *Poverty and Race* 4, no. 2 (March-April 1995): 15–17.

Goldberg, David T. "Made in the USA." In *American Mixed Race: The Culture of Microdiversity,* ed. Naomi Zack, 237–255. Lanham, Md.: Rowman and Littlefield, 1995.

Goodman, Alan. "The Race Pit." *Anthropology Newsletter* 39, no. 5 (May 1998): 52.

Gould, Stephen Jay. *The Mismeasure of Man.* New York: W. W. Norton, 1981.

_____. "The Geometer of Race." *Discover,* November 1994, 64–69.

Graham, Susan. "Grassroots Advocacy." In *American Mixed Race: The Culture of Microdiversity,* ed. Naomi Zack, 185–189. Lanham, Md.: Rowman and Littlefield, 1995.

_____. "The Real World." In *The Multiracial Experience: Racial Borders As the New Frontier,* ed. Maria P. P. Root, 37–48. Thousand Oaks, Calif.: Sage Publications, 1996.

Gramsci, Antonio. *An Antonio Gramsci Reader: Selected Writings, 1916–1935.* Ed. David Forgacs. New York: Schocken Books, 1988.

Hahn, Robert A., and Donna F. Stroup. "Race and Ethnicity in Public Health Surveillance: Criteria for the Scientific Use of Social Categories." *Public Health Reports* 109, no. 1 (January-February 1994): 7–15.

Haley, Alex. *Roots: The Saga of an American Family.* Garden City, N.Y.: Doubleday, 1974.

Hannaford, Ivan. "The Idiocy of Race." *Wilson Quarterly* 2 (Spring 1994): 8–35.

Hansen, Chris. "Race/Ethnicity and Data Collection." *Poverty and Race* 4, no. 2 (March-April 1995): 17–18.

Harding, Sandra, ed. *The Racial Economy of Science: Toward a Democratic Future.* Bloomington and Indianapolis: Indiana University Press. 1993.

Harper, Frances E. W. *Iola Leroy, or Shadows Uplifted.* 2d ed. Philadelphia: Garrigues, 1893. Reprint, Oxford: Oxford University Press, 1988.

Harris, Cheryl I. "Whiteness As Property." *Harvard Law Review* 106, no. 8 (June 1993): 1707–1791.

Harris, Marvin. *Patterns of Race in the Americas.* Westport, Conn.: Greenwood Press, 1964.

Harris, Marvin, and Conrad Kotak. "The Structural Significance of Brazilian Racial Categories." *Sociologia* 25 (1963): 203–209.

Hegel, Georg W. F. *Hegel's Philosophy of Right.* Trans. T. M. Knox. Oxford: Oxford University Press, 1967.

Hening, William Waller, ed. *The Statutes At Large; Being a Collection of All the Laws of Virginia, from the First Session of the Legislature in the Year 1619.* Vol. 3. Richmond, Va.: Samuel Pleasants, 1812.

Herrnstein, Richard J., and Charles Murray. *The Bell Curve: Intelligence and Class Structure in American Life.* New York: The Free Press, 1994.

Hoetink, Herman. *The Two Variants in Caribbean Race Relations.* Oxford: Oxford University Press, 1967.

Home Mortgage Disclosure. U.S. Code. Vol. 5, secs. 2801–2811 (1994).

Hurst, Fannie. *Imitation of Life.* New York: Harper, 1933.

Jones, Lisa. *Bulletproof Diva: Tales of Race, Sex, and Hair.* New York: Doubleday, 1994.

Jones, Nicholas. "Mixed-Race Identity Formation: Hearing from Young Mixed-Race Adults." Paper presented at the Colorlines in the Twenty-First Century conference, Chicago, September 26, 1998.

Jordan, Winthrop D. *White over Black: American Attitudes Toward the Negro, 1550–1812.* New York: W. W. Norton, 1977.

Kawash, Samira. *Dislocating the Color Line: Identity, Hybridity, and Singularity in African-American Literature.* Stanford: Stanford University Press, 1997.

King, Rebecca C., and Kimberly M. DaCosta. "Changing Face, Changing Race: The Remaking of Race in the Japanese American and African American Communities." In *The Multiracial Experience: Racial Borders As the New Frontier,* ed. Maria P. P. Root, 227–244. Thousand Oaks, Calif.: Sage Publications, 1996.

Korenbot, Carol C. "Racial/Ethnic Categories: Do They Matter to Health?" *Poverty and Race* 4, no. 2 (March-April 1995): 14–15.

Lawrence, Cecile A. "Racelessness." In *American Mixed Race: The Culture of Microdiversity,* ed. Naomi Zack, 5–37. Lanham, Md.: Rowman and Littlefield, 1995.

Lawyers' Committee for Civil Rights Under Law, National Association for the Advancement of Colored People, National Urban League, and Joint Center for Political and Economic Studies. *Coalition Statement on Proposed Modification of OMB Directive No. 15.* Fall 1994.

Leland, John, and Gregory Beals. "In Living Colors." *Newsweek,* May 5, 1997, 58–60.

Littlefield, Alice, Leonard Lieberman, and Larry T. Reynolds. "Redefining Race: The Potential Demise of a Concept in Physical Anthropology." *Current Anthropology* 23, no. 6 (1982): 641–655.

Livingstone, Frank B. "On the Nonexistence of Human Races." In *The Racial Economy of Science: Toward a Democratic Future,* ed. Sandra Harding, 133–141. Bloomington and Indianapolis: Indiana University Press. 1993.

López, Ian F. Haney. "The Social Construction of Race." In *Critical Race Theory: The Cutting Edge,* ed. Richard Delgado, 191–203. Philadelphia: Temple University Press, 1995.

Lott, Juanita T. "Policy Purposes of Race and Ethnicity: An Assessment of Federal Racial and Ethnic Categories." *Ethnicity and Disease* 3, no. 3 (Summer 1993): 221–228.

———. "The Limitations of Directive 15." *Poverty and Race* 4, no. 1 (January-February 1995): 9–11.

Lowry, Roye L. "Race and Color Designations in Federal Statistics." *Statistical Reporter* 70, no. 3 (September 1969): 37–38.

Marshall, Gloria A. "Racial Classifications: Popular and Scientific." In *The Racial Economy of Science: Toward a Democratic Future,* ed. Sandra Harding, 116–127. Bloomington and Indianapolis: Indiana University Press, 1993.

Mathews, Linda. "More Than Identity Rides on a New Racial Category." *New York Times,* July 6, 1996, A1, A7.

McCafferty, Dennis. "No Resting in Peace for Infant." *Atlanta Journal-Constitution,* March 28, 1996, D1.

―――. "Racial Burial Conflict Shakes Up Town." *Atlanta Journal-Constitution,* March 29, 1996, E2.

McKenney, Nampeo R., and Claudette E. Bennette. "Issues Regarding Data on Race and Ethnicity: The Census Bureau Experience." *Public Health Reports* 109, no. 1 (January-February 1994): 16–25.

McRoy, Ruth G., and Edith Freeman. "Racial-Identity Issues Among Mixed-Race Children." *Social Work in Education* 8, no. 3 (Spring 1986): 164–174.

Mencke, John G. *Mulattoes and Race Mixture: American Attitudes and Images, 1865–1918.* Ann Arbor, Mich.: UMI Research Press, 1979.

Michaels, Walter Benn. "Race into Culture: A Critical Genealogy of Cultural Identity." *Critical Inquiry* 18 (Summer 1992): 655–685.

―――. "Autobiography of an Ex–White Man: Why Race Is Not a Social Construction." *Transition* 7, no. 1 (1998): 122–143.

Molnar, Stephen. *Human Variation: Races, Types, and Ethnic Groups.* 4th ed. Upper Saddle River, N.J.: Prentice Hall, 1998.

Montagu, Ashley. *Man's Most Dangerous Myth: The Fallacy of Race.* 6th ed. Walnut Creek, Calif.: AltaMira Press, 1997.

Moore, David C. "Routes: Alex Haley's *Roots* and the Rhetoric of Genealogy." *Transition,* n.s., 64 (1995): 4–21.

Morgenau, Tom. "What Color Is Black?" *Newsweek,* February 13, 1995, 62–65.

Myers, Samuel L., Jr. "The Error of the Third Type." *Poverty and Race* 4, no. 1 (January-February 1995): 13–14.

Myrdal, Gunnar. *An American Dilemma: The Negro Problem and Modern Democracy.* New York: Harper and Brothers, 1944.

Nakashima, Cynthia L. "An Invisible Monster: The Creation and Denial of Mixed-Race People in America." In *Racially Mixed People in America,* ed. Maria P. P. Root, 162–180. Newbury Park, Calif.: Sage Publications, 1992.

―――. "Voices from the Movement: Approaches to Multiraciality." In *The Multiracial Experience: Racial Borders As the New Frontier,* ed. Maria P. P. Root, 79–97. Thousand Oaks, Calif.: Sage Publications, 1996.

National Affordable Housing. U.S. Code. Vol. 5, secs. 12701–12899 (1994).

National Marrow Donor Program. *Chance of a Lifetime: Questions and Answers About Unrelated Marrow Transplants.* Minneapolis: National Marrow Donor Program, 1996.

National Research Council. Committee on National Statistics. *Spotlight on Heterogeneity: The Federal Standards for Racial and Ethnic Classification, Summary of a Workshop.* Ed. Barry Edmonston, Joshua Goldstein, and Juanita T. Lott. Washington, D.C.: National Academy Press, 1996.

National Research Council. Committee on National Statistics. Panel on Census Requirements in the Year 2000 and Beyond. *Modernizing the U.S. Census.* Ed. Barry Edmonston and Charles Schultze. Washington, D.C.: National Academy Press, 1995.

Njeri, Itabari. "Sushi and Grits: Ethnic Identity and Conflict in a Newly Multicultural America." In *Lure and Loathing: Essays on Race, Identity, and the Ambivalence of Assimilation,* ed. Gerald Early, 13–40. New York: Penguin, 1993.

Norment, Lynn. "Am I Black, White, or In Between?" *Ebony,* August 1995, 108–112.

Omi, Michael, and Howard Winant. *Racial Formation in the United States: From the 1960s to the 1990s.* 2d ed. New York: Routledge, 1994.

Paperwork Reduction Act of 1980. U.S. Statutes at Large 94 (1980).

Park, Robert E. "Mentality of Racial Hybrids." *American Journal of Sociology* 36 (1930-1931): 534–551.

Patureau, Alan. "Principal Called Mixed-Race Pupil a 'Mistake.'" *Atlanta Journal-Constitution,* March 10, 1994, A3.

Peterson, Jonathan. "Stakes Raised in Civil Rights Fight." *Las Vegas Review-Journal,* January 19, 1998, A1.

Peterson, Paul E., ed. *Classifying By Race.* Princeton: Princeton University Press, 1995.

Peterson, William. "Politics and the Measurement of Ethnicity." In *The Politics of Numbers,* ed. William Alonso and Paul Starr, 187–233. New York: Russell Sage Foundation, 1987.

Piana, Libero D. "Categories Count." *Poverty and Race* 4, no. 1 (January-February 1995): 11–12.

Pinderhughes, Elaine. "Biracial Identity: Asset or Handicap?" In *Racial and Ethnic Identity: Psychological Development and Creative Expression,* ed. Herbert W. Harris, Howard C. Blue, and Ezra E. H. Griffith, 73–93. New York: Routledge, 1995.

Piper, Adrian. "Passing for White, Passing for Black." *Transition,* n.s., 58 (1992): 4–32.

Poe, Janita. "Multiracial People Want a Single Name That Fits." *Chicago Tribune,* May 3, 1993, sec. 1, 1, 13.

_____. "Woods Spotlights Multiracial Identity." *Chicago Tribune,* April 21, 1997, sec. 2, 1–2.

Poverty and Race Research Action Council. "Racial/Ethnic Categories: Do They Matter?" *Poverty and Race* 3, no. 6 (November-December 1994): 1–9.

Powell, John. "Who Thought of Dropping Racial Categories, and Why?" *Poverty and Race* 4, no. 1 (January-February 1995): 12–13.

President. Executive Order. "To Facilitate Coordination of Federal Education Programs, Executive Order 11185." *Code of Federal Regulations, Title 3: The President, 1964 and 1965 Compilation* (1967): 259–261.

_____. "Equal Employment Opportunity, Executive Order 11246." *Code of Federal Regulations, Title 3: The President, 1964 and 1965 Compilation* (1967): 339–348.

_____. "Providing for the Coordination by the Attorney General of Enforcement of Title VI of the Civil Rights Act of 1964, Executive Order 11247." *Code of Federal Regulations, Title 3: The President, 1964 and 1965 Compilation* (1967): 348–349.

_____. "Coordination of Federal Education Programs, Executive Order 11761." *Weekly Compilation of Presidential Documents* 10, no. 3 (January 19, 1974): 40–42.

_____. "Relating to the Transfer of Certain Statistical Policy Functions, Executive Order 12013." *Federal Register* 42, no. 197 (October 12, 1977): 54931–54933.

Rabin, Steve A. "A Private Sector View of Health, Surveillance, and Communities of Color." *Public Health Reports* 109, no. 1 (January-February 1994): 42–45.

Reddy, Maureen T. *Crossing the Color Line: Race, Parenting, and Culture.* New Brunswick, N.J.: Rutgers University Press, 1994.

Region in Brief. "Interracial Couples at the Prom? No Way, Says Principal in Alabama." *Atlanta Journal-Constitution,* February 26, 1994, A4.

Reuter, Donald G. "Bibliography of Edward Byron Reuter, 1880–1946." *American Journal of Sociology* 52, no. 2 (1946): 106–111.

Reuter, Edward B. "The Superiority of the Mulatto." *American Journal of Sociology* 23, no. 1 (July 1917): 83–106.

_____. *The Mulatto in the United States: Including a Study of the Rôle of Mixed-Blood Races Throughout the World.* Boston: Richard G. Badger, 1918. Reprint, New York: Negro Universities Press, 1969.

_____. *Race Mixture: Studies in Intermarriage and Miscegenation.* New York: McGraw-Hill, 1931. Reprint, New York: Johnson Reprint Corporation, 1970.

_____. "Racial Theory." *American Journal of Sociology* 50, no. 6 (May 1945): 452–461.

_____. *The American Race Problem.* Rev. ed. New York: Thomas Y. Crowell, 1970.

Reuter, Edward B., ed. *Race and Culture Contacts.* New York: McGraw-Hill, 1934.

Root, Maria P. P. "The Multiracial Contribution to the Psychological Browning of America." In *American Mixed Race: The Culture of Microdiversity,* ed. Naomi Zack, 231–236. Lanham, Md.: Rowman and Littlefield, 1995.

_____. "Mixed-Race Women." In *Race/Sex: Their Sameness, Difference, and Interplay,* ed. Naomi Zack, 157–172. New York: Routledge, 1997.

Root, Maria P. P., ed. *Racially Mixed People in America.* Newbury Park, Calif.: Sage Publications, 1992.

_____. *The Multiracial Experience: Racial Borders As the New Frontier.* Thousand Oaks, Calif.: Sage Publications, 1996.

Satris, Stephen. "'What Are They?'" In *American Mixed Race: The Culture of Microdiversity,* ed. Naomi Zack, 53–59. Lanham, Md.: Rowman and Littlefield, 1995.

Sauer, Norman J. "Applied Anthropology and the Concept of Race: A Legacy of Linnaeus." *NAPA Bulletin* 13, *Race, Ethnicity, and Applied Bioanthropology* (1993): 79–84.

Scott, Jeffry. "Race, Labels, and Identity." *Atlanta Journal-Constitution,* May 6, 1997, D1.

Sheehan, Neil. *A Bright Shining Lie: John Paul Vann and America in Vietnam.* New York: Random House, 1988.

Shepard, Paul. "Year 2000 May Bring Census with New Mixed-Race Category." *Atlanta Journal-Constitution,* April 3, 1997, A8.

Shrage, Laurie. "Passing Beyond the Other Race or Sex." In *Race/Sex: Their Sameness, Difference, and Interplay,* ed. Naomi Zack, 183–190. New York: Routledge, 1997.

Shreeve, James. "Terms of Estrangement." *Discover,* November 1994, 56–63.

Smedley, Audrey. *Race in North America: Origin and Evolution of a Worldview.* 2d ed. Boulder: Westview Press, 1999.

Snowden, Frank M. *Before Color Prejudice: The Ancient View of Blacks.* Cambridge: Harvard University Press, 1983.

Sollors, Werner. *Neither Black Nor White Yet Both: Thematic Explorations of Interracial Literature.* Oxford: Oxford University Press, 1997.

Spencer, Rainier. "Race in the Face." *Interrace,* June-July 1994, 26.

_____. "Notes from the Struggle Against Racial Categorization: Challenge or Collaboration?" *Interrace,* October-November 1994, 18–22.

_____. "Race and Mixed-Race: A Personal Tour." In *As We Are Now: Mixblood Essays on Race and Identity,* ed. William S. Penn, 126–139. Berkeley: University of California Press, 1997.

Spickard, Paul R. *Mixed Blood: Intermarriage and Ethnic Identity in Twentieth-Century America.* Madison: University of Wisconsin Press, 1989.

_____. "The Illogic of American Racial Categories." In *Racially Mixed People in America,* ed. Maria P. P. Root, 12–23. Newbury Park, Calif.: Sage Publications, 1992.

Stampp, Kenneth M. *The Peculiar Institution: Slavery in the Ante-Bellum South.* New York: Vintage Books, 1956.

Stonequist, Everett V. *The Marginal Man: A Study in Personality and Culture Conflict.* New York: Charles Scribner's Sons, 1937. Reprint, New York: Russell and Russell, 1961.

Sundiata, Ibrahim K. "At the Races: The Multiracial Proposal." *Poverty and Race* 4, no. 2 (March-April 1995): 13–14.

Thomas, Deborah A. "Black, White, or Other?" *Essence,* July 1993, 118.

Tilles, Marc C. "'Multiracial' Can Only Mean Further Racial Division." *Michigan Chronicle,* June 14-20, 1995, 1A, 4A.

_____. "Multiracial Category Becomes Law." *Michigan Chronicle,* September 20-26, 1995, 1A.

Tizard, Barbara, and Ann Phoenix. *Black, White, or Mixed Race? Race and Racism in the Lives of Young People of Mixed Parentage.* London: Routledge, 1993.

Townsel, Lisa Jones. "Neither Black Nor White: Would a New Census Category Be a Dangerous Diversion or a Step Forward?" *Ebony,* November 1996, 45–50.

U.S. Commission on Civil Rights. *Federal Title VI Enforcement to Ensure Nondiscrimination in Federally Assisted Programs.* Washington, D.C., June 1996.

U.S. Department of Commerce. Bureau of the Census. "Transfer of Responsibility for Certain Statistical Standards from OMB to Commerce," by Juanita M. Kreps. *Federal Register* 43, no. 87 (May 4, 1978): 19260–19273.

_____. *Challenges of Measuring an Ethnic World: Science, Politics, and Reality. Proceedings of the Joint Canada–United States Conference on the Measurement of Ethnicity, April 1–3, 1992.* Washington, D.C., 1993.

_____. "1996 Race and Ethnic Targeted Test (RAETT) and Its Content Reinterview, Also Identified As the 1996 Census Survey," by Gerald Taché. *Federal Register* 60, no. 231 (December 1, 1995): 62010–62015.

_____. *Findings on Questions on Race and Hispanic Origin Tested in the 1996 National Content Survey,* Population Division Working Paper no. 16. Washington, D.C., December 1996.

_____. *Results of the 1996 Race and Ethnic Targeted Test,* Population Division Working Paper no. 18. Washington, D.C., May 1997.

_____. *Questions on Race and Ethnicity for the Census 2000 Dress Rehearsal.* Washington, D.C., November 3, 1997.

U.S. Department of Commerce. Office of Federal Statistical Policy and Standards. *Statistical Policy Handbook.* Washington, D.C., 1978.

U.S. Department of Education. National Center for Education Statistics. *Racial and Ethnic Classifications Used by Public Schools,* NCES 96-092, by Nancy Carey and Elizabeth Farris. Project officer Judi Carpenter. Washington, D.C., 1996.

U.S. Department of Labor. Bureau of Labor Statistics. *A Test of Methods for Collecting Racial and Ethnic Information: May 1995,* USDL 95-428. Washington, D.C., October 26, 1995.

_____. *Statistical Note Number 40. Testing Methods of Collecting Racial and Ethnic Information: Results of the Current Population Survey Supplement on Race and Ethnicity,* by Clyde Tucker, et al. Washington, D.C., 1996.

U.S. Executive Office of the President. Bureau of the Budget. "Exhibit A: Standards for Statistical Surveys." *Circular no. A-46: Statistical Procedures* (March 28, 1952).

_____. "Exhibit K: Amendment to Circular no. A-46, Race and Color Designations in Federal Statistics." Transmittal Memorandum no. 8, August 8, 1969.

U.S. Executive Office of the President. Office of Management and Budget. "Exhibit F: Race and Color Designations in Federal Statistics." *Circular no. A-46: Standards and Guidelines for Federal Statistics* (May 3, 1974).

————. "Exhibit F (Revised May 12, 1977): Race and Ethnic Standards for Federal Statistics and Administrative Reporting." *Circular no. A–46: Standards and Guidelines for Federal Statistics* (May 3, 1974).

————. *Federal Statistics: Coordination, Standards, Guidelines,* May 1976.

————. Letter to the Heads of Executive Departments and Establishments. "Subject: Rescission of Office of Management and Budget Circulars nos. A-39, A-46, A-65, and A-91," signed by James T. McIntyre Jr., April 13, 1978.

————. "Transfer of Responsibility for Certain Statistical Standards from OMB to Commerce," by Velma N. Baldwin. *Federal Register* 43, no. 87 (May 4, 1978): 19308.

————. "Guidelines for Federal Statistical Activities," by Wendy L. Gramm. *Federal Register* 53, no. 12 (January 20, 1988): 1542–1552.

————. "Standards for the Classification of Federal Data on Race and Ethnicity," by Sally Katzen. *Federal Register* 59, no. 110 (June 9, 1994): 29831–29835.

————. "Standards for the Classification of Federal Data on Race and Ethnicity," by Sally Katzen. *Federal Register* 60, no. 166 (August 28, 1995): 44673–44693.

————. "Recommendations from the Interagency Committee for the Review of the Racial and Ethnic Standards to the Office of Management and Budget Concerning Changes to the Standards for the Classification of Federal Data on Race and Ethnicity," by Sally Katzen. *Federal Register* 62, no. 131 (July 9, 1997): 36874–36946.

————. "Revisions to the Standards for the Classification of Federal Data on Race and Ethnicity," by Sally Katzen. *Federal Register* 62, no. 210 (October 30, 1997): 58782–58790.

U.S. Federal Interagency Committee on Education. *Report of the Ad Hoc Committee on Racial and Ethnic Definitions.* Washington, D.C., April 1975.

U.S. General Accounting Office. General Government Division. *Federal Data Collection: Agencies' Use of Consistent Race and Ethnic Definitions,* GAO/GGD-93-95, by L. Nye Stevens. Washington, D.C., December 1992.

————. *Census Reform: Early Outreach and Decisions Needed on Race and Ethnic Questions,* GAO/GGD-93-96, by L. Nye Stevens. Washington, D.C., January 1993.

U.S. House. *A Bill to Amend the Paperwork Reduction Act.* 104th Cong., 2d sess., H.R. 3920. *Congressional Record,* 142, no. 114, daily ed. (July 30, 1996): H8982.

————. *A Bill to Amend the Paperwork Reduction Act.* 105th Cong., 1st sess., H.R. 830. *Congressional Record,* 143, no. 21, daily ed. (February 25, 1997): H628.

U.S. House Subcommittee on Census, Statistics, and Postal Personnel. Committee on Post Office and Civil Service. *Hearings on the Review of Federal Measurements of Race and Ethnicity.* 103d Cong., 1st sess., April 14, June 30, July 29, and November 3, 1993.

————. *Hearings on the Review of Federal Measurements of Race and Ethnicity.* Testimony by Reynolds Farley on April 14, 1993. 103d Cong., 1st sess., April 14, June 30, July 29, and November 3, 1993, 47–70.

————. *Hearings on the Review of Federal Measurements of Race and Ethnicity.* Testimony by Juanita T. Lott on April 14, 1993. 103d Cong., 1st sess., April 14, June 30, July 29, and November 3, 1993, 36–47, 65–70.

_____. *Hearings on the Review of Federal Measurements of Race and Ethnicity*. Testimony by Marvin C. Arnold on June 30, 1993. 103d Cong., 1st sess., April 14, June 30, July 29, and November 3, 1993, 159–171.

_____. *Hearings on the Review of Federal Measurements of Race and Ethnicity*. Testimony by Steven Carbo on June 30, 1993. 103d Cong., 1st sess., April 14, June 30, July 29, and November 3, 1993, 178–182, 189–196.

_____. *Hearings on the Review of Federal Measurements of Race and Ethnicity*. Testimony by Susan Graham on June 30, 1993. 103d Cong., 1st sess., April 14, June 30, July 29, and November 3, 1993, 105–125, 165–171.

_____. *Hearings on the Review of Federal Measurements of Race and Ethnicity*. Testimony by Carlos Fernández on June 30, 1993. 103d Cong., 1st sess., April 14, June 30, July 29, and November 3, 1993, 125–157, 165–171.

_____. *Hearings on the Review of Federal Measurements of Race and Ethnicity*. Testimony by Sonia M. Pérez on June 30, 1993. 103d Cong., 1st sess., April 14, June 30, July 29, and November 3, 1993, 171–178, 189–196.

_____. *Hearings on the Review of Federal Measurements of Race and Ethnicity*. Testimony by Rachel A. Joseph on July 29, 1993. 103d Cong., 1st sess., April 14, June 30, July 29, and November 3, 1993, 235–245.

_____. *Hearings on the Review of Federal Measurements of Race and Ethnicity*. Testimony by Sally Katzen on July 29, 1993. 103d Cong., 1st sess., April 14, June 30, July 29, and November 3, 1993, 213–229.

_____. *Hearings on the Review of Federal Measurements of Race and Ethnicity*. Testimony by Thomas Sawyer on July 29, 1993. 103d Cong., 1st sess., April 14, June 30, July 29, and November 3, 1993, 197–198.

_____. *Hearings on the Review of Federal Measurements of Race and Ethnicity*. Testimony by Norma V. Cantú on November 3, 1993. 103d Cong., 1st sess., April 14, June 30, July 29, and November 3, 1993, 261–267, 272–282.

_____. *Hearings on the Review of Federal Measurements of Race and Ethnicity*. Testimony by Arthur A. Fletcher on November 3, 1993. 103d Cong., 1st sess., April 14, June 30, July 29, and November 3, 1993, 248–261, 272–282.

_____. *Hearings on the Review of Federal Measurements of Race and Ethnicity*. Testimony by Tony E. Gallegos on November 3, 1993. 103d Cong., 1st sess., April 14, June 30, July 29, and November 3, 1993, 285–294.

_____. *Hearings on the Review of Federal Measurements of Race and Ethnicity*. Testimony by Paul Williams on November 3, 1993. 103d Cong., 1st sess., April 14, June 30, July 29, and November 3, 1993, 267–282.

U.S. House Subcommittee on Government Management, Information, and Technology. Committee on Government Reform and Oversight. *Hearings on Federal Measures of Race and Ethnicity and the Implications for the 2000 Census*. 105th Cong., 1st sess., April 23, May 22, and July 25, 1997.

_____. *Hearings on Federal Measures of Race and Ethnicity and the Implications for the 2000 Census*. Testimony by Sally Katzen on April 23, 1997. 105th Cong., 1st sess., April 23, May 22, and July 25, 1997, 45–115.

_____. *Hearings on Federal Measures of Race and Ethnicity and the Implications for the 2000 Census*. Testimony by Thomas Petri on April 23 and July 25, 1997. 105th Cong., 1st sess., April 23, May 22, and July 25, 1997, 223–227, 523–524.

_____. *Hearings on Federal Measures of Race and Ethnicity and the Implications for the 2000 Census.* Testimony by Ramona Douglass on May 22, 1997. 105th Cong., 1st sess., April 23, May 22, and July 25, 1997, 382–396, 433–439.

_____. *Hearings on Federal Measures of Race and Ethnicity and the Implications for the 2000 Census.* Testimony by Carlos Fernández on May 22 and July 25, 1997. 105th Cong., 1st sess., April 23, May 22, and July 25, 1997, 389–391, 557–576.

_____. *Hearings on Federal Measures of Race and Ethnicity and the Implications for the 2000 Census.* Testimony by Susan Graham on May 22 and July 25, 1997. 105th Cong., 1st sess., April 23, May 22, and July 25, 1997, 282–297, 327–382, 546–556.

_____. *Hearings on Federal Measures of Race and Ethnicity and the Implications for the 2000 Census.* Testimony by Stephen Horn on July 25, 1997. 105th Cong., 1st sess., April 23, May 22, and July 25, 1997, 507–509.

_____. *Hearings on Federal Measures of Race and Ethnicity and the Implications for the 2000 Census.* Testimony by Carrie Meek on July 25, 1997. 105th Cong., 1st sess., April 23, May 22, and July 25, 1997, 537–538.

_____. *Hearings on Federal Measures of Race and Ethnicity and the Implications for the 2000 Census.* Testimony by Thomas Sawyer on July 25, 1997. 105th Cong., 1st sess., April 23, May 22, and July 25, 1997, 517–522.

Vagas, Raymond J. "A Box of Many Colors: Wrestling with a Multiracial Category." *California Tomorrow,* Winter 1989, 15.

Voting Rights Act of 1965. U.S. Statutes at Large 79 (1965).

Voting Rights Act of 1965 (Amendment to). U.S. Statutes at Large 106 (1992).

Wallman, Katherine K., and John Hodgdon. "Race and Ethnic Standards for Federal Statistics and Administrative Reporting." *Statistical Reporter* 77, no. 10 (July 1977): 450–454.

Warren, Reuben C., Robert A. Hahn, Lonnie Bristow, and Elena S. H. Yu. "The Use of Race and Ethnicity in Public Health Surveillance." *Public Health Reports* 109, no. 1 (January-February 1994): 4–6.

Waugh, Dexter. "Census Bureau to Review Mixed Category." *San Francisco Chronicle,* April 21, 1991, B5.

Webster, Yehudi. *The Racialization of America.* New York: St. Martin's Press, 1992.

White, Jack E. "'I'm Just Who I Am.'" *Time,* May 5, 1997, 32–36.

White, Walter. *Rope and Faggot: A Biography of Judge Lynch.* Salem, N.H.: Ayer Company, 1928.

Wiegman, Robyn. *American Anatomies: Theorizing Race and Gender.* Durham, N.C.: Duke University Press, 1995.

Williams, David R., Risa Lavizzo-Mourey, and Rueben C. Warren. "The Concept of Race and Health Status in America." *Public Health Reports* 109, no. 1 (January-February 1994): 26–41.

Williams, Teresa K. "Race As Process: Reassessing the 'What Are You?' Encounters of Biracial Individuals." In *The Multiracial Experience: Racial Borders As the New Frontier,* ed. Maria P. P. Root, 191–210. Thousand Oaks, Calif.: Sage Publications, 1996.

Williamson, Joel. *New People: Miscegenation and Mulattoes in the United States.* New York: The Free Press, 1980.

Wills, Christopher. "The Skin We're In." *Discover,* November 1994, 76–81.

Wilson, Anne. *Mixed Race Children: A Study of Identity.* Boston: Allen and Unwin, 1987.

Winant, Howard. "Racial Dualism at Century's End." In *The House That Race Built: Black Americans, U.S. Terrain,* ed. Wahneema Lubiano, 87–115. New York: Pantheon, 1997.

Wise, Paul H. "Confronting Racial Disparities in Infant Mortality: Reconciling Science and Politics." *Racial Differences in Preterm Delivery: Developing a New Research Paradigm* (supplement). *American Journal of Preventive Medicine* 9, no. 6 (November-December 1993): 7–16.

Worthington, Rogers. "'Multiracial' Census Category Is Sought." *Chicago Tribune,* July 13, 1994, sec. 1, 15–16.

Wright, Lawrence. "One Drop of Blood." *New Yorker,* July 25, 1994, 46–55.

Younge, Gary. "Multiracial Citizens Divided on Idea of Separate Census Classification." *Washington Post,* July 19, 1996, A3.

Yzaguirre, Raúl, and Sonia M. Pérez. "Accurate Racial/Ethnic Data Should Drive Category Review." *Poverty and Race* 4, no. 1 (January-February 1995): 7–9.

Zack, Naomi. *Race and Mixed Race.* Philadelphia: Temple University Press, 1993.

_____. "On Being and Not-Being Black and Jewish." In *The Multiracial Experience: Racial Borders As the New Frontier,* ed. Maria P. P. Root, 140–151. Thousand Oaks, Calif.: Sage Publications, 1996.

Zack, Naomi, ed. *American Mixed Race: The Culture of Microdiversity.* Lanham, Md.: Rowman and Littlefield, 1995.

_____. *Race/Sex: Their Sameness, Difference, and Interplay.* New York: Routledge, 1997.

Index